# VMware vCenter Cookbook

Over 65 hands-on recipes to help you efficiently manage
your vSphere environment with VMware vCenter

**Konstantin Kuminsky**

[PACKT]
PUBLISHING

enterprise 🕸
professional expertise distilled

BIRMINGHAM - MUMBAI

# VMware vCenter Cookbook

First published: May 2015

Production reference: 1270515

Published by Packt Publishing Ltd.
Livery Place
35 Livery Street
Birmingham B3 2PB, UK.

ISBN 978-1-78355-397-6

www.packtpub.com

# Credits

**Author**

Konstantin Kuminsky

**Reviewers**

Ravi Kishore Angajala

Sébastien Brochet

Greg Mefford

Ranjit Singh "RJ" ThakurRatan

**Commissioning Editor**

Kunal Parikh

**Acquisition Editor**

Usha Iyer

**Content Development Editor**

Samantha Gonsalves

**Technical Editor**

Madhunikita Sunil Chindarkar

**Copy Editor**

Adithi Shetty

**Project Coordinator**

Sanchita Mandal

**Proofreaders**

Stephen Copestake

Safis Editing

**Indexers**

Hemangini Bari

Priya Sane

**Graphics**

Sheetal Aute

**Production Coordinator**

Komal Ramchandani

**Cover Work**

Komal Ramchandani

# Foreword

Virtualization is becoming a central component of data center strategies and as a result, it is an increasingly important aspect of the information technology strategy of many organizations. Organizations across many different sectors and of varying sizes are working to deploy more sophisticated computing infrastructures that use virtualization in order to maximize resource utilization. Virtualization provides organizations with a number of advantages, including better efficiency, better resource utilization, an improved ability to scale solutions and services while often achieving cost savings, and significant return on investment.

However, supporting a highly virtualized computing infrastructure can be challenging for many organizations. Managing and deploying many virtual machines can be a challenge, and managing the many different configurations can be overwhelming, especially for heterogeneous computing environments comprised of different kinds of servers with different processors, cores, memory, and so on. For enterprises making use of virtualized environments to serve core enterprise applications and house critical data, ensuring availability and reliability in a virtualized environment can be daunting.

As the leading virtualization company, VMware too has recognized the challenges in managing complex, enterprise datacenters and computing environments. To address these challenges and associated complexities, it introduced vCenter and vSphere to help administrators manage complex virtualized environments. Like many commercial software products, vCenter and vSphere are really a suite of software components that come in a number of different versions. While they make life easier for the administrator, they too are complex software products.

As in many situations, learning to use a complex software suite often requires assistance and sometimes, it is best done through examples. This book plays an important role in helping to fill an administrator's understanding and use of vCenter and vSphere. This book assumes that the reader/user will have access to vCenter that is deployed and has hosts and datastores. This book notes that this could be a trial license, which should be sufficient to allow the reader to explore vCenter and vSphere. For those in the process of acquiring vCenter, this is a useful suggestion as it will help determine versions of vSphere that may be needed.

# Overview and informational elements

The key focus is on vCenter and vSphere and the key functions and capabilities of the suite of software. This book covers a number of different requirements of virtualized environments—not all environments will have all the requirements. Thus, the text can be used by administrators across a range of environments; readers can "pick-and-choose" the chapters that are most relevant to their needs.

The core focus of the text covers the means of dealing with key enterprise needs: Availability, Scalability, Efficiency, and Optimization (chapters 2 to 5). The other chapters are useful as well. *Chapter 1*, covers basic vCenter tasks and examines different vSphere editions (I found this chapter particularly useful). *Chapters 6* and *7* cover basic administrative tasks and ways to improve the manageability of the virtual environment.

This book is very well written and there is consistent organization throughout the chapters. There are numerous step-by-step instructions on how to do certain tasks and many of these are accompanied by screenshots. This gives the book a "cookbook" flavor as there are many recipes (in fact, the text refers to many of the steps as "recipes") for tasks, and coupling this with the actual use of the software provides an excellent learning model.

# The content

This book falls into three logical sections: *Chapter 1*, basics of vCenter and vSphere; chapters 2-5, central enterprise tasks; *Chapters 6* and *7*, basic tasks and manageability.

## Chapter 1 – vCenter basis tasks and features

This chapter provides a discussion and comparison of various vSphere editions, what software components and kits are included under the different licenses, what each license covers (for example, CPUs), and so on. There is a very nice walk-through of the different editions, licenses, and options, and it can be very helpful in making a choice that is most appropriate for your organization. This chapter covers a number of basic vCenter tasks, such as booting a VM from a virtual CD, using hosts with different CPUs in one cluster, running vCenter on a VM, accessing hosts via SSH, and so on. There are, of course, screenshots to help the reader. I found this chapter to be particularly useful, since it clearly explained the different vSphere editions.

# Chapter 2 – Increasing environment availability

This chapter covers vCenter's approach in dealing with availability. It covers how to configure and tune the High Availability (HA) and Fault Tolerance (FT) options. Different scenarios are reviewed, including prioritizing VMs for recovery, admission control, backup, and replication. There are useful discussions on resource consumption for HA and FT, particularly on network traffic, memory, and disk. There are also some useful "tips" or best practices since HA and FT can impact available resources. Another useful element of this chapter is that it explains some of the messages that the administrator may get while configuring HA and FT, and it explains why these messages are being generated.

# Chapter 3 – Increasing environment scalability

For many organizations, one main advantage of virtualized data centers is the ability to scale. This chapter covers some of the options and features available in vCenter to improve the administrator's efficiency. This includes templates, customizations, host profiles, and other solutions designed to automate and simplify VM, host deployment, and configuration. Templates enable an administrator to take a set of tasks used for the deployment of virtual servers and package them. With this template, the administrator can deploy as many servers as needed and perform only tasks that are different from each other. In situations where there is a requirement to deploy many VMs in a short period of time, the process can be automated using scripts; the use of PowerCLI scripts is covered as an alternative way to deploy or upgrade hosts.

# Chapter 4 – Improving environment effiiency

This chapter describes some features and enhancements offered by vCenter along with vSphere 5, designed to increase environment efficiency. This includes new virtual hardware, SCSI controllers and network cards, efficient space utilization, power consumption, and the utilization of flash memory to make hosts and VMs faster. Of particular interest is the portion of this chapter that covers features of vSphere that enable a reduction in power consumption during off-peak hours, including Distributed Power Management (DPM), which allows certain hosts to be placed in the standby mode. This chapter also provides a discussion on how to leverage nonuniform memory access (NUMA) in modern server memory design.

# Chapter 5 – Optimizing resource usage

This chapter looks at resource usage and the options available in vSphere to optimize resource consumption. The common strategies in this area include better distribution of load between hosts and datastores, prioritization of resource consumers according to their importance and needs, as well as limiting resource usage, including CPU, memory, network, and storage I/O. Ensuring that there are enough resources, limiting resources, and balancing loads between hosts are the responsibilities of the Distributed Resource Scheduler (DRS). The Storage Distributed Resource Scheduler (SDRS) has been introduced in vSphere 5 to deal with storage performance. The common tasks utilizing both of these is covered.

## Chapter 6 – Basic administrative tasks

Tasks covered in this chapter, as the title suggests, are basic administrative tasks that will help administrators increase control and visibility of their environment. These tasks include setting up rules for virtual machine placement, setting alarms and e-mail alerts, automating basic tasks with a scheduler (for example, powering on/off, cloning), and controlling the space and location of snapshots. It also discusses automating VM placement with an affinity, which is related to optimization issues discussed in *Chapter 5*.

## Chapter 7 – Improving environment manageability

A variety of useful administrative tasks, which can make an administrator's life easier, are covered in this chapter. These tasks can improve the overall manageability of the environment. This chapter covers Tagging, a new feature introduced in vSphere 5, which can help categorize objects in the environment. There is also a section that covers a new command-line interface, esxcli, which has been introduced in vSphere 5; it offers improved syntax and additional functionality, including network and security policies, firewall, and VIN management.

# Wrapping up

This is an excellent text for those just getting into vCenter as well as more experienced administrators moving into more complex environments. With recipes for tasks coupled with screenshots, it is a very useful "desk side" companion.

**Michael Bauer**
Professor
Department of Computer Science
The University of Western Ontario

# About the Author

**Konstantin Kuminsky** is a VMware-, Microsoft-, and Cisco-certified IT professional with over 10 years of experience in different areas of the IT industry, including virtualization, networking, and security. His experience includes the support of Tier 3 Data Centre, the management of private Clouds, the administration of second- and third-level help desk and on-call support, as well as the deployment and support of various redundant systems and environments with high security requirements.

Konstantin is also the author of *Implementing vCenter Server*, published by Packt Publishing, which covers general aspects of vCenter implementation and usage.

I would like to thank my better half for all the support and patience throughout my work on this book. Truly, this book would not have been possible without you, Yelena. I admire your love and understanding.

# About the Reviewers

**Ravi Kishore Angajala** is currently working as an instructional student assistant for Virtualization Technologies while simultaneously pursing his master's in software engineering degree at San Jose State University. His main focus is on cloud and virtualization technologies.

> I would like to take this opportunity to express my gratitude to all my friends for their help and support. I would also like to thank my parents for their unceasing encouragement, support, and attention.

**Sébastien Brochet** has been working for 20 years in both software development and infrastructure positions and describes himself as half-dev/half-ops. From real-time embedded software, secure driving license, and ATM protocol to video games, electronic surveys, and healthcare, he has already lived many lives. He has a lot of experience with VMware products he leveraged with success, especially vSphere, which he has recently worked with to script basic tasks and orchestrate a full DRP using the vSphere API. He is active in the Devops community and co-organizes Devopsdays Paris 2015. He also helps start-ups develop their digital products or online services while enjoying life with his wonderful wife and two children.

**Greg Mefford** works in a leading IT infrastructure team supporting a VMware vCenter environment, among many other technologies. In his spare time, he enjoys learning new things, writing Ruby code, and playing board games.

**Ranjit Singh "RJ" ThakurRatan** is a VMware vExpert (2014 and 2015) and works as a Cloud Solutions Architect specializing in architecting Enterprise Cloud solutions. He works for Rackspace—the world leader in managed hosting and home of the fanatical support, which is based out of San Antonio, Texas.

Ranjit "RJ" Singh holds a master's degree in information technology-infrastructure assurance and an engineering degree in computer science, and he has over 10 years of hands-on IT experience. He has presented at numerous VMUG UserCon sessions, including Boston, Washington DC, New York, Denver, and Dallas. He also runs a technology blog, `www.rjapproves.com,` and can be reached via his twitter handle at @RJAPPROVES.

I would like to thank my parents, Jagat Singh and Thakur Sindhu Kumari, for making me the man I am today, and my brothers, Jagjit Singh and Manjit Singh, for being supportive all along. Lastly, thanks to my lovely dog, "Shyla Singh", who shares selfless love and has kept me going.

# www.PacktPub.com

## Support files, eBooks, discount offers, and more

For support files and downloads related to your book, please visit www.PacktPub.com.

Did you know that Packt offers eBook versions of every book published, with PDF and ePub files available? You can upgrade to the eBook version at www.PacktPub.com and as a print book customer, you are entitled to a discount on the eBook copy. Get in touch with us at service@packtpub.com for more details.

At www.PacktPub.com, you can also read a collection of free technical articles, sign up for a range of free newsletters and receive exclusive discounts and offers on Packt books and eBooks.

https://www2.packtpub.com/books/subscription/packtlib

Do you need instant solutions to your IT questions? PacktLib is Packt's online digital book library. Here, you can search, access, and read Packt's entire library of books.

## Why subscribe?

- ▸ Fully searchable across every book published by Packt
- ▸ Copy and paste, print, and bookmark content
- ▸ On demand and accessible via a web browser

## Free access for Packt account holders

If you have an account with Packt at www.PacktPub.com, you can use this to access PacktLib today and view 9 entirely free books. Simply use your login credentials for immediate access.

## Instant updates on new Packt books

Get notified! Find out when new books are published by following @PacktEnterprise on Twitter or the *Packt Enterprise* Facebook page.

# Table of Contents

# Preface

This book will become your assistant in the day-to-day administration of the VMware virtual environment with vCenter Server.

My goal was to make this book as practical as possible. Each chapter is focused on detailed steps on how to perform administrative tasks and implement solutions. The intention was to provide the minimum amount of theory, just enough to understand what a feature does and why it can be useful.

While there is no lack of literature about vCenter, this topic is quite broad and can't be completely covered in one book. The selection of advice and solutions included here has been made based on daily tasks I was challenged with during my work. So with high probability, most of these tasks will be useful for other administrators who work with vSphere and vCenter.

Also, one of the goals of this book was to make each recipe self-sufficient so that there is no need to read a bunch of other articles and tips to implement a particular feature or setting. That's why you will not be required to read each chapter from top to bottom. A reader should be able to open a particular device and implement the solution if it suits their requirements.

Easier recipes will be useful for administrators who are just starting to work with vCenter. More advanced administrators may benefit from solutions related to scripting and new features introduced in vSphere 5.

With Web Client, this became available in vSphere 5 and many administrators are just starting to learn it. As this transition is happening, I have focused my attention on both Web Client and traditional vSphere Client, unless it's a new feature that can be configured only in Web Client.

Finally, beside recipes with step-by-step instructions, there is general advice about NUMA and virtual CPUs more related to planning. The principles described here are important to keep in mind each time you create a new virtual machine.

Enjoy reading!

# What this book covers

*Chapter 1, vCenter Basic Tasks and Features*, covers some basic solutions administrators may need to implement while working with vCenter.

*Chapter 2, Increasing Environment Availability*, covers availability solutions offered by vCenter, including High Availability (HA), Fault Tolerance (FT), Admission Control, backup, and replication.

*Chapter 3, Increasing Environment Scalability*, describes vCenter features that can improve an administrator's efficiency. These features include templates, customizations, and host profiles.

*Chapter 4, Improving Environment Efficiency*, covers enhancements designed to improve an environment's efficiency.

*Chapter 5, Optimizing Resource Usage*, discovers options available to administrators to improve resource usage. These include Distributed Resource Scheduler (DRS) and Storage DRS, VM shares, limits and reservations, and network and storage I/O control.

*Chapter 6, Basic Administrative Tasks*, covers administrative tasks that allow increasing an administrator's control and visibility in the environment.

*Chapter 7, Improving Environment Manageability*, includes advice to improve an environment's manageability by utilizing tags, new commands, netdump, virtual switch backup, and PowerCLI.

# What you need for this book

All recipes in this book assume that you already have vCenter deployed and that it already has some hosts and datastores connected. You may be running vCenter with a trial license, which will work just fine if you decide to try some of the solutions described. All features and settings mentioned in this book exist in any vSphere 5 version, unless otherwise noted.

# Who this book is for

VMware vCenter Cookbook is intended for system administrators who have some experience with virtualization and already use VMware vCenter. This book will be helpful for those looking for tips or shortcuts for common administration tasks as well as work-arounds for pain points of vSphere administration.

# Sections

In this book, you will find several headings that appear frequently (Getting ready, How to do it, How it works, There's more, and See also).

To give clear instructions on how to complete a recipe, we use these sections as follows:

## Getting ready

This section tells you what to expect in the recipe, and describes how to set up any software or any preliminary settings required for the recipe.

## How to do it...

This section contains the steps required to follow the recipe.

## How it works...

This section usually consists of a detailed explanation of what happened in the previous section.

## There's more...

This section consists of additional information about the recipe in order to make the reader more knowledgeable about the recipe.

## See also

This section provides helpful links to other useful information for the recipe.

# Conventions

In this book, you will find a number of text styles that distinguish between different kinds of information. Here are some examples of these styles and an explanation of their meaning.

Code words in text, database table names, folder names, filenames, file extensions, pathnames, dummy URLs, user input, and Twitter handles are shown as follows: "Locate the image profile using the `Get-EsxImageProfile` cmdlet."

Any command-line input or output is written as follows:

```
$targetHost = "esxi6"
New-VM -vmhost $targetHost ...
```

**New terms** and **important words** are shown in bold. Words that you see on the screen, for example, in menus or dialog boxes, appear in the text like this: " To do that, close the current dialog and click on **Enable VM Storage policies per compute resource** icon, select a cluster from the list, and click on **Enable**."

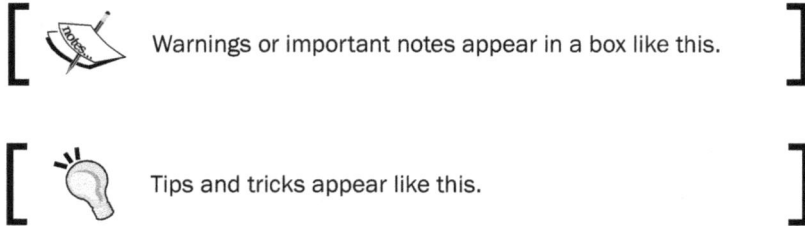

[ Warnings or important notes appear in a box like this. ]

[ Tips and tricks appear like this. ]

# Reader feedback

Feedback from our readers is always welcome. Let us know what you think about this book—what you liked or disliked. Reader feedback is important for us as it helps us develop titles that you will really get the most out of.

To send us general feedback, simply e-mail feedback@packtpub.com, and mention the book's title in the subject of your message.

If there is a topic that you have expertise in and you are interested in either writing or contributing to a book, see our author guide at www.packtpub.com/authors.

# Customer support

Now that you are the proud owner of a Packt book, we have a number of things to help you to get the most from your purchase.

## Downloading the color images of this book

We also provide you with a PDF file that has color images of the screenshots/diagrams used in this book. The color images will help you better understand the changes in the output. You can download this file from https://www.packtpub.com/sites/default/files/downloads/3976EN_ColoredImages.pdf..

## Errata

Although we have taken every care to ensure the accuracy of our content, mistakes do happen. If you find a mistake in one of our books—maybe a mistake in the text or the code—we would be grateful if you could report this to us. By doing so, you can save other readers from frustration and help us improve subsequent versions of this book. If you find any errata, please report them by visiting http://www.packtpub.com/submit-errata, selecting your book, clicking on the **Errata Submission Form** link, and entering the details of your errata. Once your errata are verified, your submission will be accepted and the errata will be uploaded to our website or added to any list of existing errata under the Errata section of that title.

To view the previously submitted errata, go to https://www.packtpub.com/books/content/support and enter the name of the book in the search field. The required information will appear under the **Errata** section.

## Piracy

Piracy of copyrighted material on the Internet is an ongoing problem across all media. At Packt, we take the protection of our copyright and licenses very seriously. If you come across any illegal copies of our works in any form on the Internet, please provide us with the location address or website name immediately so that we can pursue a remedy.

Please contact us at copyright@packtpub.com with a link to the suspected pirated material.

We appreciate your help in protecting our authors and our ability to bring you valuable content.

## Questions

If you have a problem with any aspect of this book, you can contact us at questions@packtpub.com, and we will do our best to address the problem.

# 1
# vCenter Basic Tasks and Features

In this chapter, we will cover the follow recipes:

- ▸ Choosing the right vSphere and vCenter edition
- ▸ Booting a VM from a virtual CD-ROM
- ▸ Using hosts with different CPUs in one cluster
- ▸ Fixing VMware tools to autostart after Linux updates
- ▸ Running vCenter on a VM
- ▸ Managing several vCenter Servers from one client
- ▸ Accessing new vCenter features
- ▸ Accessing hosts via SSH
- ▸ Securing host management access
- ▸ Storing host logs on a shared datastore
- ▸ Configuring remote logging

## Introduction

This chapter covers some basic tasks and features administrators may need to use while working with vCenter. Most of the tips and advices in this chapter as well as in this book assume that you already have vCenter deployed and that it already has some hosts and datastores connected. You may be running vCenter with a trial license, which will work just fine if you decide to try some of the how-tos in this chapter. All features and settings described in this chapter exist in any vSphere 5 version unless otherwise noted.

# Choosing the right vSphere and vCenter editions

The vCenter edition required for a particular environment is very much determined by the vSphere edition in use. The vSphere edition in turn is chosen based on the size of the environment and features that will be used.

## How to do it...

To choose the vCenter edition that's right for your environment you need to:

1. Determine the vSphere features required.
2. Choose the vSphere edition based on environment size, features required, and growth expected.
3. Select the vCenter edition if it's not included in the chosen vSphere edition.

### vSphere editions

A vSphere license can be bought as part of a kit or separately. Kits include a vCenter license while other vSphere editions require a separate vCenter license. When choosing a vSphere edition, it may be a good idea to take a look at its kits first. An included vCenter license will save costs. If you determine that none of the available kits include the required features and capacity, select one of the separate vSphere editions.

The following table compares five main kits available and shows the features that are included in each kit:

| Features | Essentials kits | | Operations management kits (vSOM) | | |
|---|---|---|---|---|---|
| | Essentials | Essentials Plus | Standard | Enterprise | Enterprise Plus |
| Physical CPUs included | 6 | 6 | 6 | 6 | 6 |
| Hypervisor | + | + | + | + | + |
| vMotion | | + | + | + | + |
| High Availability (HA) | | + | + | + | + |
| Data Protection (DP) | | + | + | + | + |
| vSphere Replication (VR) | | + | + | + | + |
| Operations monitoring, optimization and visibility | | | + | + | + |
| Fault Tolerance (FT) | | | + | + | + |

| Features | Essentials kits | | Operations management kits (vSOM) | | |
|---|---|---|---|---|---|
| | **Essentials** | **Essentials Plus** | **Standard** | **Enterprise** | **Enterprise Plus** |
| Storage vMotion | | | + | + | + |
| Distributed Resource Scheduler (DRS) | | | | + | + |
| Distributed Power Management (DPM) | | | | + | + |
| Storage DRS | | | | | + |
| Distributed switch | | | | | + |
| Flash Read Cache | | | | | + |

Kit editions are meant for smaller environments and have their limitations. Six processors included determine that the environment cannot be larger than three servers with two physical processors each. As a result, if there is a plan to grow the environment in the near future, choose one of the separate vSphere editions.

The following table shows the available vSphere editions and features included:

| Features | Standard | Enterprise | Enterprise Plus | Standard with vSOM | Enterprise with vSOM | Enterprise Plus with vSOM |
|---|---|---|---|---|---|---|
| Physical CPUs included (per-CPU license entitlement) | 1 | 1 | 1 | | | |
| Hypervisor (basic virtualization capabilities) | + | + | + | | | |
| Operations monitoring, optimization and visibility | | | | + | + | + |
| vMotion | + | + | + | + | + | + |
| High Availability (HA) | + | + | + | + | + | + |

| Features | Standard | Enterprise | Enterprise Plus | Standard with vSOM | Enterprise with vSOM | Enterprise Plus with vSOM |
|---|---|---|---|---|---|---|
| Data Protection (DP) | + | + | + | + | + | + |
| vSphere Replication (VR) | + | + | + | + | + | + |
| Fault Tolerance (FT) | + | + | + | + | + | + |
| Storage vMotion | + | + | + | + | + | + |
| Distributed Resource Scheduler (DRS) | | + | + | | + | + |
| Distributed Power Management (DPM) | | + | + | | + | + |
| Storage DRS | | | + | | | + |
| Distributed switch | | | + | | | + |
| Flash Read Cache | | | + | | | + |

Remember that vSphere 5 is licensed per physical CPU. For instance, two physical servers with two CPUs each will require four vSphere 5 CPU licenses. If DRS is a requirement, four Enterprise licenses will be needed. To take advantage of the Storage DRS, you will need four Enterprise Plus licenses in this case.

Both the preceding tables include only the main features we believe are necessary to make a decision. A full feature comparison can be found on the Compare VMware vSphere Editions page at `http://www.vmware.com/products/vsphere/compare`.

Additional information on the existing features and editions as well as upgrade paths from vSphere 4 can be found at the following link: `http://www.vmware.com/files/pdf/vsphere_pricing.pdf`

# vCenter editions

Each of the following vSphere kit editions includes one instance of vCenter:

- ▸ Essentials
- ▸ Essentials Plus
- ▸ vSOM Standard
- ▸ vSOM Enterprise
- ▸ vSOM Enterprise Plus

Other vSphere editions do not include a vCenter license, and if a separate vSphere edition has been chosen, there are two options for the vCenter edition:

- ▸ vCenter Server Foundation
- ▸ vCenter Server Standard

It is important to know that according to the End User License Agreement, customers licensed under Essentials or Essentials Plus are not allowed to purchase any other vCenter addition. If you need to manage more hosts, then the solution is to upgrade the existing license to vSphere Standard or above and purchase vCenter Standard.

The following table compares vCenter editions:

| Feature | Essentials (part of Essentials or Essentials Plus kit) | Foundation | Standard |
|---|---|---|---|
| Maximum number of hosts that can be managed | 3 | 3 | 1,000 |
| Management service | + | + | + |
| Database server | + | + | + |
| Inventory service | + | + | + |
| vSphere Clients | + | + | + |
| vCenter APIs | + | + | + |
| Single Sign-On | + | + | + |
| vCenter Orchestrator | | | + |
| Linked Mode | | | + |

## There's more...

There is also an option to purchase a support plan from VMware along with the software. The two available options include:

▶ **Basic**: Provides support during business hours

▶ **Production**: Provides 24 x 7 support

The production support plan is recommended for critical environments. Both plans include an unlimited number of support cases. Any of the preceding subscriptions are required for at least one year.

VMware also offers an option for per incident support, which can be purchased in 1, 3, or 5-incident packs. This option is available for vSphere Essentials kit only.

# Booting a VM from a virtual CD-ROM

If a VM has just been created and you are trying to install the operating system from a virtual CD-ROM, you can turn the VM on, connect the ISO image to the operating system, and reboot the VM. It will start booting from the CD-ROM right away.

If the operating system has already been installed and you need to boot this VM from the CD-ROM, it may be challenging, as the option to press *Esc* for **Boot Menu** is displayed for a very short period of time:

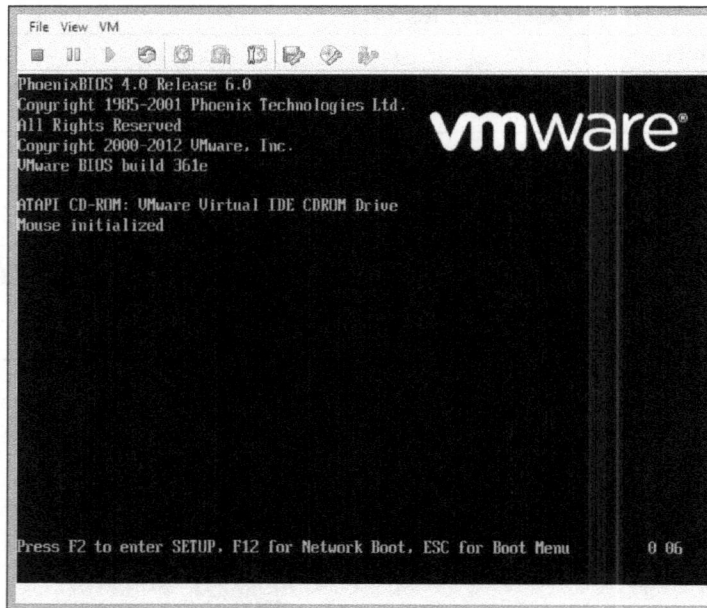

## How to do it...

To increase the time for which this option is displayed so that you can press *Esc*, you'll need to change the **Power On Boot Delay** value. To do that, perform the following steps:

1. Go to **VM Settings** | **Options** | **Boot Options**.

2. Select the **Power On Boot Delay** option.

3. Set the value to 3,000 so that the VM waits for 3 seconds for Esc.

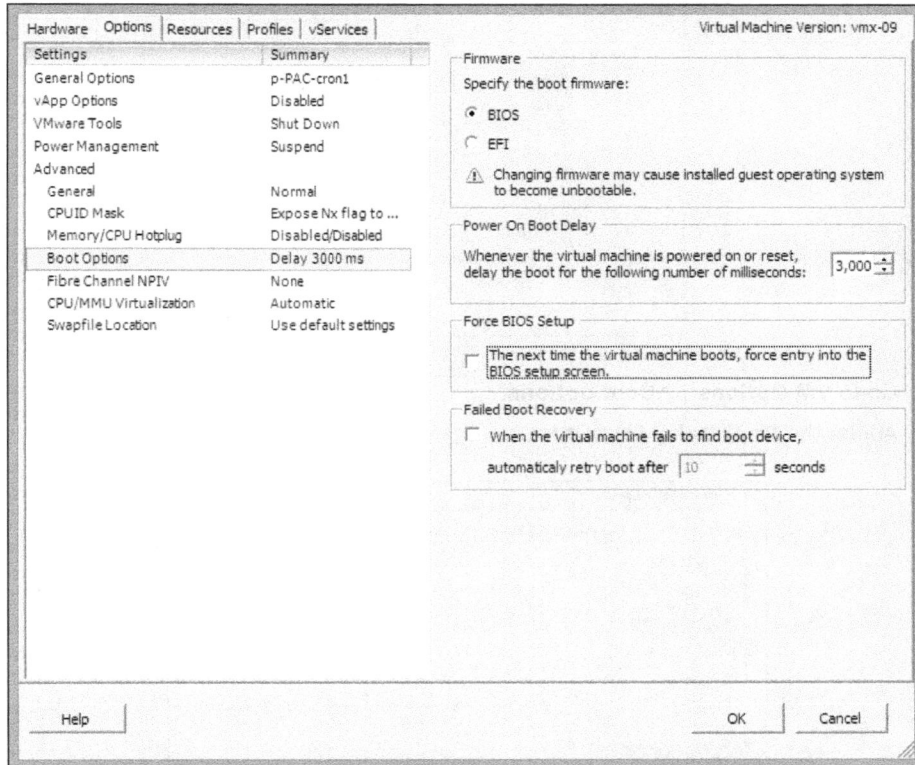

| Hardware | Options | Resources | Profiles | vServices | | Virtual Machine Version: vmx-09 |

| Settings | Summary |
| --- | --- |
| General Options | p-PAC-cron1 |
| vApp Options | Disabled |
| VMware Tools | Shut Down |
| Power Management | Suspend |
| Advanced | |
| General | Normal |
| CPUID Mask | Expose Nx flag to ... |
| Memory/CPU Hotplug | Disabled/Disabled |
| Boot Options | Delay 3000 ms |
| Fibre Channel NPIV | None |
| CPU/MMU Virtualization | Automatic |
| Swapfile Location | Use default settings |

Firmware

Specify the boot firmware:

- BIOS
- EFI

⚠ Changing firmware may cause installed guest operating system to become unbootable.

Power On Boot Delay

Whenever the virtual machine is powered on or reset, delay the boot for the following number of milliseconds: `3,000`

Force BIOS Setup

☐ The next time the virtual machine boots, force entry into the BIOS setup screen.

Failed Boot Recovery

☐ When the virtual machine fails to find boot device, automatically retry boot after `10` seconds

| Help | | OK | Cancel |

4. The location of this setting in vCenter Web Client is similar:

   ❑ Right-click on a VM

❑   Go to **Edit Settings...**

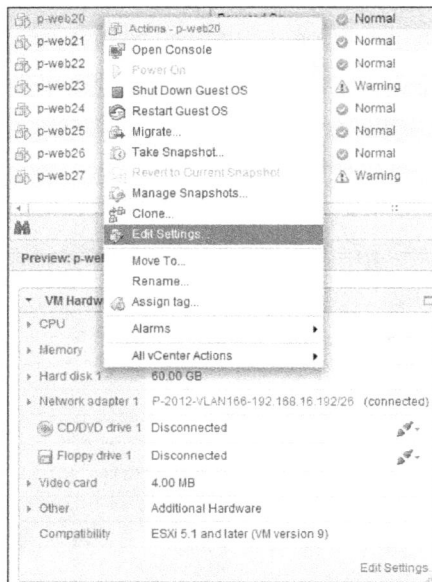

5.   Go to **VM Options | *Boot options**.

6.   Adjust the **Boot Delay (*)** setting.

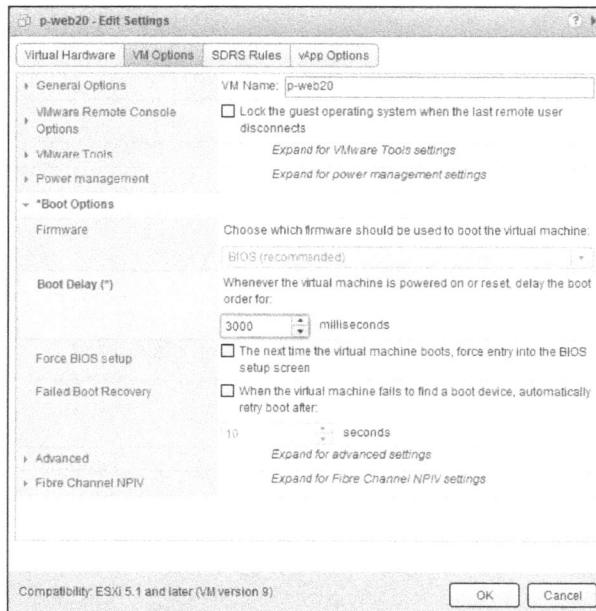

## How it works...

Once *Esc* has been pressed, you'll get the **Boot Menu** options to choose from. Connect the ISO image, host or local CD-ROM in **VM Settings**, and choose **CD-ROM drive** from the **Boot Menu**:

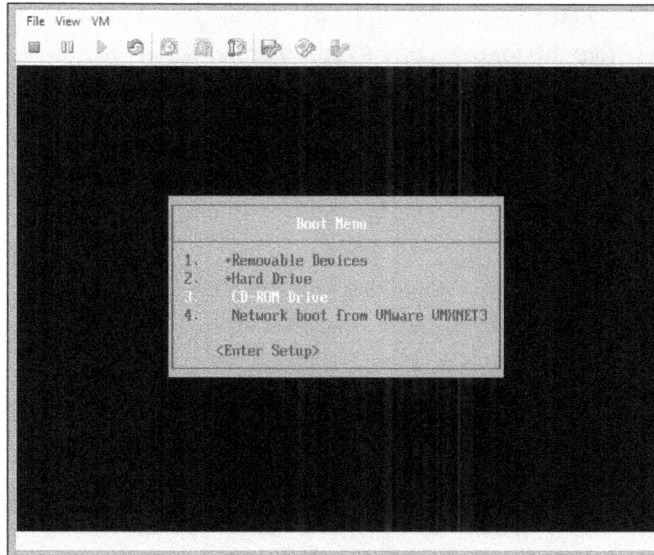

# Using hosts with different CPUs in one cluster

One of the core vSphere features is vMotion. It allows administrators to move a running virtual machine from one host to another without interruption.

Unfortunately, one of the requirements for vMotion is to use hosts with the same processors so that the virtual machine that has been moved can keep running on a new host. This is due to the fact that newer processors, even within the same family, typically have additional features. New generations of processors can also have a different set of instructions. When features or instructions an application is using are not available, the application will crash.

Clusters consisting of hosts with different CPU generations can use **Enhanced vMotion Compatibility** (**EVC**) mode. In this mode, vCenter hides CPU features and instructions that are not available on older hosts. This way, it makes all hosts' CPUs in the cluster look like they are the same.

The obvious downside of using this feature is that the cluster's processors will all be the same or lower than the oldest host's CPU.

## Getting ready

Things to consider before enabling the feature are as follows:

- ▶ All hosts must have either Intel or AMD processors.
- ▶ All cluster VMs running on hosts where EVC mode will be enabled must be shut down before the feature can be turned on.

## How to do it...

To enable EVC:

1. Switch to the **Hosts and Clusters** view.

2. Right-click on your cluster and choose **Edit Settings**.

3. Go to **VMware EVC** and click on **Change EVC Mode**.

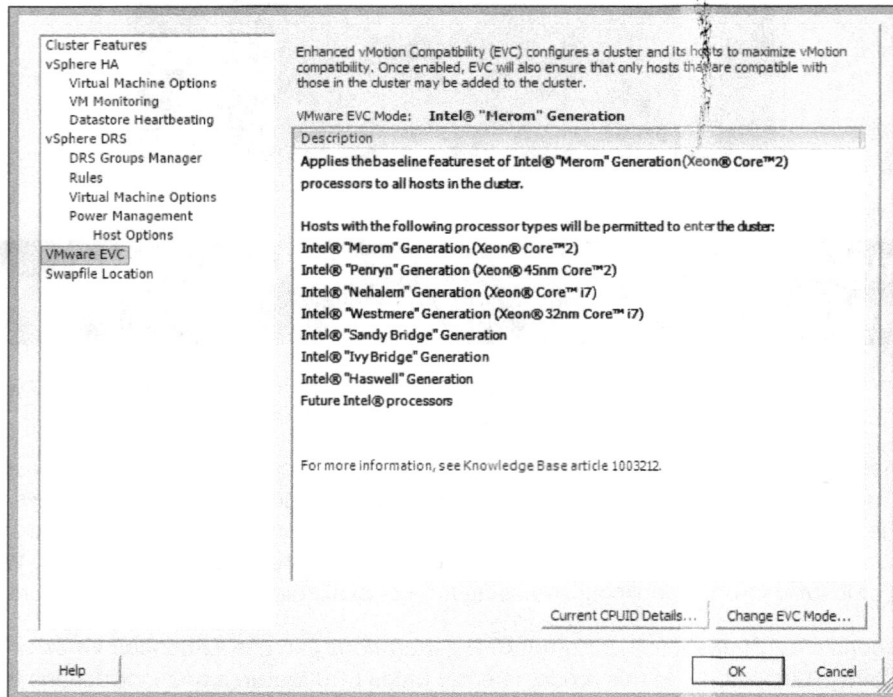

4. Choose `AMD` or `Intel` depending on the host's CPU.

5. Choose the best available option for processor generation.

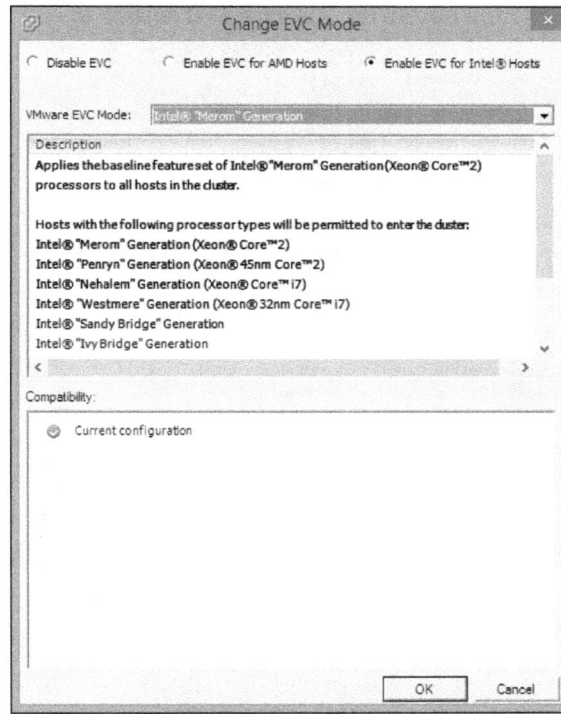

6. In vCenter Web Client, this setting can be found by going to **vCenter** | **Cluster** | **Manage** | **Settings** | **VMware EVC**:

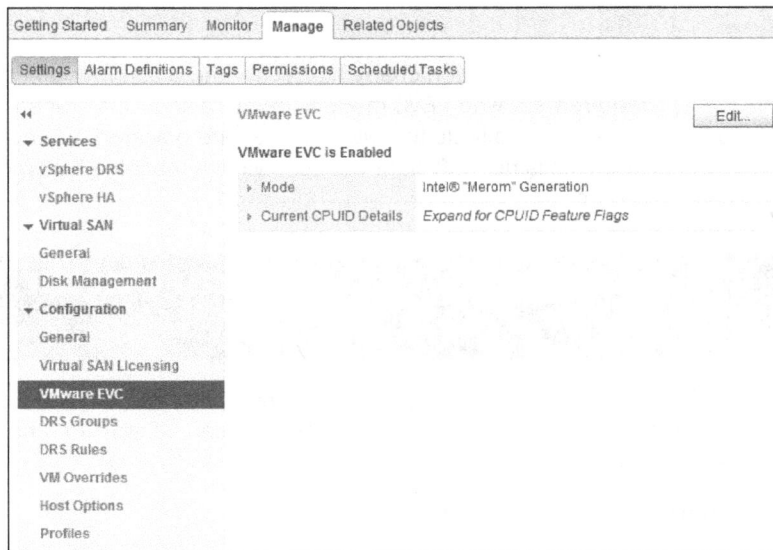

7.  Press the **Edit...** button next to the **VMware EVC** section to change EVC mode:

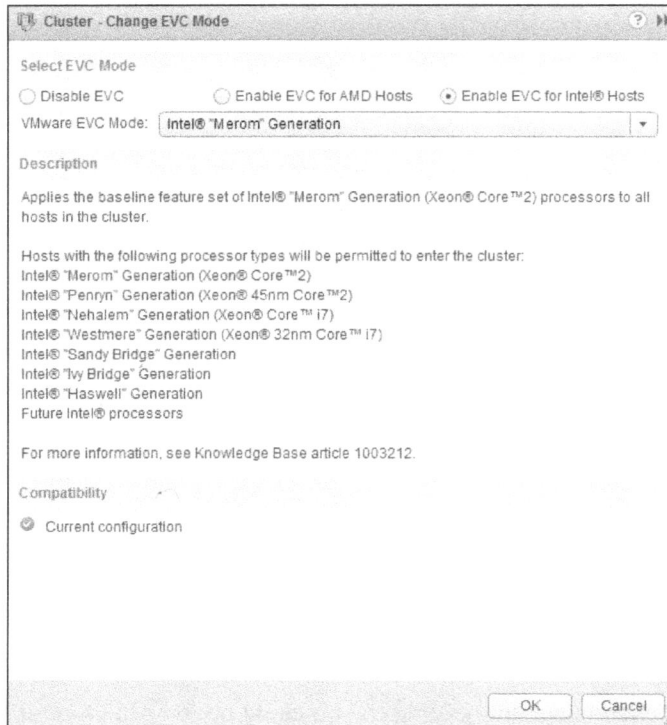

## There's more...

Virtual machines always have to be off when changing EVC mode to an older processor generation. This is not a requirement when EVC mode is being raised. Unfortunately, in this case, new CPU features will not be available to VMs until they are powered off and back on. Suspending or restarting VMs is not sufficient because virtual machine EVC mode is determined when it's turned on.

# Fixing VMware tools to autostart after Linux updates

From time to time, VMware tools that have been working fine before refuse to start automatically when the Linux guest is rebooted. VMware tools can be started manually using the following command:

```
# /etc/vmware-tools/services.sh start
```

> The preceding command and other commands in this book assume RHEL or CentOS and can be different for Debian or other Linux distributions.

The following error message may be displayed:

```
Checking acpi hot plug                                    [  OK  ]
Starting VMware Tools services in the virtual machine:
    Switching to guest configuration:                     [  OK  ]
    VM communication interface:                           [FAILED]
    VM communication interface socket family:             [FAILED]
    Guest operating system daemon:                        [  OK  ]
```

In most cases, this issue is related to recent OS updates; in particular, the Linux kernel update, which breaks the existing VMware tools installation.

As servers are not rebooted often, it may be hard to correlate the issue of VMware tools not starting automatically and OS updates.

## How to do it...

To fix the issue, simply reinstall VMware tools the same way they were installed the first time. The following commands have been tested on CentOS 5 and depending on the Linux distribution, the commands you use and their sequence may be different.

1.  Initiate the VMware tools installation by going to **VM** menu and then navigating to **Guest | Install/Upgrade VMware Tools**:

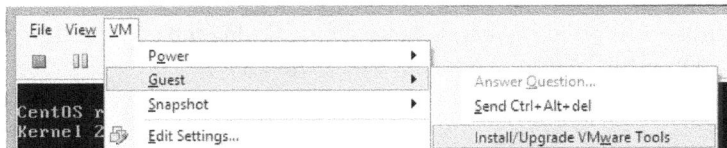

2.  For Linux guest, the **Automatic** option will not be available. Click on **OK**.

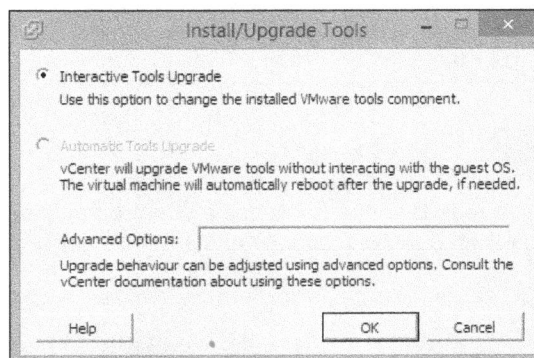

3. The VMware tools ISO image from the ESXi host will be connected to the virtual CD-ROM of the VM.

4. Mount the image as follows:

```
# mount /dev/cdrom /mnt/cdrom
```

5. Extract the archive with VMware tool's installation files:

```
# tar xzvf /mnt/cdrom/VMwareTools-<x.x.x-xxxx>.tar.gz -C /tmp/
```

6. Start the installation. Switch –d is for the unattended installation with default settings:

```
# cd /tmp/vmware-tools-distrib/
# ./vmware-install.pl -d
```

7. Reboot the virtual machine. VMware tools should start automatically as soon as the guest OS is back up:

```
# shutdown -r now0
```

## There's more...

Additional details about the issue can be found in the VMware KB 2050592 article on the VMware Knowledge Base website at `http://kb.vmware.com/kb/2050592`.

# Running vCenter on a VM

Administrators have three options when it comes to deploying the vCenter Server. vCenter can be imported as a Linux-based virtual appliance or it can be installed on a physical or virtual Windows Server.

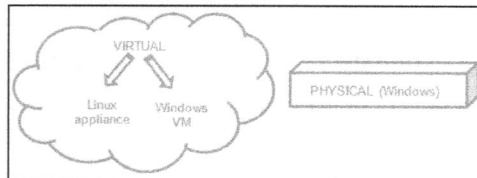

## How to do it...

For smaller environments, it makes sense to choose a vCenter appliance. Its installation and configuration is easier than deploying your own vCenter Server:

1. Download the vCenter Server Appliance from `my.vmware.com`.

2. Deploy the appliance from a template using the **Deploy OVF Template...** option from the **File** menu.

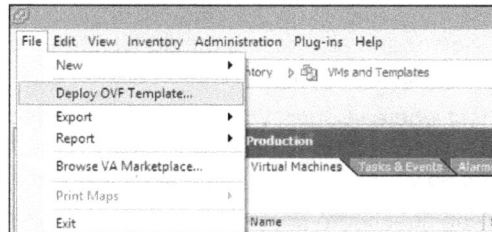

File | Edit | View | Inventory | Administration | Plug-ins | Help
- New
- Deploy OVF Template...
- Export
- Report
- Browse VA Marketplace...
- Print Maps
- Exit

3. Open your web browser and go to `http://<ip address of virtual appliance>:5480`.

4. Log in using the default credentials to configure vCenter:

   ❑ Username: `root`

   ❑ Password: `vmware`

5. After logging in, go through the steps of the configuration wizard to start using the appliance.

## There's more...

vCenter Appliance has its limitations. First of all, if an embedded database is used, this server will be able to manage only up to five hosts and up to 50 virtual machines. In vSphere 5.5, this limit has been increased to 100 hosts and 3,000 virtual machines.

Also, this solution doesn't support the Linked Mode configuration. More information about the supported services and limitations can be found in the Knowledge Base article KB2002531 at `http://kb.vmware.com/kb/2002531`.

### vCenter Server on a VM

Running the vCenter Server on a virtual machine offers all virtualization advantages:

- No additional hardware is needed, which means savings and flexibility.
- Administrators can take advantage of using high availability features offered by vSphere—HA or FT.
- vMotion offers additional flexibility and higher uptime.
- Snapshots can be utilized as a rollback option.

Virtual machines are easier to manage but at the same time, there are a few concerns related to this approach:

1. The main concern is that issues with the vSphere environment potentially can affect the vCenter Server and as a result, the administrator's ability to manage the environment and troubleshoot issues.

   For example, if a host where vCenter VM is running becomes unavailable, vCenter is not accessible until it's restarted and comes back online. In certain cases, HA fails to restart some VMs so vCenter may become unavailable for a longer time.

   The administrator can connect to hosts directly using the vSphere Client but in this case, the core features offered by vCenter will not be available.

2. Another concern is related to environments that have only one host. Certain tasks such as ESXi updates require host maintenance mode, which means that all VMs need to be turned off. In this case, the vCenter Server has to be shut down and thus, Update Manager can't be used.

   Updating ESXi from the command line can be more time consuming and challenging in certain cases. In other words, running the vCenter Server on a VM in environments with only one ESXi host can introduce some administrative difficulties.

> In general, a single ESXi host with vCenter Server VM is not a recommended design option for the enterprise environment.

# Managing several vCenter Servers from one client

There is a way to manage more than one vCenter Server from the same vCenter client. This is accomplished by using **Linked Mode groups**. Linked Mode group is a group of vCenter Servers that allows managing other members by connecting to any one of them.

## Getting ready

This feature is available only in vCenter Server Standard edition and cannot be used with **vCenter Server Appliance (vCSA)**.

The main requirement is that all group members must run the same version of vCenter. Other requirements are as follows:

▶ Members must belong to the same Active Directory domain or different domains that have two-way trust relationships with each other.

▶ DNS has to be operational for Linked Mode groups to work properly.

▶ vCenter must be licensed or in evaluation mode.

▶ The domain account is the local administrator on both vCenter Servers—the one that is being joined to the group and the target server.

## How to do it...

To be able to manage additional vCenter Servers, they need to be joined to the Linked Mode group.

### Joining vCenter to a group

The vCenter Server can be joined to a group either during installation or any time after. The Linked Mode group is created when the first member is being joined to a group that doesn't exist.

To join the running vCenter Server to the existing Linked Mode group, follow the ensuing steps:

1. On the vCenter Server, go to **Start | All Programs | VMware**.

2. Run **vCenter Server Linked Mode Configuration**.

3. Select **Modify linked mode configuration**.

4. Click on **Join this vCenter server instance to an existing linked mode group or another instance**.

5. Click on **Next**.

6. Enter the FQDN of an existing member and LDAP port.

7. In case role conflict has been detected, choose a way to resolve it. You can either let vCenter rename the group or you can rename it yourself.

8. Restart the vCenter Server.

If a member that is being joined to the Linked Mode group is running an older version of vCenter than other members of the group it has to be upgraded. Also, if vCenter on a member is upgraded, it will be disconnected from the group.

### Removing vCenter from a group

To remove vCenter from a Linked Mode group, execute the following steps:

1. On the vCenter Server, go to **Start | All Programs | VMware**.

2. Run **vCenter Server Linked Mode Configuration**.

3. Choose **Modify linked mode configuration**.

4. Select **Isolate this vCenter server instance from linked mode group** and click on **Next**.

5. Click on **Continue** and then on **Finish**.

6. Reboot the vCenter Server.

## Accessing new vCenter features

vSphere 5 introduced a new web client, which can be used to manage the environment along with the traditional vSphere Client we used before.

**vCenter Web Client** is just another way to access the environment using a web browser. Three major browsers—Internet Explorer, Firefox, and Chrome—are supported.

Web Client becomes the main administrative interface starting with vSphere 5.1 and while vSphere Client can still be used, a lot of new features introduced in vSphere 5 are available only through Web Client.

Some of these new features are:

- Datastore cluster and Storage DRS
- vSphere Replication
- vSphere Data Protection
- Enhanced vMotion
- Drag-and-drop actions as well as bulk operations for vSphere objects

## How to do it...

1. To access your vSphere environment using Web Client, open your web browser and point it to `https://<vCenter Server IP address>:9443/vsphere-client`.

2. On the VMware vSphere welcome page, click on the **Log in to vSphere Web Client** link.

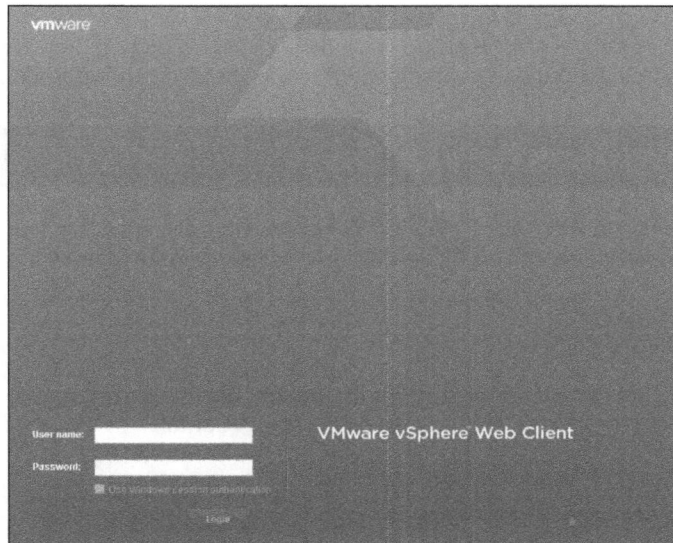

3. From this page, you will be able to log in to vCenter using the same credentials that work for older clients.

## There's more...

Take a look at the following error message:

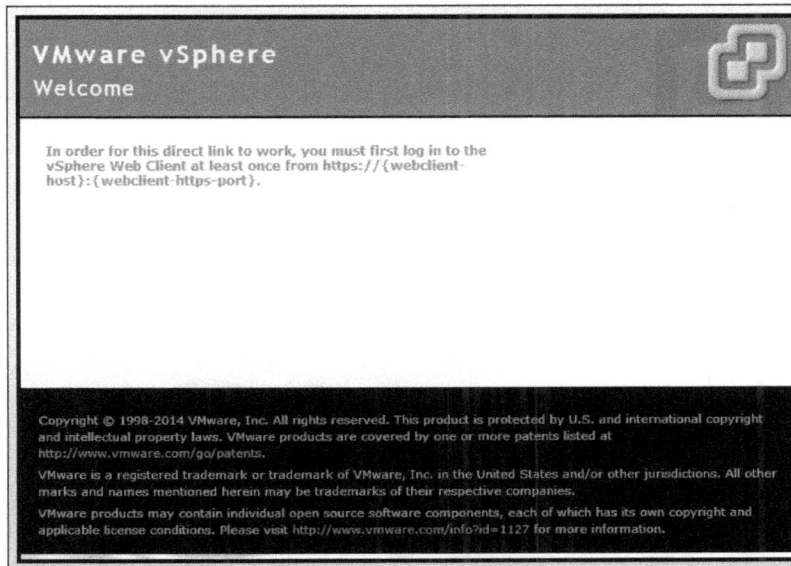

If the preceding error message is displayed, add port 9443 after the vCenter Server address or name in the URL: `https://<vcenter-server>:9443/vsphere-client/`. This will take you to the same login page, assuming vCenter was installed with default port settings.

# Accessing hosts via SSH

In certain cases, you may need to access the ESXi host via SSH. This may be needed to run a script, troubleshoot an issue, or use a command or a feature not available via vSphere Client.

## How to do it...

SSH access to ESXi hosts is disabled by default and can be enabled using the ESXi console and command line or through vCenter. To enable it from vCenter:

1. Allow SSH port through the host's firewall.
2. Start the SSH service on the host.

### Opening the SSH port on the firewall

To allow the SSH port through the firewall on the ESXi host, execute the following steps:

1. Go to the **Hosts and Clusters** view.
2. Select the host and go to the **Configuration** tab.
3. Click on **Security Profile** on the left.

4. Click on the **Properties...** link next to the **Firewall** section.

**Hardware**

- Processors
- Memory
- Storage
- Networking
- Storage Adapters
- Network Adapters
- Advanced Settings
- Power Management

**Software**

- Licensed Features
- Time Configuration
- DNS and Routing
- Authentication Services
- Power Management
- Virtual Machine Startup/Shutdown
- Virtual Machine Swapfile Location
- ▸ Security Profile
- Host Cache Configuration
- System Resource Allocation
- Agent VM Settings
- Advanced Settings

**Security Profile**

**Services**                                                    Refresh    Properties...

I/O Redirector (Active Directory Service)
snmpd
Network Login Server (Active Directory Service)
lbtd
vSphere High Availability Agent
vpxa
ESXi Shell
xorg
Local Security Authentication Server (Active Directory Service)
NTP Daemon
vprobed
SSH
Direct Console UI
CIM Server

**Firewall**                                                    Refresh    Properties...

Incoming Connections

| | | |
|---|---|---|
| CIM Secure Server | 5989 (TCP) | All |
| SSH Server | 22 (TCP) | All |
| CIM Server | 5988 (TCP) | All |
| DHCP Client | 68 (UDP) | All |
| NFC | 902 (TCP) | All |
| vSphere Web Access | 80 (TCP) | All |
| vMotion | 8000 (TCP) | All |
| vSphere High Availability Agent | 8182 (TCP,UDP) | All |
| DNS Client | 53 (UDP) | All |
| Fault Tolerance | 8100,8200,8300 (TCP,UDP) | All |
| SNMP Server | 161 (UDP) | All |
| vSphere Client | 902,443 (TCP) | All |
| CIM SLP | 427 (UDP,TCP) | All |

Outgoing Connections

| | | |
|---|---|---|
| Software iSCSI Client | 3260 (TCP) | All |
| NTP Client | 123 (UDP) | All |
| WOL | 9 (UDP) | All |
| HBR | 31031,44046 (TCP) | All |
| DHCP Client | 68 (UDP) | All |
| NFC | 902 (TCP) | All |
| vMotion | 8000 (TCP) | All |
| vSphere High Availability Agent | 8182 (TCP,UDP) | All |
| DNS Client | 53 (UDP,TCP) | All |
| Fault Tolerance | 80,8100,8200,8300 (TCP,UDP) | All |
| VMware vCenter Agent | 902 (UDP) | All |
| CIM SLP | 427 (UDP,TCP) | All |

5. The Firewall Properties window will open. Check **SSH Server** under the **Secure Shell** section.

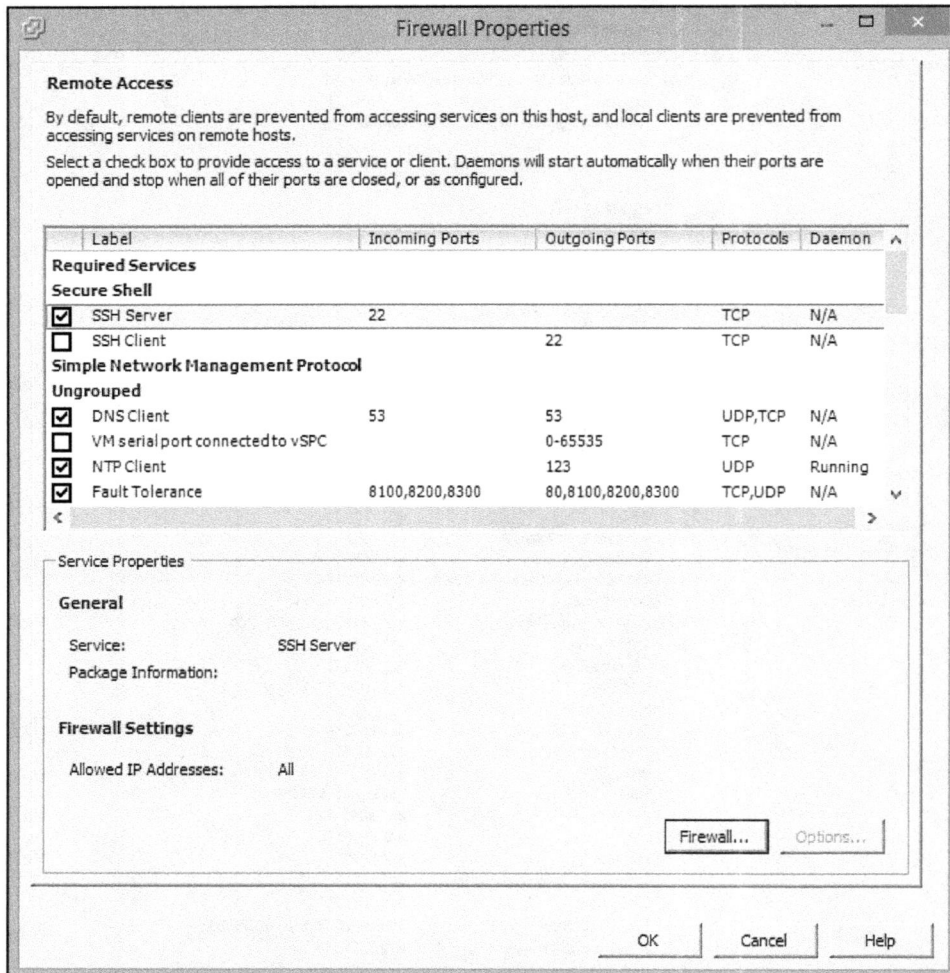

**Firewall Properties**

**Remote Access**

By default, remote clients are prevented from accessing services on this host, and local clients are prevented from accessing services on remote hosts.

Select a check box to provide access to a service or client. Daemons will start automatically when their ports are opened and stop when all of their ports are closed, or as configured.

| Label | Incoming Ports | Outgoing Ports | Protocols | Daemon |
|---|---|---|---|---|
| **Required Services** | | | | |
| **Secure Shell** | | | | |
| ☑ SSH Server | 22 | | TCP | N/A |
| ☐ SSH Client | | 22 | TCP | N/A |
| **Simple Network Management Protocol** | | | | |
| **Ungrouped** | | | | |
| ☑ DNS Client | 53 | 53 | UDP,TCP | N/A |
| ☐ VM serial port connected to vSPC | | 0-65535 | TCP | N/A |
| ☑ NTP Client | | 123 | UDP | Running |
| ☑ Fault Tolerance | 8100,8200,8300 | 80,8100,8200,8300 | TCP,UDP | N/A |

**Service Properties**

**General**

Service:          SSH Server

Package Information:

**Firewall Settings**

Allowed IP Addresses:     All

Firewall...     Options...

OK          Cancel          Help

6. Click on the **Firewall** button to allow only certain IP addresses to connect. Click on **OK** when finished to apply the changes.

In Web Client, perform the following steps:

1. Select a host.

2. Go to **Manage | Settings | Security Profile**.

3. Click on the **Edit...** button next to the **Firewall** section.

4. Select the **SSH Server** option and click on **OK** as shown in the next screenshot.

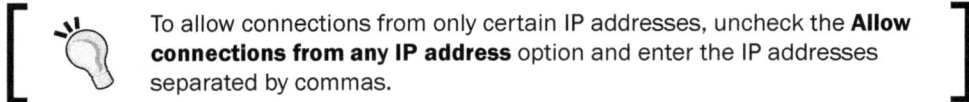

> To allow connections from only certain IP addresses, uncheck the **Allow connections from any IP address** option and enter the IP addresses separated by commas.

| Name | Incoming Ports | Outgoing Ports | Protocols | Daemon |
|---|---|---|---|---|
| p-esxi1: Edit Security Profile | | | | |

To provide access to a service or client, check the corresponding box.
By default, daemons will start automatically when any of their ports are opened, and stop when all of their ports are closed.

| Name | Incoming Ports | Outgoing Ports | Protocols | Daemon |
|---|---|---|---|---|
| Required Services | | | | |
| Secure Shell | | | | |
| ☐ SSH Client | | 22 | TCP | N/A |
| ☑ SSH Server | 22 | | TCP | N/A |
| Simple Network Man... | | | | |
| Ungrouped | | | | |

| | |
|---|---|
| ▾ Service Details | N/A |
| Status | N/A |
| ▾ Allowed IP Addresses | Allow connections from any IP address |
| IP Addresses | ☑ Allow connections from any IP address |

Enter a comma-separated list of IP addresses. E.g.: 111.111.111.111, 111.111.111/222

OK    Cancel

## Starting an SSH service

To start an SSH service on the host from the same place under **Configuration | Security Profile**:

1. Click on the **Properties...** link next to the **Services** section.

2. Select **SSH** in the list of services and click on **Options...**.

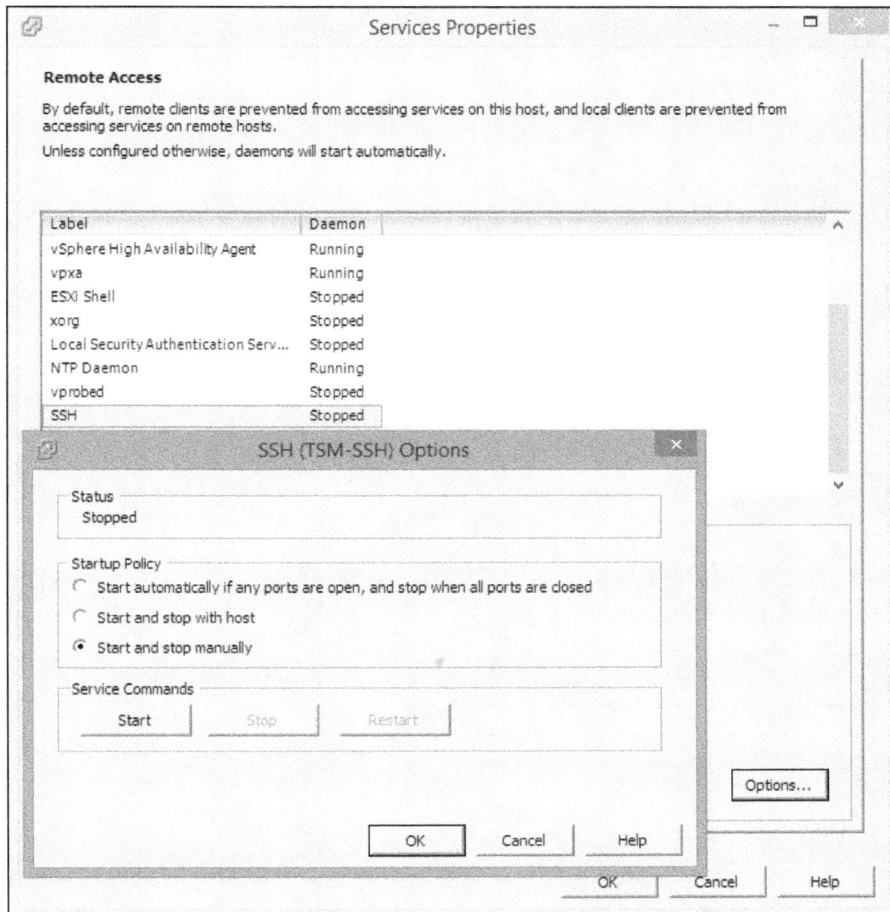

3. Click on the **Start** button.
4. Once the service starts, both windows can be closed.

From Web Client, perform the following steps:

1. Select a host.
2. Go to **Manage | Settings | Security Profile**.

3. Scroll down to the **Services** section.

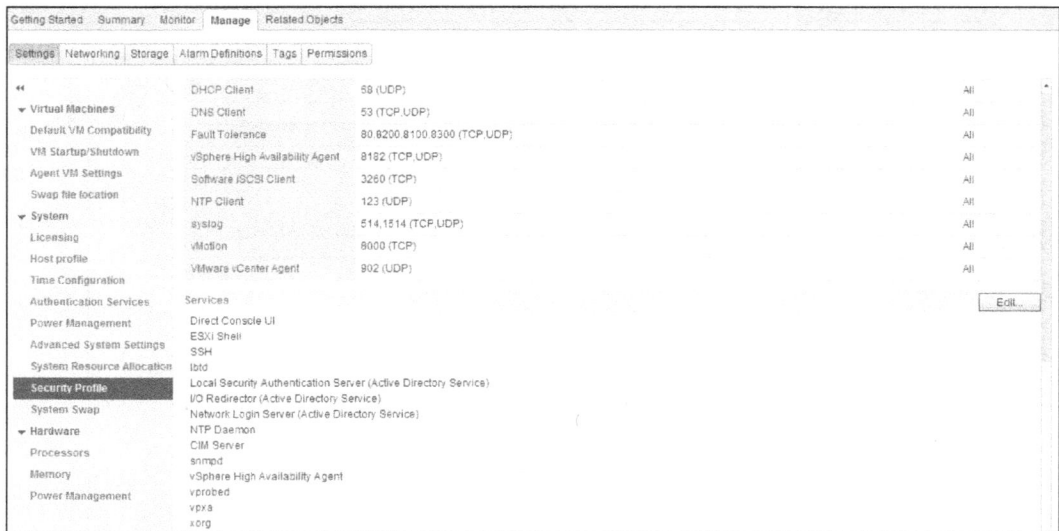

4. Click on the **Edit** button.
5. Select **SSH** from the list.
6. Click on **Start**.

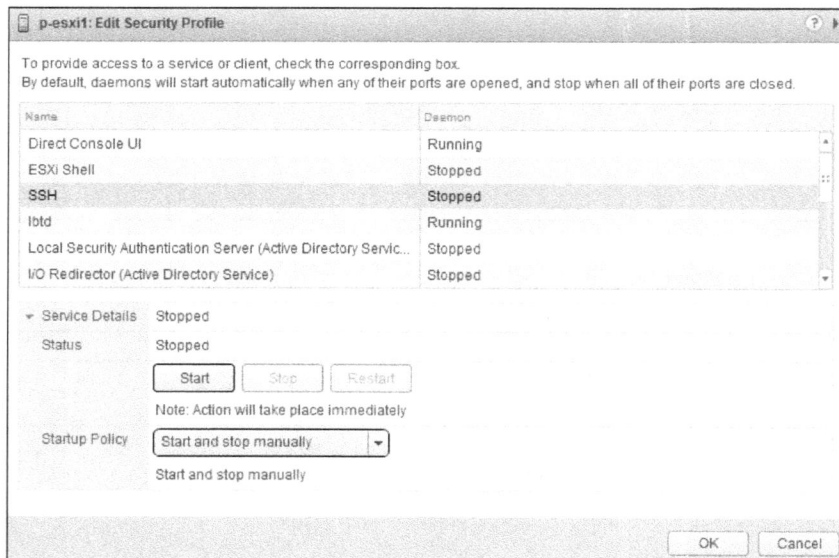

## There's more...

Now you will be able to access the ESXi command line using the SSH client.

> Note that when SSH service is running on the host, vCenter marks it with a yellow exclamation mark as it is a configuration issue. Enabling SSH is considered to be an insecure practice.

| p-esxi1 | | | | |
|---|---|---|---|---|
| p-esxi2 | **Configuration Issues** | | | |
| p-esxi3 | SSH for the host has been enabled | | | |
| p-esxi4 | | | | |
| p-esxi5 | **General** | | **Resources** | |
| p-esxi6 | | | | |
| Custom | Manufacturer: | Dell Inc. | CPU usage: **4819 MHz** | Capacity |
| High CF | Model: | PowerEdge 1950 | | 8 x 2.826 GHz |
| High M | CPU Cores: | 8 CPUs x 2.826 GHz | Memory usage: **20225.00 MB** | Capacity |
| Low CP | Processor Type: | Intel(R) Xeon(R) CPU | | 32762.87 MB |
| Normal | | E5440 @ 2.83GHz | | |

# Securing host management access

When it comes to managing ESXi hosts, there are a few interfaces available to perform management tasks:

►  **Common Information Model** (**CIM**), which is used for vCenter Server access.

►  **Direct Console User Interface** (**DCUI**), which is also known as the ESXi console.

►  **Tech Support Mode** (**TSM**)

  ❑  Local—console access to the ESXi command line.

  ❑  Remote—SSH access to the ESXi command line.

►  **vSphere Application Programming Interface** (**API**) such as vSphere Client, PowerCLI, vCLI, and so on.

Remote TSM has been covered in the *Accessing hosts via SSH* recipe in this chapter. Local TSM and DCUI are console options available if you have physical access to the host or remote console access such as iDRAC.

All interfaces except vSphere API can be managed from vCenter under host **Configuration** | **Security Profile** | **Services**:

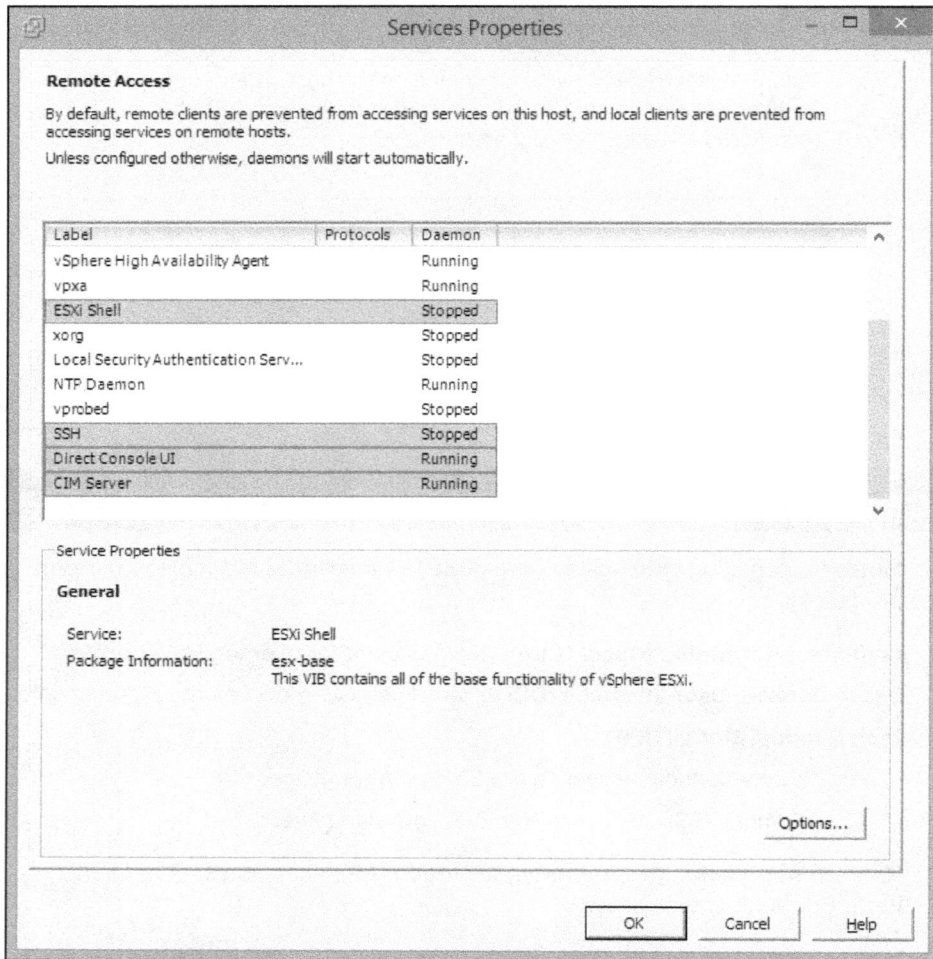

| Services Properties | | | |
| --- | --- | --- | --- |

**Remote Access**

By default, remote clients are prevented from accessing services on this host, and local clients are prevented from accessing services on remote hosts.

Unless configured otherwise, daemons will start automatically.

| Label | Protocols | Daemon |
| --- | --- | --- |
| vSphere High Availability Agent | | Running |
| vpxa | | Running |
| ESXi Shell | | Stopped |
| xorg | | Stopped |
| Local Security Authentication Serv... | | Stopped |
| NTP Daemon | | Running |
| vprobed | | Stopped |
| SSH | | Stopped |
| Direct Console UI | | Running |
| CIM Server | | Running |

Service Properties

**General**

| Service: | ESXi Shell |
| --- | --- |
| Package Information: | esx-base |
| | This VIB contains all of the base functionality of vSphere ESXi. |

Options...

OK    Cancel    Help

Both TSM options can also be configured from the DCUI console.

The following table summarizes different management interfaces and where each one can be configured:

| Management interface | Description | Configuration from vCenter | Configuration from DCUI |
|---|---|---|---|
| CIM | vCenter access | Host's Services | |
| DCUI | ESXi console | Host's Services | |
| Local TSM | Console CLI | Host's Services | Troubleshooting menu |
| Remote TSM | SSH access to CLI | Host's Services | Troubleshooting menu |
| APIs | vSphere Client, PowerCLI, vCLI | | |

VMware offers a way to secure management access to hosts called **Lockdown mode**.

**Lockdown mode** is a security feature, which limits the administrator's ability to manage the ESXi host only through vCenter. When a host is in this mode, the administrator cannot use the command line or run scripts. Also, any third-party software cannot get or change any settings on this host.

> User root will still be able to access DCUI but not TSM.

The following table summarizes each management interface's behavior in Normal and Lockdown modes:

| Management interface | Normal mode | Lockdown mode |
|---|---|---|
| CIM | User and group permissions | Only vCenter server |
| DCUI | User root and users with administrator rights | Only root user |
| Local TSM | Only root user | None |
| Remote TSM | Only root user | None |
| APIs | User and group permissions | Only vCenter vpxuser |

Additional security always means inconvenience. If the vCenter VM crashed or didn't come up after the reboot, and access to vCenter has been lost, ESXi has to be reinstalled on hosts that are in Lockdown mode to restore access.

## How to do it...

To enable lockdown mode from vCenter, execute the following steps:

1. Lockdown mode can be enabled per host by going to **Configuration** | **Security Profile**:

2. Click on **Edit** next to **Lockdown Mode**, select **Enable Lockdown Mode**, and click on **OK**:

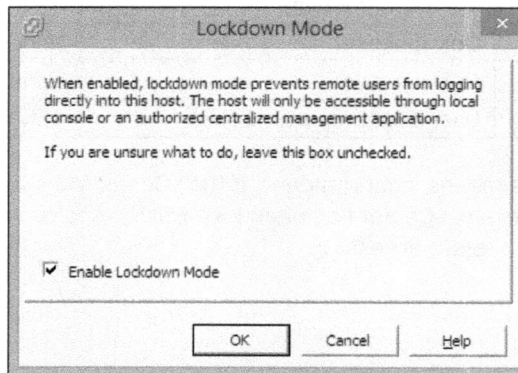

> All the existing vCenter Client connections to the host will be dropped immediately.
>
> Users that are currently logged in to DCUI or TSM will still have access after Lockdown mode has been enabled until they log off. Logged in users will not be able to switch Lockdown mode off in this case.
>
> All the existing user and group permissions will be restored once Lockdown mode is disabled if it was enabled from vCenter.

To enable Lockdown Mode from Web Client, execute the following steps:

1. Select a host.
2. Go to **Manage** | **Settings** | **Security Profile**.
3. Scroll down to the **Lockdown Mode** section.
4. Click on the **Edit** next to the section.
5. Check **Enable Lockdown Mode**.
6. Click on **OK**.

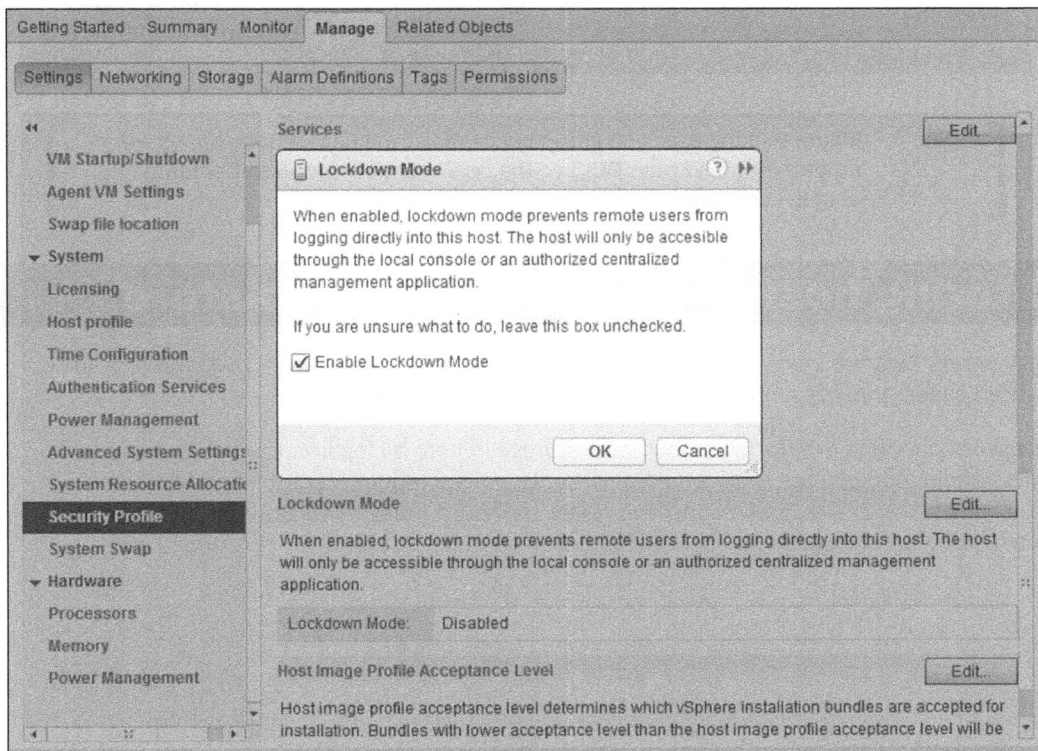

## Enable Lockdown mode from the ESXi console

To enable Lockdown mode from DCUI, press *F2*, log in with the root user, move the cursor to the **Configure Lockdown Mode** item, and press *Enter*.

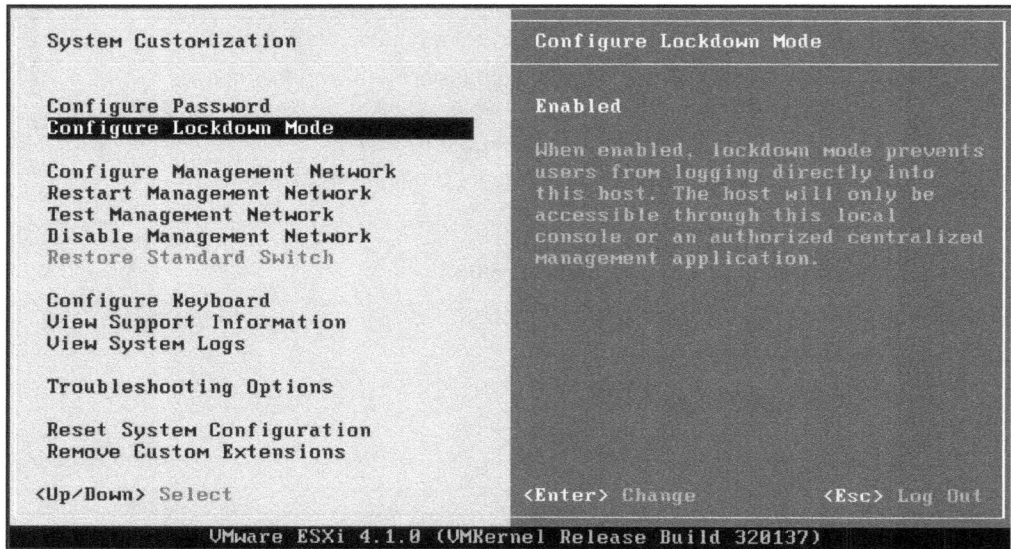

```
System Customization              Configure Lockdown Mode

Configure Password                Enabled
Configure Lockdown Mode
                                  When enabled, lockdown mode prevents
Configure Management Network      users from logging directly into
Restart Management Network        this host. The host will only be
Test Management Network           accessible through this local
Disable Management Network        console or an authorized centralized
Restore Standard Switch           management application.

Configure Keyboard
View Support Information
View System Logs

Troubleshooting Options

Reset System Configuration
Remove Custom Extensions

<Up/Down> Select                  <Enter> Change          <Esc> Log Out

              VMware ESXi 4.1.0 (VMKernel Release Build 320137)
```

All the existing user and group permissions will be lost once Lockdown mode is enabled from DCUI so the best practice is to use vCenter to enable Lockdown.

# Storing host logs on a shared datastore

ESXi server logs are stored locally by default on each host in the /var/log directory. In certain cases, there is a requirement to store logs on a datastore.

Possible scenarios are hosts without local storage, where all locally stored logs disappear after reboot, compliance requirements where there is a requirement to store logs in an alternative location, or space concerns where there are many hosts and the administrator has to keep older logs.

## How to do it...

vCenter allows redirecting ESXi logs to one of the datastores accessible to the host. This can be accomplished by going to **Configuration** | **Advanced Settings** | **Syslog** by changing the variable `Syslog.global.logDir` to an appropriate value [Datastore]/Folder:

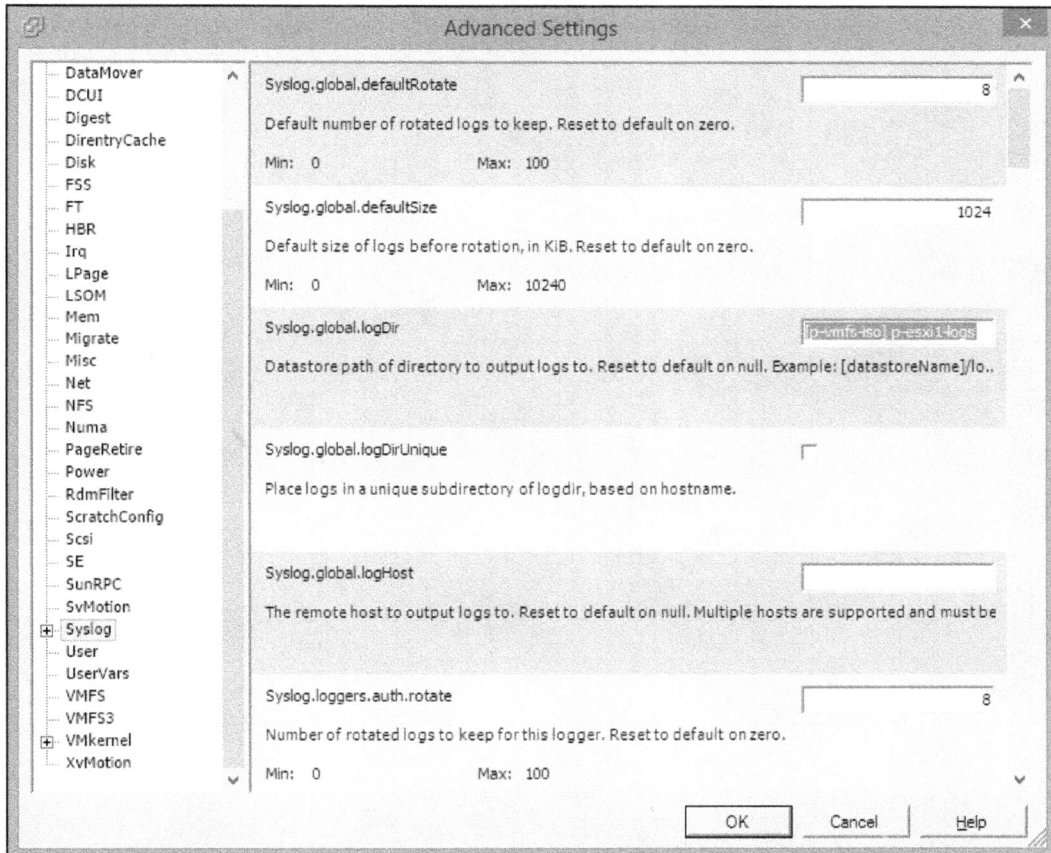

In vCenter Web Client, these options can be found by going to **Host** | **Manage** | **Settings** | **Advanced System Settings,** as shown in the following figure:

| Getting Started | Summary | Monitor | **Manage** | Related Objects |
|---|---|---|---|---|

| Settings | Networking | Storage | Alarm Definitions | Tags | Permissions |
|---|---|---|---|---|---|

Advanced System Settings

**Virtual Machines**
- Default VM Compatibility
- VM Startup/Shutdown
- Agent VM Settings
- Swap file location

**System**
- Licensing
- Host profile
- Time Configuration
- Authentication Services
- Power Management
- **Advanced System Settings**
- System Resource Allocation
- Security Profile
- System Swap

**Hardware**
- Processors
- Memory
- Power Management

| Name | Value |
|---|---|
| Scsi.TimeoutTMThreadMin | 1 |
| Scsi.TimeoutTMThreadMax | 16 |
| Scsi.TimeoutTMThreadExpires | 1800 |
| Scsi.TimeoutTMThreadRetry | 2000 |
| Scsi.TimeoutTMThreadLatency | 2000 |
| Scsi.ScsiRestartStalledQueueLatency | 500 |
| Scsi.CompareLUNNumber | 1 |
| Scsi.UseAdaptiveRetries | 1 |
| Scsi.ChangeQErrSetting | 1 |
| Scsi.ScanSync | 0 |
| Scsi.FailVMIOonAPD | 0 |
| SunRPC.WorldletAffinity | 2 |
| SunRPC.MaxConnPerIP | 4 |
| SunRPC.SendLowat | 25 |
| SvMotion.SvMotionAvgDisksPerVM | 8 |
| Syslog.global.defaultRotate | 8 |
| Syslog.global.defaultSize | 1024 |
| Syslog.global.logDir | [p-vmfs-iso] p-esxi1-systemlogs |
| Syslog.global.logDirUnique | false |
| Syslog.global.logHost | udp://192.168.15.81:514 |
| Syslog.loggers.Xorg.rotate | 8 |

## There's more...

Once this change is made, you will see log files created in the configured folder if you browse the datastore.

From the same **Advanced Settings** section, you can configure the additional logging options:

| Option | Description |
|---|---|
| Syslog.global.logDirUnique | If chosen the ESXi syslog will create a separate folder for this host in the specified logging folder. The folder will be named with the ESXi hostname. |
| | This option is helpful when the logging folder is shared between more than one host. |
| Syslog.global.defaultRotate | This is the maximum number of log files to keep after rotation. |
| Syslog.global.defaultSize | This is the maximum log file size in kilobytes. Once reached, the log file will be rotated. |

The same logging parameters can also be configured from the ESXi command line using the `esxcli system syslog` command.

For example, to validate logging settings configured from vCenter use:

```
esxcli system syslog config get
```

VMware KB 2003322 gives more details about configuring syslog, including CLI command sequence, which is available at `http://kb.vmware.com/kb/2003322`.

# Configuring remote logging

For compliance and security reasons, administrators may need to redirect ESXi logs to a remote syslog server.

## How to do it...

This configuration is done by going to **Configuration** | **Advanced Settings** | **Syslog** and changing the variable `Syslog.global.logHost` to `<protocol>://<syslog host>:<port>` as shown in the following screenshot:

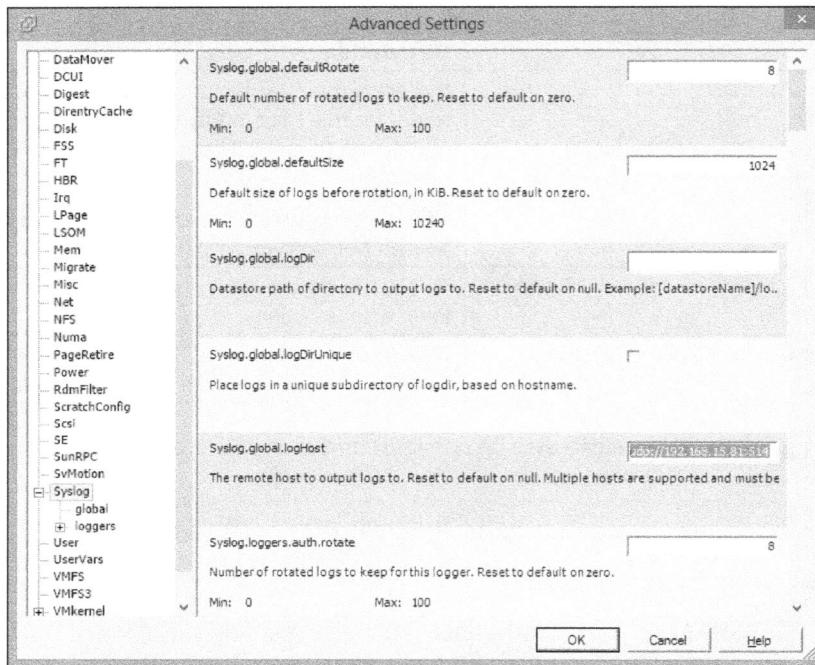

From Web Client, perform the following steps:

1. Go to **Manage** | **Settings** | **Advanced System Settings**.

2. Select the **Syslog.global.logHost** option in the list.

3. Click on the **Edit** button above the list.

4. Adjust the value of the **Syslog.global.logHost** option.

5. Click on **OK**.

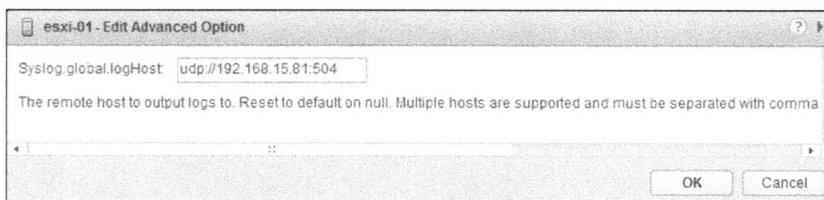

> In most cases, syslog uses UDP and that's why in case of high logging volume or high network utilization, some log entries may be lost. Consider this when planning the logging infrastructure.
>
> You can configure the syslog and datastore logging mentioned in storing host logs on a shared datastore at the same time for each host.

Also, administrators may need to configure the ESXi firewall to allow outbound syslog traffic. This is done by going to **Configuration** | **Security Profile** | **Firewall** and performing the following steps:

1. Click on **Properties** next to the **Firewall** section.

2. Make sure **syslog** is chosen.

3. Click on **OK**.

Alternatively, from Web Client, perform the following steps:

1.  Select a host.

2.  Go to **Manage | Settings | Security Profile**.

3.  Click on the **Edit** button next to the **Firewall** section.

4.  Select **syslog** in the list.

5.  Click on **OK**.

| Name | Incoming Ports | Outgoing Ports | Protocols | Daemon |
|---|---|---|---|---|
| ☐ VM serial port con... | 1024, 23 | 0 | TCP | N/A |
| ☑ SNMP Server | 161 | | UDP | Stopped |
| ☑ syslog | | 514, 1514 | TCP, UDP | N/A |
| ☐ vCenter Update M... | | 80, 9000 | TCP | N/A |
| ☑ vMotion | 8000 | 8000 | TCP | N/A |
| ☐ VM serial port con... | | 0 | TCP | N/A |

p-esxit Edit Security Profile

To provide access to a service or client, check the corresponding box.
By default, daemons will start automatically when any of their ports are opened, and stop when all of their ports are closed.

- Service Details    N/A
  Status    N/A
- Allowed IP Addresses   Allow connections from any IP address
  IP Addresses   ☑ Allow connections from any IP address

Enter a comma-separated list of IP addresses. E.g.: 111.111.111.111, 111.111.111/222

OK    Cancel

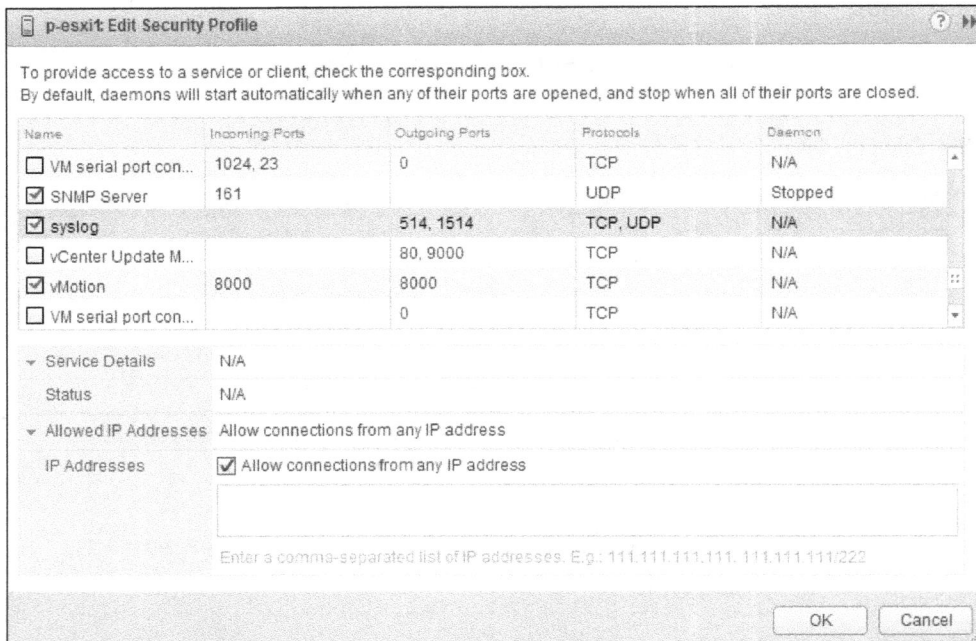

Once this configuration is completed the remote syslog server will start receiving logging data.

# 2
# Increasing Environment Availability

In this chapter, we will cover the following topics:

- ► Configuring the HA feature
- ► Prioritizing VMs for recovery
- ► Tuning up vSphere HA
- ► Ensuring 100 percent uptime for critical VMs
- ► Protecting host redundancy for equally sized hosts
- ► Protecting host redundancy for significantly different hosts
- ► Protecting host redundancy with failover hosts
- ► Backing up/restoring .vmdk files
- ► Restoring VM backup without vCenter
- ► Configuring the backup retention policy
- ► Protecting the vCenter VM

## Introduction

This chapter covers the availability solutions offered by vCenter. We will look at configuring and tuning **High Availability** (**HA**) and **Fault Tolerance** (**FT**), reviewing different scenarios of using admission control, backup, and replication. You may be running vCenter with a trial license, which will work just fine if you decide to try some of these recipes.

# Configuring the HA feature

The vSphere HA feature offers additional protection for virtual machines running on a cluster. There are three scenarios it can handle:

- Restart VMs on another host in case of host failure; this requires **host monitoring**.
- Restart a VM in case of guest OS failure; this requires **VM monitoring**.
- Reset a VM in case of application failure; this requires **application monitoring**.

HA is a cluster setting that applies to all running VMs. Once enabled, it protects all virtual machines and allows administrators to adjust additional settings such as VM prioritization and monitoring settings.

vCenter Server is required to configure the feature. It's not required for HA to operate and once the feature is enabled, it works even if vCenter is down.

Host monitoring prevents ESXi host failure. When it's enabled, HA monitors the host's heartbeats. If heartbeats are not received within a certain period of time, HA restarts VMs on another host.

VM monitoring is a protection against guest OS failure. When this option is turned on, HA monitors VMware tools heartbeats on a VM. If heartbeats are not received, HA assumes that the guest OS has crashed or has become unresponsive and restarts the VM after the configured timeout. Prior to a restart, a screenshot of VM's console is taken and saved in the virtual machine folder. This is done in case important information related to the crash was displayed, for example, **Blue Screen of Death** (**BSOD**) for Windows OS.

Application monitoring allows restarting a VM when an application running on it becomes unresponsive or crashes. If an application that is being monitored does not support VMware application monitoring, the administrator will be required to obtain the appropriate **Software Development Kit** (**SDK**). It can then be leveraged to configure customized heartbeats for the application.

## How to do it...

Before any type of monitoring can be enabled, vSphere HA must be turned on for the cluster. It also has to be turned on before admission control and FT are available.

To do this, execute the following steps:

1. Go to the **Hosts and Clusters** view.
2. Right-click on a cluster and choose **Edit Settings**.

3. Go to **Cluster Features** and check **Turn On vSphere HA**.

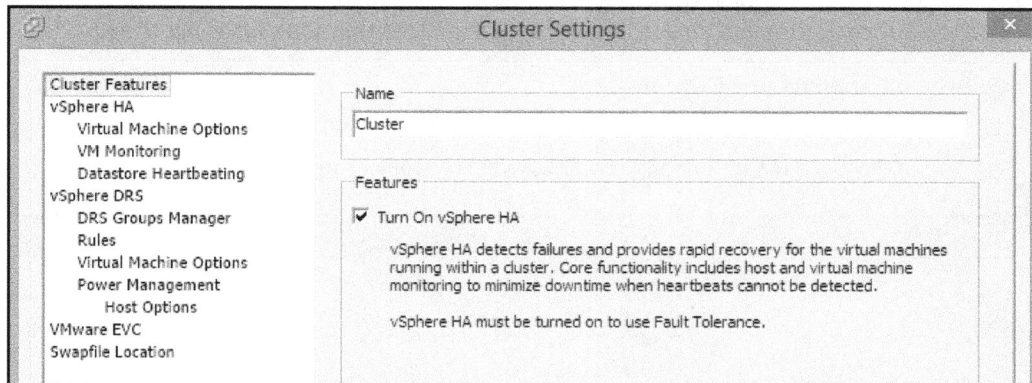

In Web Client, to enable these options, execute the following steps:

1. Select a cluster.
2. Go to **Manage | Settings | vSphere HA**.
3. Click on the **Edit** button.
4. Select **Turn ON vSphere HA**.

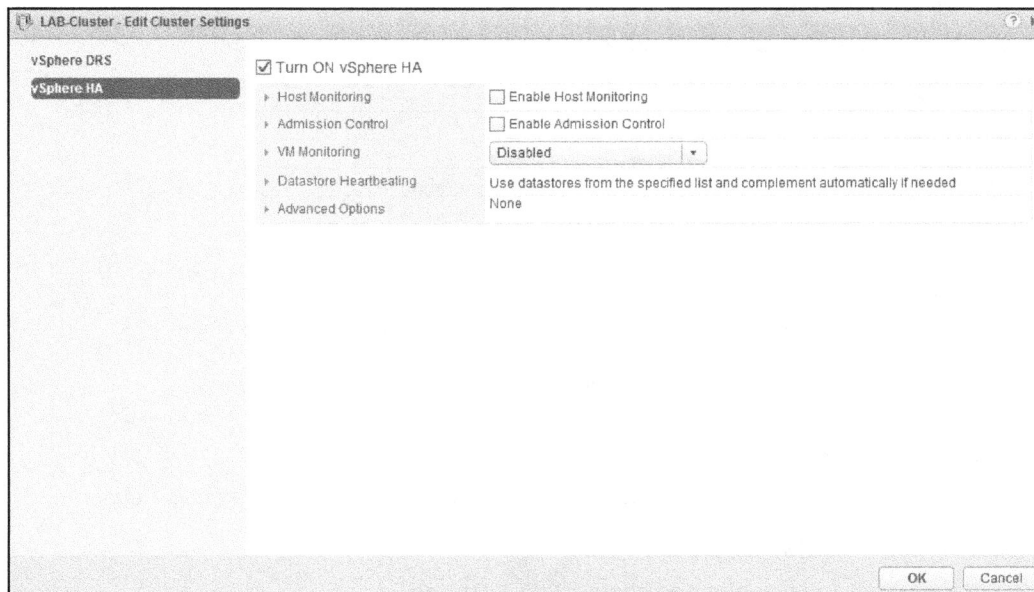

## Enabling host protection

Host protection will be enabled by default once vSphere HA is turned on. To confirm. it's enabled so that it protects VMs in case of host failure, perform the following steps:

1. Go to the **Hosts and Clusters** view.

2. Right-click on a cluster and choose **Edit Settings**.

3. Go to **vSphere HA** and check the **Enable Host Monitoring** option.

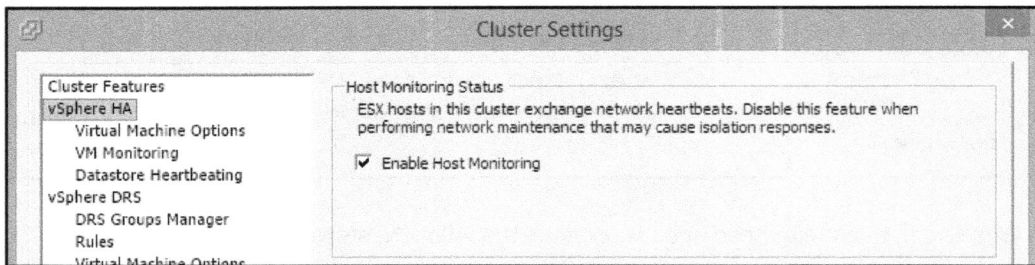

In Web Client, follow these steps:

1. Select a cluster.

2. Go to **Manage | Settings | vSphere HA**.

3. Click on the **Edit** button.

4. Select **Enable Host Monitoring**.

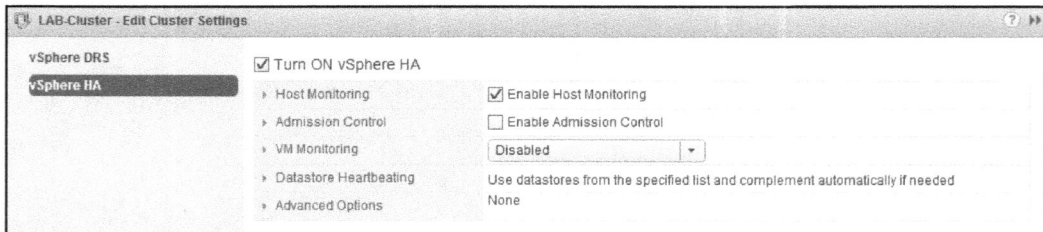

Once you press **OK**, vCenter will reconfigure the cluster and enable protection.

## Enabling VM monitoring

To enable VM protection from the OS and application failure, follow the ensuing steps:

1. Go to the **Hosts and Clusters** view.

2. Right-click on a cluster and choose **Edit Settings**.

3. Go to **vSphere HA | VM Monitoring**.

4.  In the **VM Monitoring Status** section, enable either **VM Monitoring Only** or **VM and Application Monitoring**.

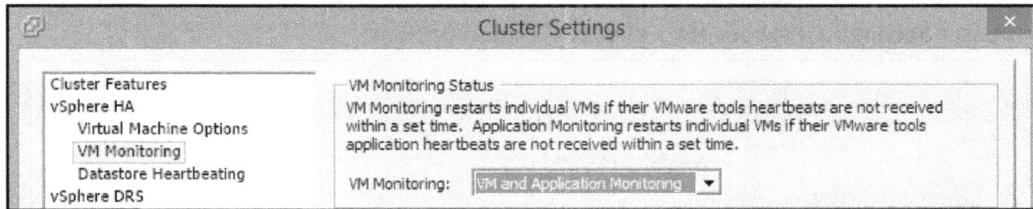

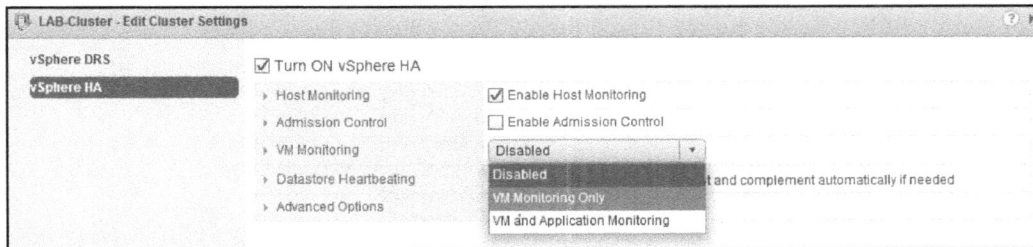

| |
| --- |

Cluster Settings

Cluster Features
vSphere HA
    Virtual Machine Options
    VM Monitoring
    Datastore Heartbeating
vSphere DRS

VM Monitoring Status
VM Monitoring restarts individual VMs if their VMware tools heartbeats are not received within a set time. Application Monitoring restarts individual VMs if their VMware tools application heartbeats are not received within a set time.

VM Monitoring: VM and Application Monitoring ▾

In Web Client, perform the following steps:

1.  Select a cluster.

2.  Go to **Manage** | **Settings** | **vSphere HA**.

3.  Click on the **Edit** button.

4.  Next, in the **VM Monitoring** section, enable either **VM Monitoring Only** or **VM and Application Monitoring**.

LAB-Cluster - Edit Cluster Settings

vSphere DRS
vSphere HA

☑ Turn ON vSphere HA

› Host Monitoring     ☑ Enable Host Monitoring
› Admission Control     ☐ Enable Admission Control
› VM Monitoring
› Datastore Heartbeating
› Advanced Options

Disabled ▾
Disabled
VM Monitoring Only
VM and Application Monitoring

t and complement automatically if needed

# Prioritizing VMs for recovery

vSphere HA is a cluster-wide setting. This means that once it's enabled, it protects all virtual machines that are a part of the cluster.

In most cases, there are more important virtual machines running along with less critical VMs on the same cluster, and it's desirable that more important and critical VMs are restarted first. Also, depending on cluster resources available, vCenter may not be able to restart all virtual machines on other hosts, so it becomes even more important to make sure the most important servers will be backed up first.

Each environment has critical virtual machines, which in case of host failure need to be restarted before other VMs. A good example is domain controllers, which in most cases need to be up before other servers become available. Another example is database servers, which may be required online by applications and web servers. In such cases, the ability to configure VM restart priority can be very useful.

## How to do it...

vCenter offers an additional HA setting called **VM restart priority**, which is available by going to **Cluster Settings | vSphere HA | Virtual Machine Options**:

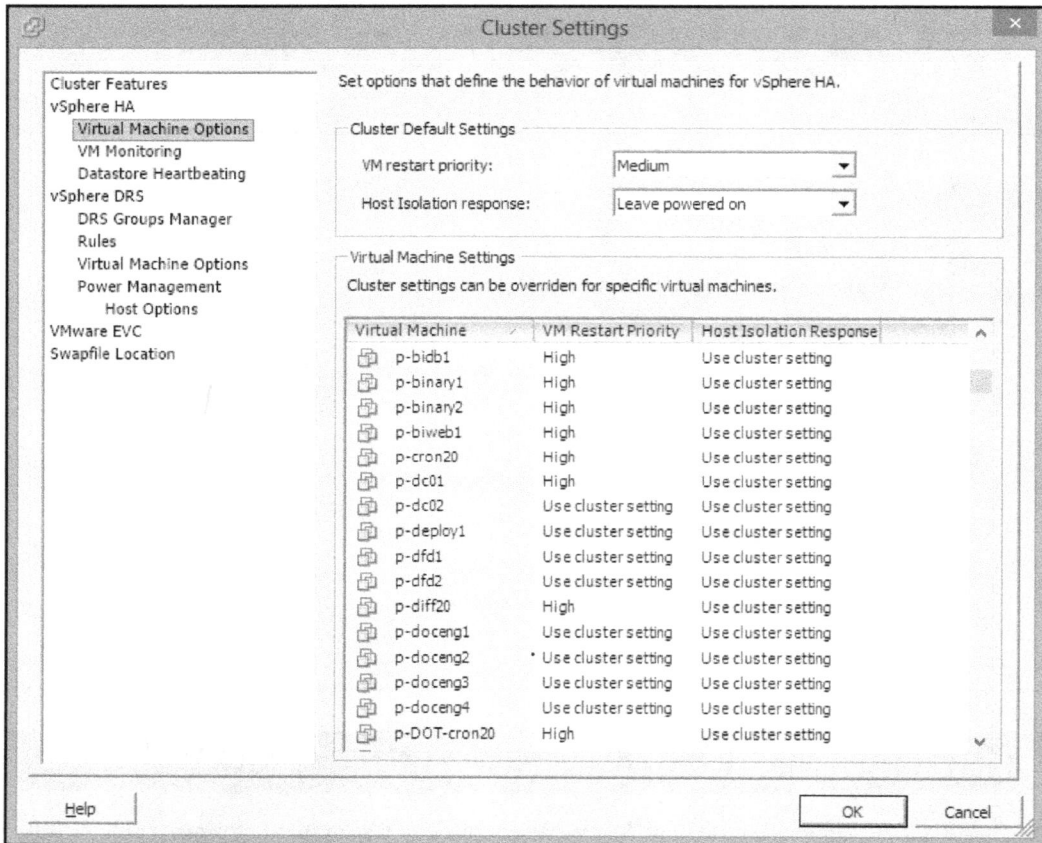

Under this menu, administrators can choose **Cluster Default Settings**, which applies to all VMs unless another setting is specified.

By default, the VM restart priority is **Medium**. In the **Virtual Machine Settings** section, you can choose VMs that will have higher or lower priority by changing the priority for each VM in the list.

There is also an option to disable **VM restart priority**, which means that this VM will never be restarted in case of host failure.

To set default options for **VM restart priority** in Web Client, follow the ensuing steps:

1. Select a cluster.

2. Go to **Manage | Settings | vSphere HA**.

3. Click on the **Edit** button.

4. Expand the **Host Monitoring** section.

5. Set values under **Virtual Machine Options**.

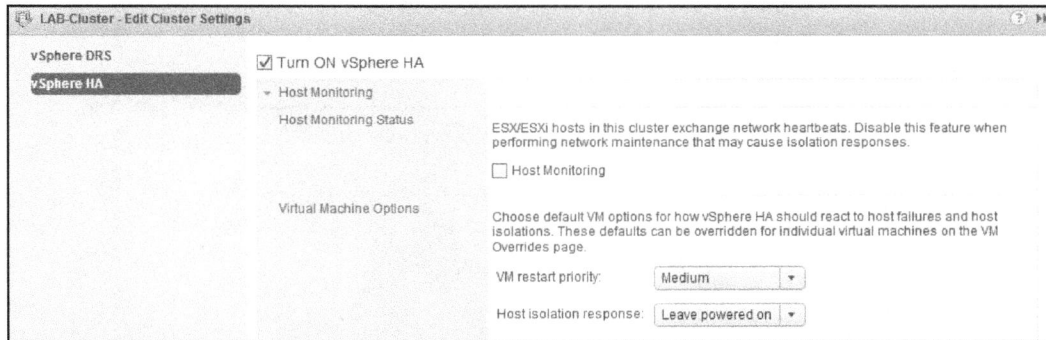

To change the individual VM settings Web Client:

1. Select a cluster.

2. Go to **Manage | Settings | VM Overrides**.

3. Select VM in the list and click on the **Edit...** button on top.

4. Change **VM restart priority** and **Host isolation response** as required.

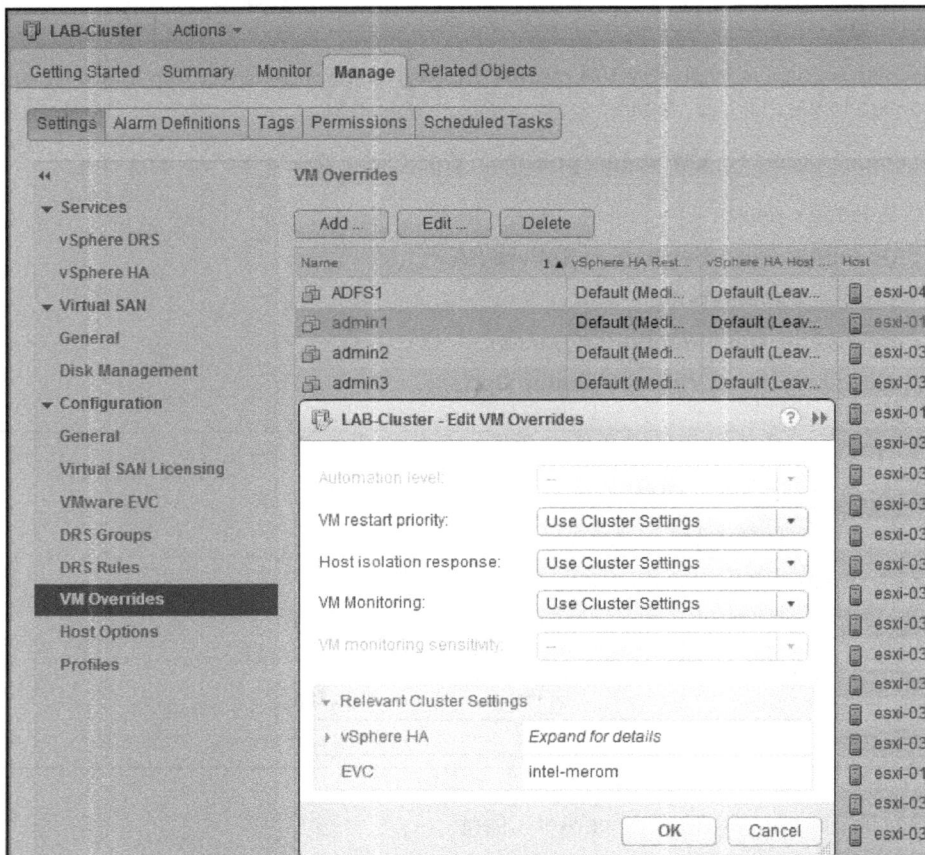

# Tuning up vSphere HA

When it comes to VM monitoring and auto-restart of individual VMs, vCenter offers an option to adjust the VM monitoring and application monitoring setting for individual VMs as well as change monitoring sensitivity.

Sensitivity can be set to low, medium, or high. These settings correspond to the following heartbeat timeout intervals: 120 seconds, 60 seconds, and 30 seconds. In other words, VM monitoring responds to missing the VMware tools heartbeat after this period of time. There is also an option to set a custom value for the timeout.

The custom option also allows you to change the following values:

- **Minimum uptime**: This is the amount of time after VM monitoring has been enabled and before it starts monitoring VMware tools heartbeats.

- **Maximum per-VM resets**: This is the amount of times a VM will be restarted within the maximum resets time window.

- **Maximum resets time window**: This is the period of time before VM reset count is zeroed on.

## How to do it...

These additional settings can be found in **Cluster Settings** under **vSphere HA | VM Monitoring**.

Under the **Default Cluster Settings** section, administrators can choose one of three predefined monitoring sensitivity levels:

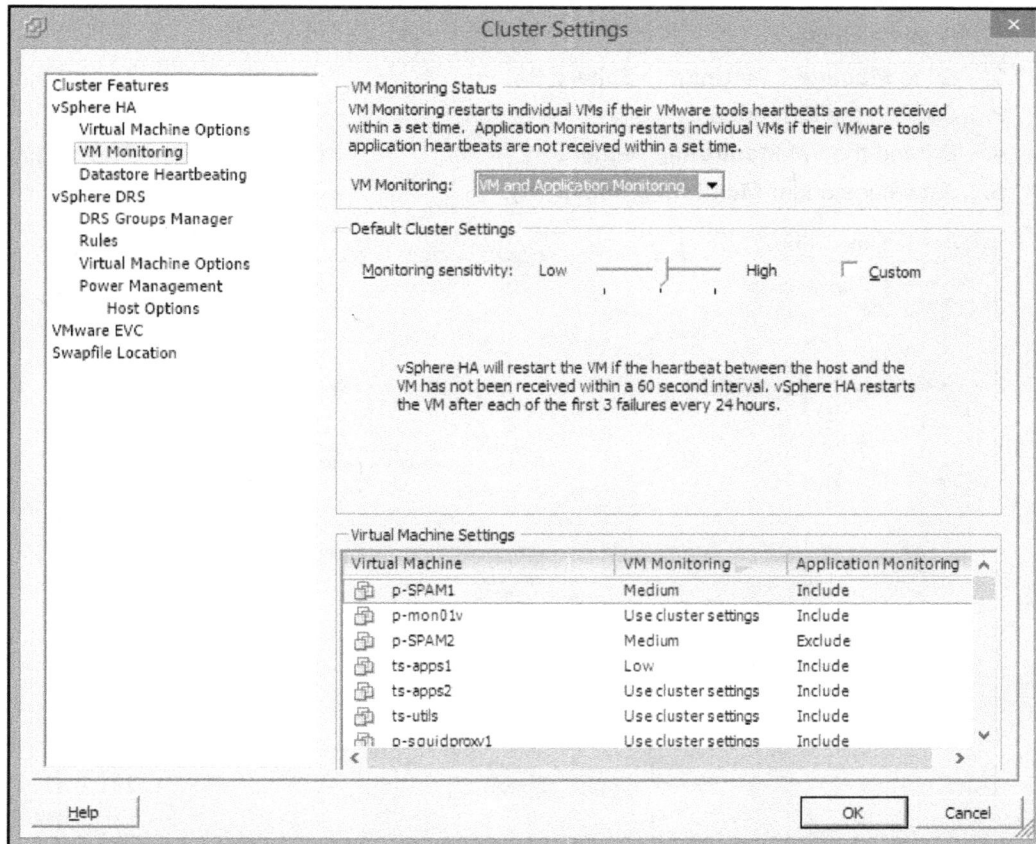

Alternatively, administrators can also adjust monitoring settings by choosing **Custom**:

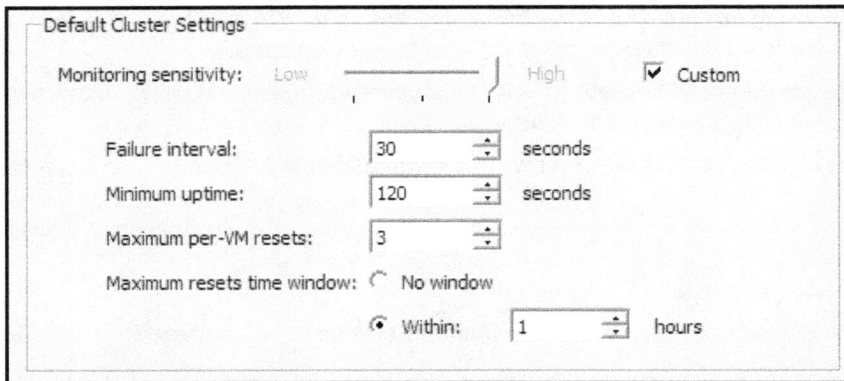

In Web Client, perform the following steps:

1. Select a cluster.
2. Go to **Manage** | **Settings** | **vSphere HA**.
3. Click on the **Edit** button.
4. Expand the **VM Monitoring** section.
5. Set values under **Monitoring Sensitivity**.

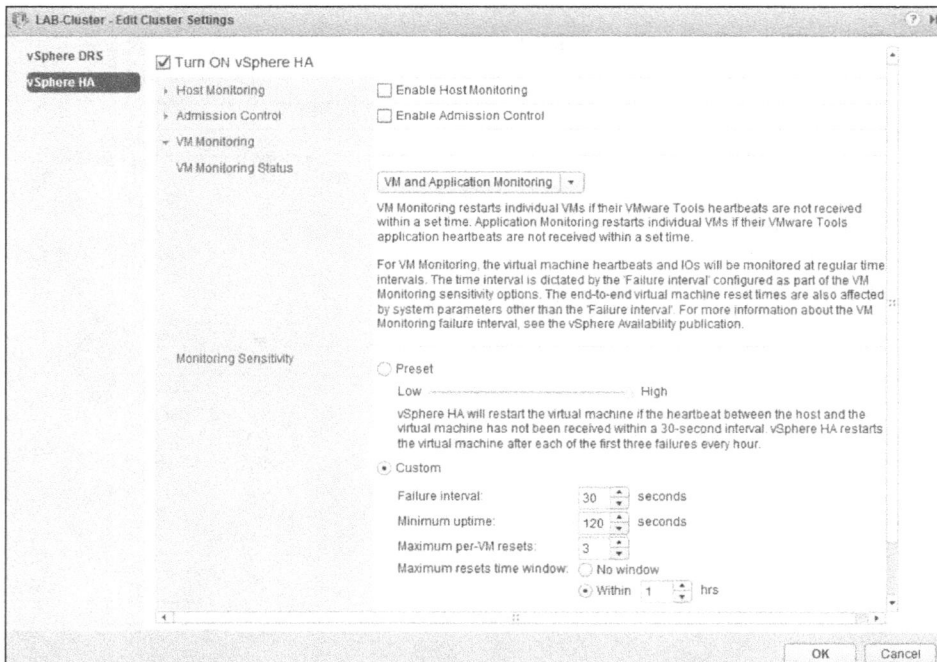

Once these cluster-wide settings have been specified under the **Virtual Machine Settings** section, monitoring sensitivity can be changed per VM. The available options are the same: high, medium, low, custom, or disabled.

In the same section, each VM can also be excluded from application monitoring.

If the **Custom** option is chosen for individual VMs for VM monitoring, you will be presented the same set of settings as in **Default Cluster Settings** custom mode:

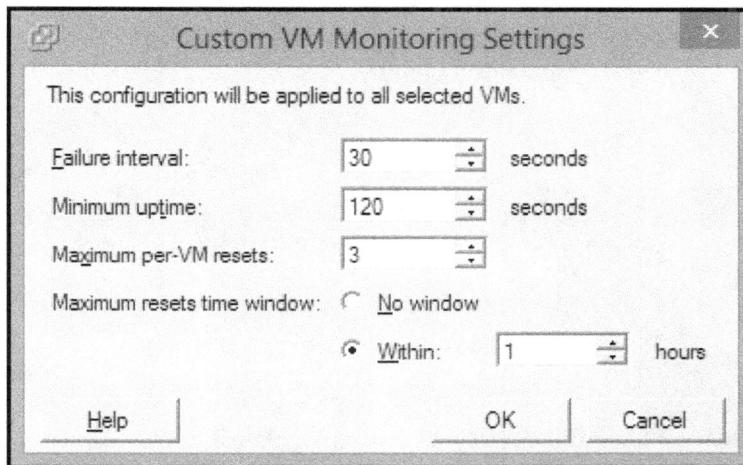

To adjust these settings per VM in Web Client:

1. Select a cluster.
2. Go to **Manage | Settings | VM Overrides**.
3. Select a VM in the list and click on the **Edit...** button on the top.

4. Change **VM restart priority** and **Host isolation response** as required.

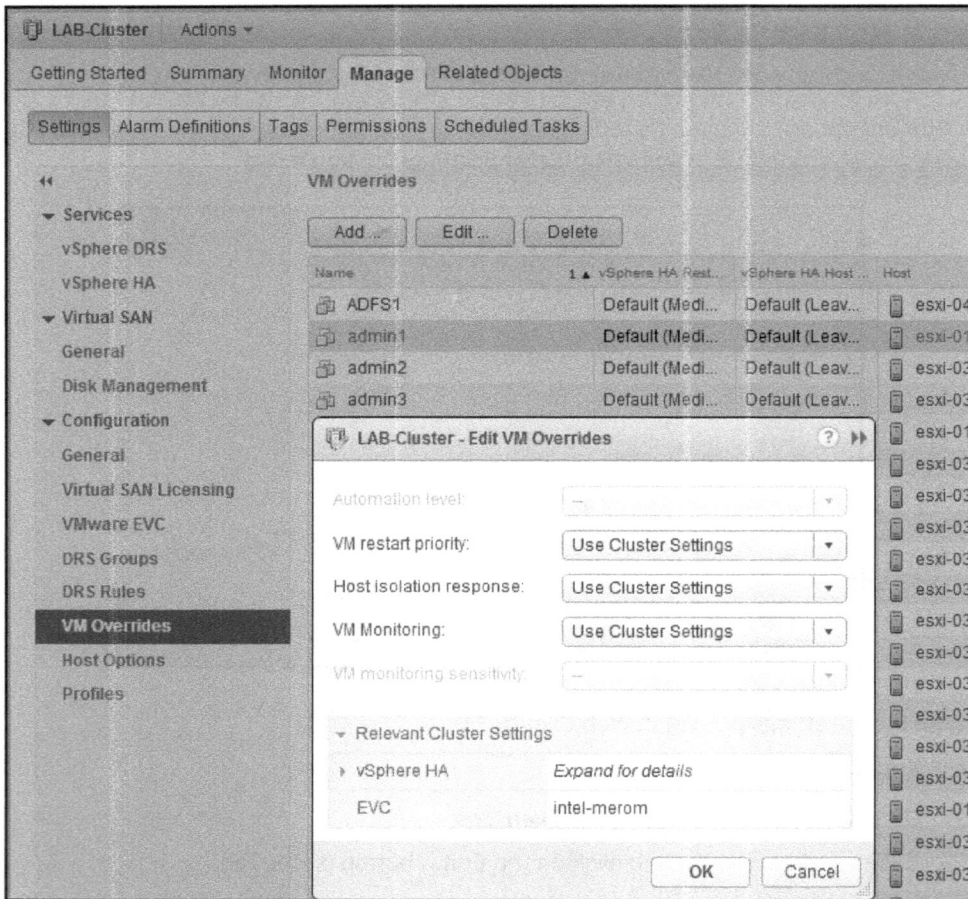

# Ensuring 100 percent uptime for critical VMs

For VMs that need to be up 100 percent of the time and do not tolerate even a brief interruption caused by a reboot as a result of host failure, vSphere offers a continuous availability option called **Fault Tolerance** (**FT**).

FT creates and maintains an exact copy of a running virtual machine—secondary VM—on another host. Both VMs exchange heartbeats to monitor each other's status.

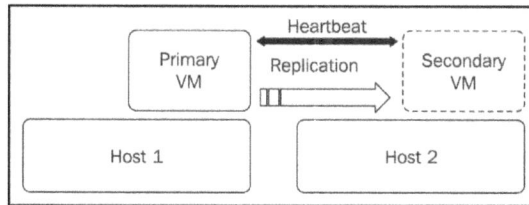

When a host with a primary VM fails, the secondary VM becomes active almost instantly. There is a little delay but clients do not see the interruption. As everything that happens on the primary VM replays on the secondary one, this failover happens transparently without the interruption of the existing network connections or in-progress transactions. The replication delay is typically less than 1 millisecond and it's unlikely that there will be transactions that have not yet been replicated. Such transactions, should they happen, will be lost.

## Getting ready

Requirements to enable FT include the following:

- ▶ vSphere HA cluster with vMotion enabled
- ▶ Shared datastores and networks
- ▶ Correct vSphere license
- ▶ Virtual machines must have one CPU
- ▶ Virtual machines must be stored on a shared storage available to all cluster hosts

> Unfortunately, FT is not compatible with snapshots, storage vMotion, VM backup, and thin provisioning.

## How to do it...

To enable FT on a VM:

1. Right-click on a VM.
2. Go to **Fault Tolerance**.

3. Click on **Turn On Fault Tolerance**.

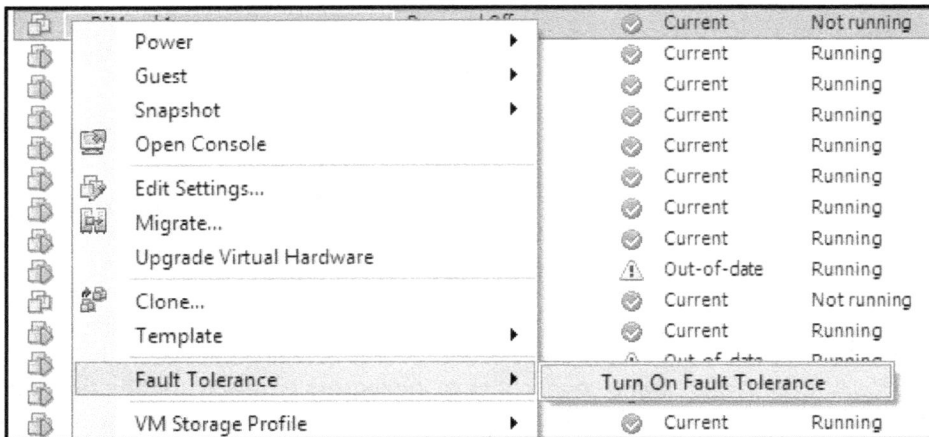

> In Web Client, this setting is available under **All vCenter Actions**.

Once this is done, this VM will become the primary one. The secondary VM will be created on another host. It will have a lighter icon and the word "secondary" in brackets after the VM name.

When enabling FT, you may also get the following error message:

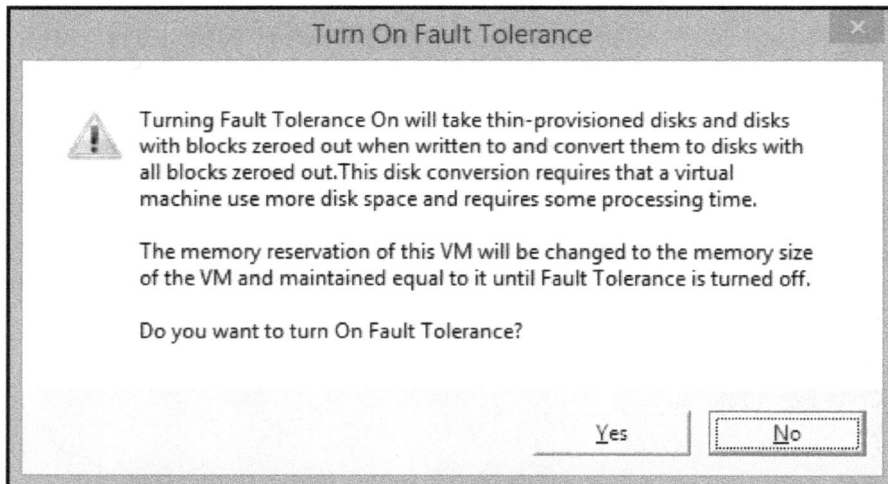

The reason for this message is that when FT is enabled, vCenter removes any memory limits set on a VM and creates a memory reservation equal to RAM allocated to this VM. This is done to prevent swap file creation, which causes unnecessary replication overhead. Reservations, limits, or shares cannot be changed when the VM is protected by FT.

Also, FT requires thick-provisioned disks, and any thin-provisioned `.vmdk` files have to be converted.

## Verifying VM FT status

The FT status for a VM can be verified under its **Summary** tab in the **Fault Tolerance** section:

1. Switch to the **Hosts and Clusters** view.

2. Select a VM from the left side.

3. Go to the **Summary** tab on the right.

admin2

| Summary | Resource Allocation | Performance | Tasks & Events | Alarms | Console | Permissions | Maps | Storage Views | Update Manager |

**General**

| | |
|---|---|
| Guest OS: | Microsoft Windows Server 2008 R2 (64-... |
| VM Version: | vmx-09 |
| CPU: | 1 vCPU |
| Memory: | 2048 MB |
| Memory Overhead: | 125.47 MB |
| VMware Tools: | Not running (Current) |
| IP Addresses: | |
| DNS Name: | WIN2008-R2-STD-Template |
| EVC Mode: | N/A |
| State: | Powered Off |
| Host: | esxi-03 |
| Active Tasks: | |
| vSphere HA Protection: | N/A |

**Commands**

- Power On
- Edit Settings
- Migrate

**Annotations**

Edit

Owner:
Notes:

**Resources**

| | |
|---|---|
| Consumed Host CPU: | 0 MHz |
| Consumed Host Memory: | 0.00 MB |
| Active Guest Memory: | 0.00 MB |
| | Refresh Storage Usage |
| Provisioned Storage: | 42.21 GB |
| Not-shared Storage: | 654.19 KB |
| Used Storage: | 40.00 GB |

| Storage | Status | Drive Type |
|---|---|---|
| NetApp-Vmware1 | Normal | Non-SSD |

| Network | Type | Sta |
|---|---|---|
| Production | Standard port group | |

**Fault Tolerance**

| | |
|---|---|
| Fault Tolerance Status: | ⚠ **Not protected** |
| | VM not Running |
| Secondary Location: | esxi-01 |
| Total Secondary CPU: | 0 MHz |
| Total Secondary Memory: | 0.00 MB |
| vLockstep Interval: | N/A |
| Log Bandwidth: | N/A |

**VM Storage Profiles**

Refresh

VM Storage Profiles:
Profiles Compliance:

In this section, you will also see the following:

▸ **Secondary Location**: This is the host where it's running.

▸ **vLockstep Interval**: This is the change replication delay in seconds.

▸ **Log Bandwidth**: This is the network capacity utilized during data transfer between VMs.

## Disabling FT

FT can be disabled from the same menu:

1. Right-click on a primary VM.

2. Go to **Fault Tolerance**.

3. From this menu, you can choose either **Disable Fault Tolerance** or **Turn off Fault Tolerance**.

The difference between these two options is that **Disable Fault Tolerance** preserves the secondary VM while the **Turn off Fault Tolerance** option deletes it.

> FT can only be disabled or turned off from the primary VM.

## There's more...

FT replication generates a lot of network traffic. It is considered the best practice to have a separate network for FT heartbeats so that the replication does not impact other traffic. VMware recommends a 10 Gbps network for this purpose.

For the same reason, it's not recommended to have more than eight FT-protected virtual machines on one host. The replication traffic may strain the FT-enabled network card.

A good approach is to have at least three hosts in the cluster with FT-protected VMs. In case a host with primary or secondary VM fails, the VM can be recreated on the third host. This way, it stays protected after host failure.

FT requires additional memory and disk space resources. The secondary VM reserves the same amount of memory as the primary one, so FT requires twice the memory. Also, as space overprovisioning is not supported, administrators should consider additional datastore space requirements.

# Protecting host redundancy for equally sized hosts

When there is more than one host in a cluster, it's usually expected that these hosts are redundant. In other words, if one or more hosts fail, the remaining should still be able to accommodate all VMs.

For this reason, each time a new VM is powered on or more memory or CPU is added to a VM, the administrator needs to be sure that the required redundant capacity is still available.

VMware offers a feature called admission control, which helps to ensure that sufficient resources are available to provide the required reservations or redundancy.

Once enabled, admission control is automatic. It is available not only for hosts but also for resource pools and vSphere HA.

Admission control monitors the environment for certain actions and decides whether they should be allowed or not based on resources that will be available after the action. This is to make sure that once the action is allowed, there are still enough resources to provide the expected redundancy.

These actions include the following:

- Powering on a VM
- Migrating a VM from one host, cluster, or resource pool to another
- Increasing the memory or CPU reservation for a VM

## How to do it...

To enable **Admission Control**, perform the following steps:

1. Go to the **Hosts and Clusters** view.
2. Right-click on a cluster.
3. Click on **Edit Settings**.
4. Go to **vSphere HA**.
5. In the **Admission Control** section, select **Enable: Disallow VM power on operations that violate availability constraints**.
6. In the **Admission Control Policy** section, switch to **Host failures the cluster tolerates** and specify the number of hosts.

7. Click on **OK**.

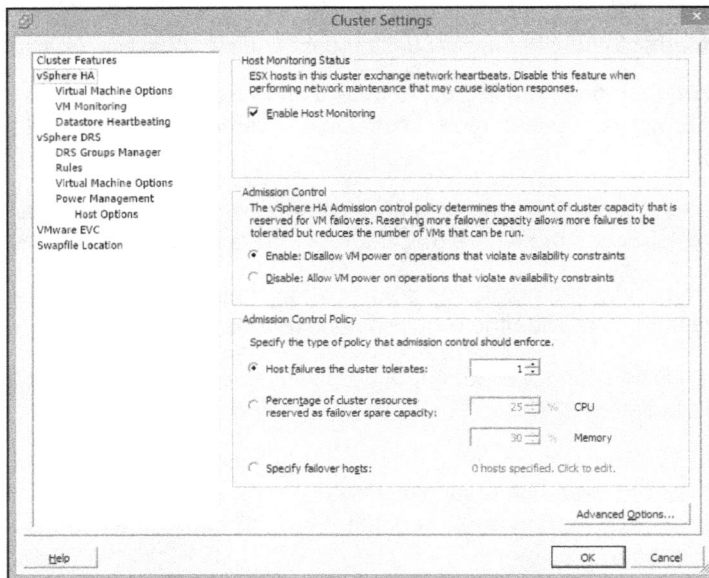

In Web Client:

1. Select a cluster.

2. Go to **Manage | Settings | vSphere HA**.

3. Click on the **Edit** button.

4. Expand the **Admission Control** section.

5. Select **Define failover capacity by static number of hosts** and then set the number of hosts as shown in the following screenshot.

6. Under this option, it's also possible to specify the available CPU and memory resources instead of choosing to protect all powered on VMs.

LAB-Cluster - Edit Cluster Settings

vSphere DRS

**vSphere HA**

☑ Turn ON vSphere HA

▸ Host Monitoring     ☐ Enable Host Monitoring

▾ Admission Control

    Policy

Admission control is a policy used by vSphere HA to ensure failover capacity within a cluster. Raising the proportion of ensured host failures increases the availability constraints and capacity reserved in the cluster.

(•) Define failover capacity by static number of hosts.

Reserved failover capacity: [ 1 ⬍ ] Hosts

Slot size policy:

(•) Cover all powered-on virtual machines

Calculate slot size based on the maximum CPU/Memory reservation and overhead of all powered-on virtual machines.

◯ Fixed slot size

Specify the slot size explicitly.

CPU slot size:    32 ⬍ MHz

Memory slot size:   4143 ⬍ MB

OK     Cancel

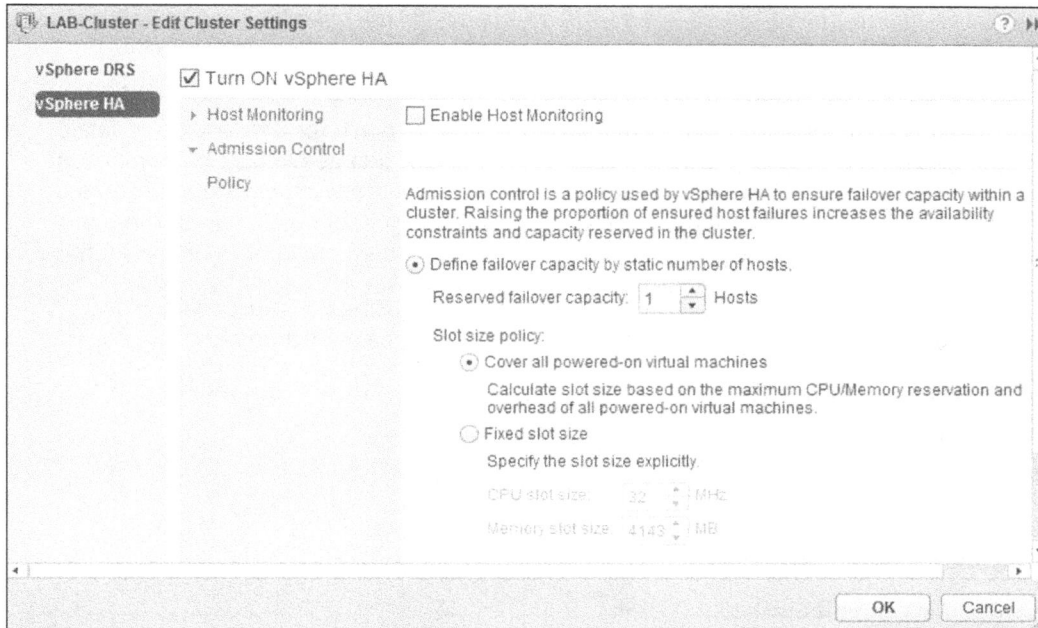

# Protecting host redundancy for significantly different hosts

Admission control helps to make sure there is spare capacity available in a cluster to keep the required level, redundancy, or reservations.

There are three types of policies available, which are as follows:

▸ Number of host failures a cluster tolerates

▸ Percentage of cluster resources reserved

▸ Specific failover hosts

When the requirement is to be able to lose one or more hosts and still be able to keep all the VMs needed running, the **Host failures cluster tolerates** option works quite well unless the hosts you are trying to protect have significantly different sizes—memory and CPU resources available.

This option for different hosts results in reserving an excessive capacity based on the size of the largest host. Reserving more capacity than required in its turn results in wasting resources.

For clusters with differently-sized hosts, VMware advice is to use the percentage of cluster resources reserved option. This option ensures that a specified percentage of memory and CPU is reserved across all hosts. The actual amount of resources to be reserved depends on the number of hosts, their size, and the acceptable number of host failures. There are no general recommendations and the values should be defined on a per-environment basis.

As this option offers more flexibility, VMware recommends using it in most cases. Combined with the HA VM priority, it may be used for all kinds of environments.

## How to do it...

To enable **Admission Control**, perform the following steps:

1. Go to the **Hosts and Clusters** view.
2. Right-click on your cluster.
3. Click on **Edit Settings**.
4. Go to **vSphere HA**.
5. In the **Admission Control** section, select **Enable: Disallow VM power on operations that violate availability constraints**.
6. In the **Admission Control Policy** section, switch to **Percentage of cluster resources reserved as failover spare capacity** and specify the required ercentage of CPU and memory.
7. Click on **OK**.

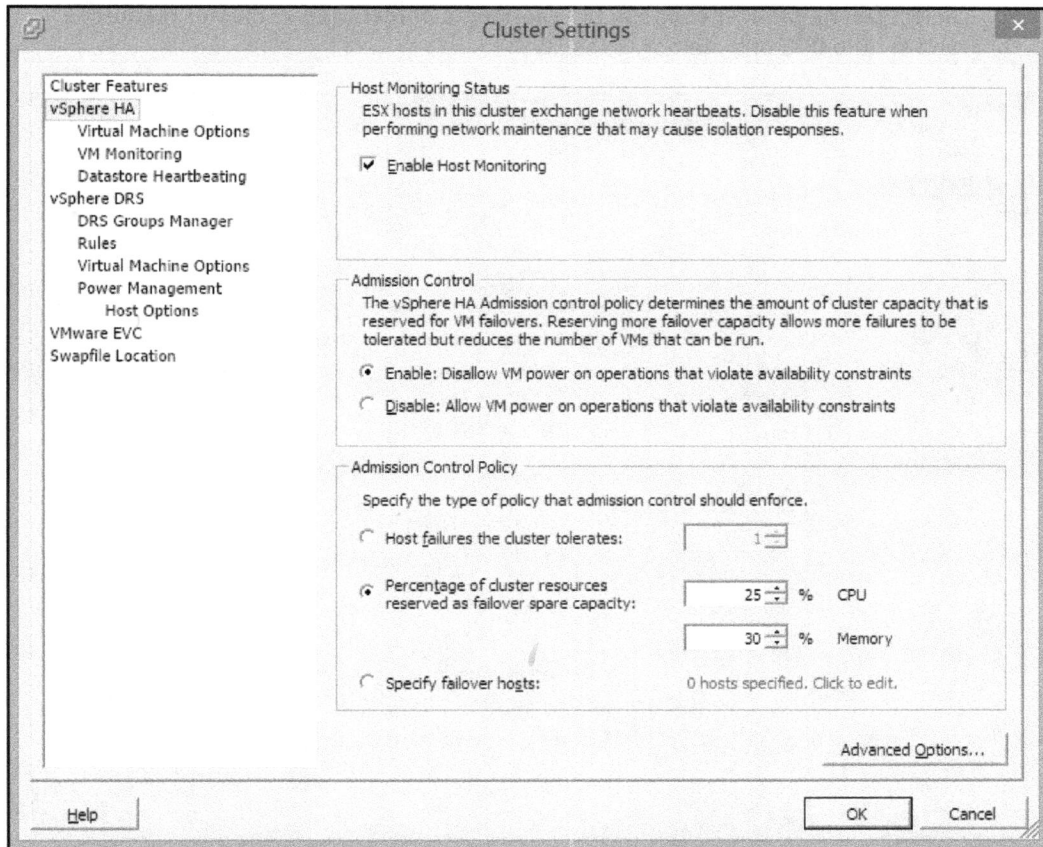

In Web Client, perform the following steps:

1. Select a cluster.
2. Go to **Manage** | **Settings** | **vSphere HA**.
3. Click on the **Edit** button.
4. Expand the **Admission Control** section.

5. Select **Define failover capacity by reserving a percentage of cluster resources**, and set the CPU and memory capacity.

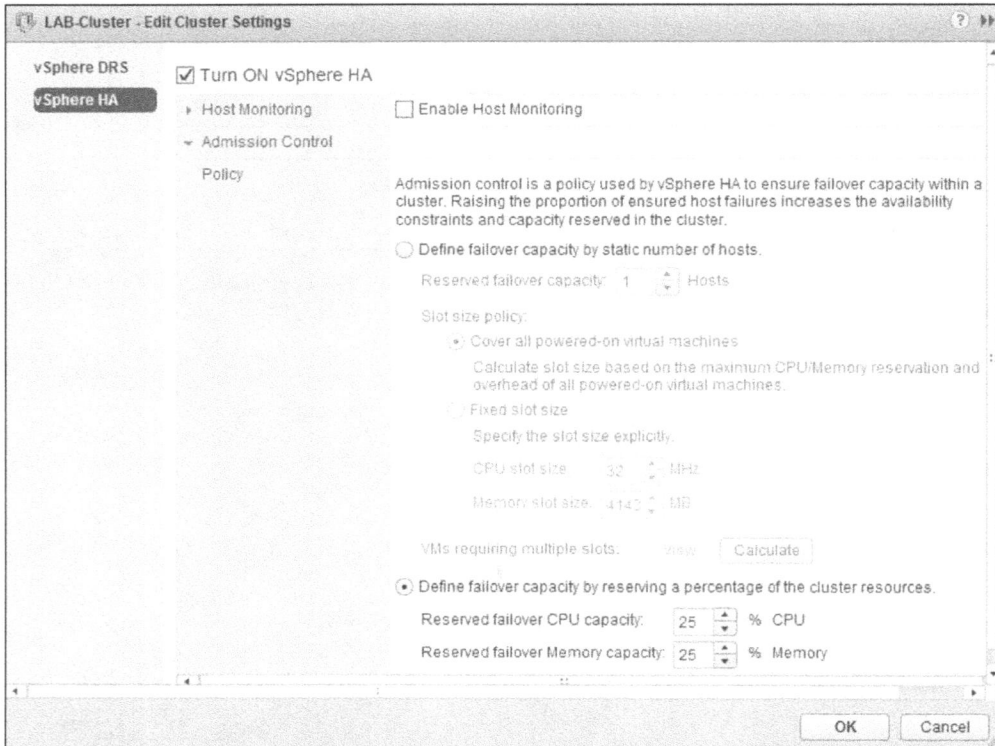

# Protecting host redundancy with failover hosts

In certain cases, administrators may decide to use a separate standby host, which will take over and accommodate VMs from a failed host. This can be accomplished by using the third available option in the **Admission Control Policy** settings—**Specify failover hosts**.

When this policy is chosen, vCenter doesn't allow any VMs on the failover host even when a VM is being migrated there. This host will be used only when a failure occurs.

One important requirement is a shared storage available to all hosts, including the failover host. VMs running on the host's local storage will not be migrated in case of host failure.

If, for some reason, the failover host cannot be used to accommodate VMs, HA will try to restart them on other available cluster hosts.

## How to do it...

To enable **Admission Control**, perform the following steps:

1. Go to the **Hosts and Clusters** view.
2. Right-click on your cluster.
3. Click on **Edit Settings**.
4. Go to **vSphere HA**.
5. In the **Admission Control** section, select **Enable**.
6. In the **Admission Control Policy** section, switch to **Specify failover hosts**.

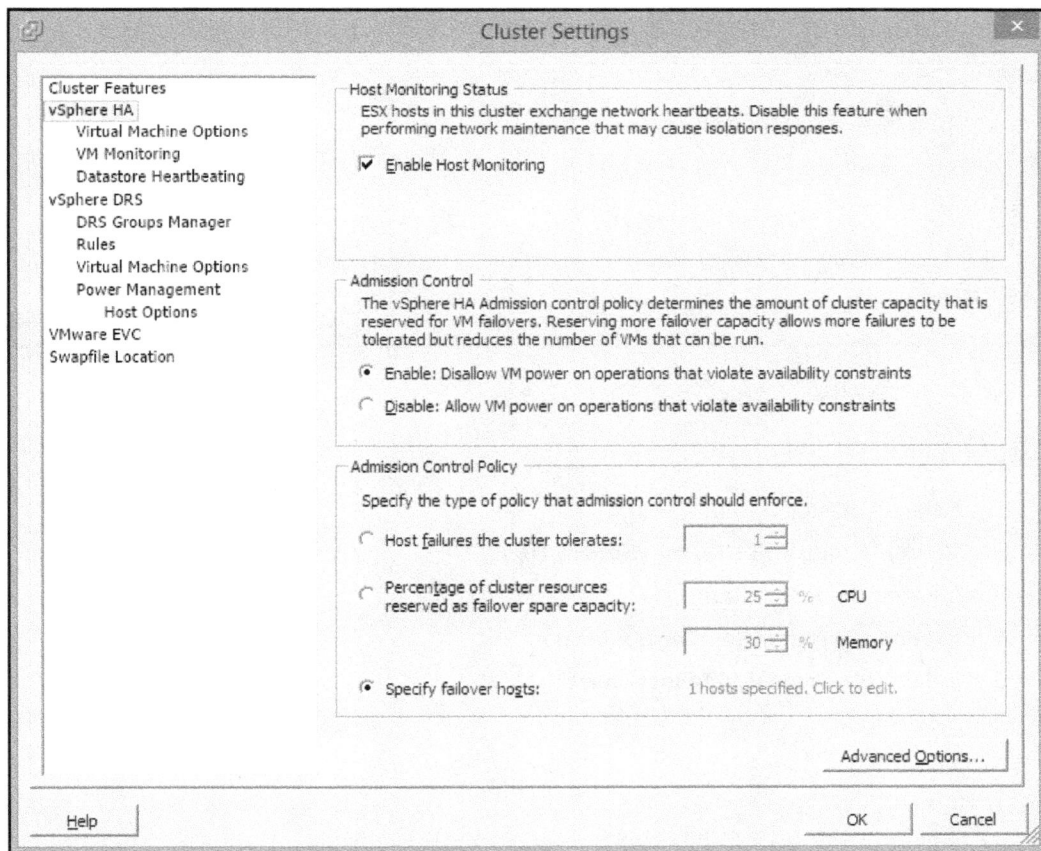

7. Click on the **Edit** link next to this option.

8. Choose one or more hosts.

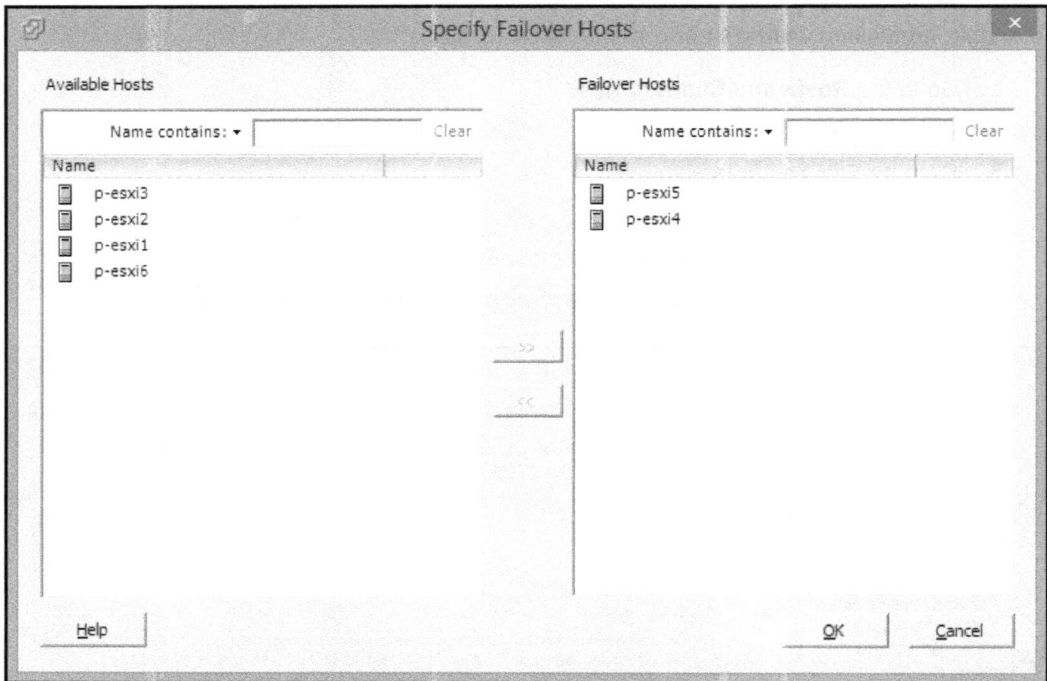

9. Click on **OK** two times.

In Web Client:

1. Select a cluster.
2. Go to **Manage | Settings | vSphere HA**.
3. Click on the **Edit** button.
4. Expand the **Admission Control** section.
5. Select **Use dedicated failover host**.

6. Click on the green plus sign, select failover hosts, and click on **OK**.

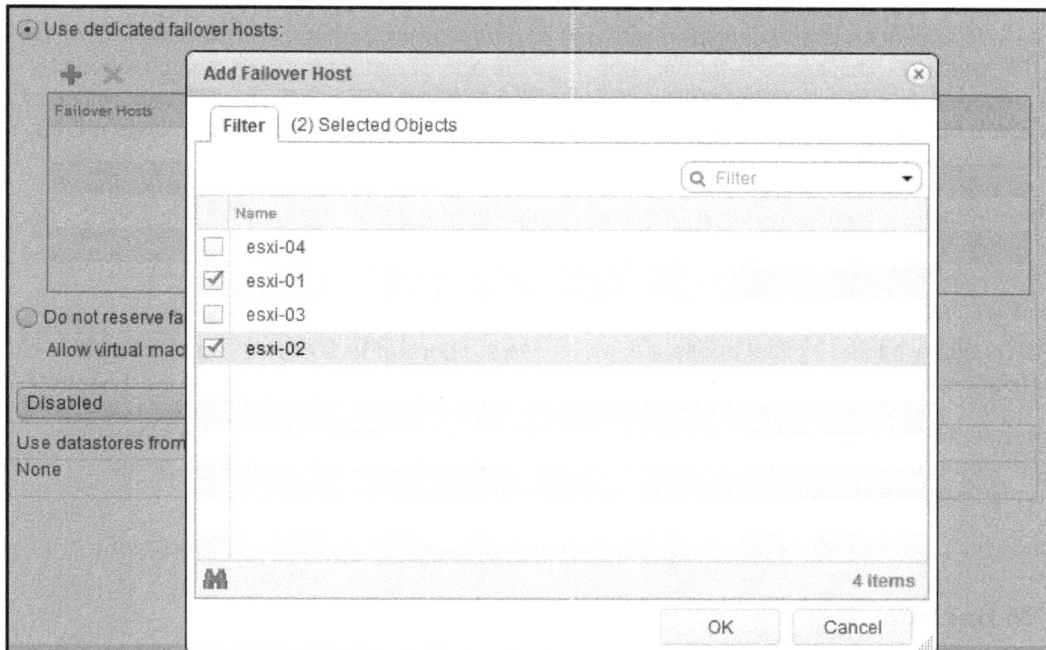

Use dedicated failover hosts:

**Add Failover Host**                                              ⊗

| Filter | (2) Selected Objects |

Q Filter ▾

Name
- ☐ esxi-04
- ☑ esxi-01
- ☐ esxi-03
- ☑ esxi-02

Do not reserve fa
Allow virtual mac

Disabled

Use datastores from
None

4 items

OK      Cancel

# Backing up/restoring .vmdk files

VMware offers a backup and recovery solution called **vSphere Data Protection** (**VDP**). While fully integrated with vCenter, this solution provides agentless disk-based backup of virtual machines.

Starting from vSphere 5.1:

▶ VDP is included in vSphere Essentials Plus Kit with a 4 TB limit for backup storage.

▶ The VDP advanced version has to be purchased separately.

Some of the core VDP features are as follows:

▶ De-duplication

▶ **Changed Block Tracking** (**CBT**) backup and restore

▶ Application awareness (MS Exchange, SQL Server, SharePoint, and so on)

## Getting ready

The VDP appliance is preconfigured with one of the following destination datastores: 0.5 TB, 1 TB, and 2 TB. This space is for backups only. The operating system, logs, and checkpoints of the appliance require additional space. According to VMware, a 0.5 TB appliance will need 850 GB of free space in total, a 1 TB appliance requires 1.57 TB of free space, while a 2 TB VDP will consume 3.02 TB of free space.

This should be considered when selecting a datastore for a VDP appliance.

## How to do it...

VDP is deployed as a virtual appliance, which can support up to 100 VMs. Up to 10 VDP appliances can be deployed per vCenter Server with a limit of 1 VDP appliance per ESXi host.

After appliance deployment has been done, use a web browser to connect to the appliance to perform the initial configuration. Open the console to see the the exact URL for the configuration interface.

Once the configuration is complete, VDP can be managed through vSphere Web Client.

### VM backup

Backup jobs can be created or edited under the **Backup** tab of VDP.

> You may need to log off and log back in to Web Client after deploying and configuring the VDP appliance to see VDP in the menu on the left.
>
> You may be required to click on **Connect**.

To add a new backup job:

1. Expand **Backup Job Actions** and choose **New**.

2. Select backing up virtual machines (**Guest Images**) or **Applications**, and click on **Next**.

3. Assuming we are backing up VMs, the next option is to choose between **Full Image** and **Individual Disks**.

4. If **Full Image** has been chosen, select **Virtual Machines** to back up and click on **Next**.

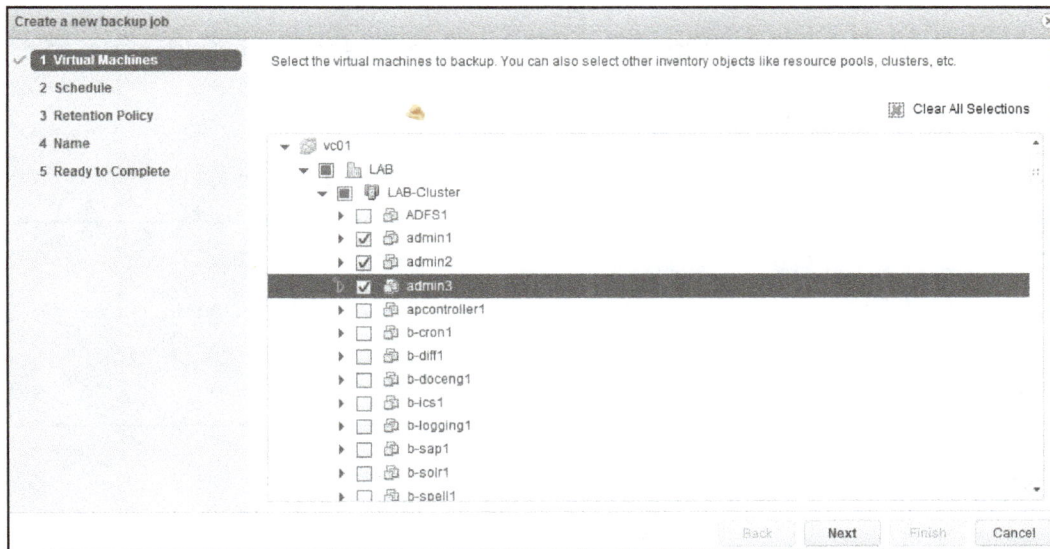

> Administrators can choose individual VMDK files if the **Individual Disks** option has been selected in the previous step. In this step, containers such as cluster or datacentre can be selected instead of individual VMs.
>
> If a container has been chosen, any VM moved off of it will not be backed up. Any new VMs will be backed up during the next backup job.

5. In the next step, configure the backup schedule. The available options are daily, weekly, or a certain day of the month:

6. Specify the retention policy. See the *Configuring backup retention policy* recipe, of this chapter, for more details.

7. Name the new policy and click on **Next** to complete the process.

You will see a new job in the list and will be able to run it manually if required.

## VM restore

To restore a VM, perform the following steps:

1. Go to the **Restore** tab.

2. Expand the backed up VM.

3. Select one or more restore points.

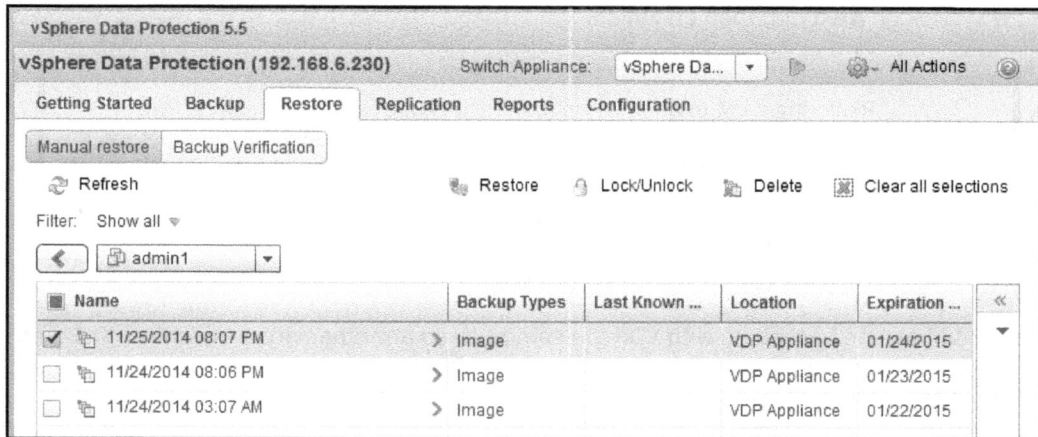

> Click on a restore point to get a list of virtual drives available for that restore point.

4. Click on **Restore**.

5. Choose whether you wish to restore to the original location or specify a new VM name and datastore.

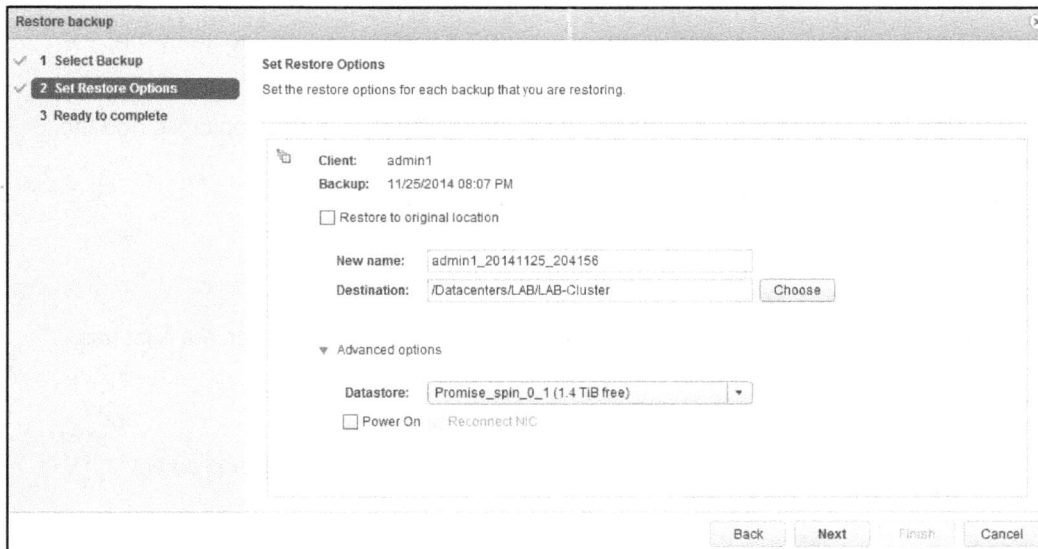

6.  Click on **Next** and then on **Finish**.

> Restoring a VM to another location results in a full image restore. When restoring to the original location, CBT chooses the fastest restore method between full image restore and restoring only blocks that have changed.

## There's more...

vCenter VM can be backed up with VDP the same way as any other virtual machine. If vCenter VM fails, the backed up virtual machines, including vCenter itself, can be restored using the direct-to-host restore option.

The procedure is described in the following recipe.

# Restoring VM backup without vCenter

VDP—backup and recovery solution from VMware—offers the so called **direct-to-host restore** option, which makes it possible to recover virtual machines without vCenter Server.

## Getting ready

Direct-to-host restore is supported starting from VDP 5.5. It is important to know the requirements for successful emergency restore:

▶  The DNS required is available and configured properly for VDP appliance and the host it's running on.

▶  The host VDP is running on has to be detached from vCenter.

## How to do it...

Make sure the host VDP appliance is running on is detached from vCenter. If a host has to be detached, execute the following steps:

1.  In vCenter Client, right-click on the host and select **Remove**.

2.  In Web Client, right-click on the host, go to **All vCenter Actions,** and select **Remove from Inventory**.

> If the host is a part of a cluster, it has to be put into maintenance mode first.

When vCenter Server is not available, which is most likely the case if direct-to-host restore is required, the host can be detached from vCenter using the vCenter Client connected directly to the host:

1. Connect directly to the host with the vCenter Client.

2. Select the host on the left.

3. Go to the **Summary** tab.

4. Under the **Host Management** section, click on **Disassociate host from vCenter Server...**.

| Summary | Virtual Machines | Resource Allocation | Performance | Configuration | Local Users & Groups | Events | Permissions |

**General**

| | |
|---|---|
| Manufacturer: | IBM |
| Model: | IBM System x3550 -[7978E... |
| CPU Cores: | 8 CPUs x 2.327 GHz |
| Processor Type: | Intel(R) Xeon(R) CPU E5345 @ 2.33GHz |
| License: | VMware vSphere 5 Enterprise - Licensed for 2 physical CP... |
| Processor Sockets: | 2 |
| Cores per Socket: | 4 |
| Logical Processors: | 8 |
| Hyperthreading: | Inactive |
| Number of NICs: | 6 |
| State: | Connected |
| Virtual Machines and Templates: | 25 |
| vMotion Enabled: | N/A |
| VMware EVC Mode: | Disabled |
| vSphere HA State | ⑦ N/A |
| Host Configured for FT: | N/A |
| Active Tasks: | |
| Host Profile: | N/A |
| Image Profile: | (Updated) ESXi-5.1.0-7997... |
| Profile Compliance: | ⑦ N/A |
| DirectPath I/O: | Not supported 🖵 |

**Resources**

CPU usage: **1457 MHz** — Capacity 8 x 2.327 GHz

Memory usage: **13016.00 MB** — Capacity 32767.30 MB

| Storage | Drive Type | Capacity |
|---|---|---|
| esxi-01:storage1 | Non-SSD | 131.50 GB |
| NetApp-Vmware1 | Non-SSD | 2.50 TB |
| NetApp-Vmware2 | Non-SSD | 2.50 TB |
| NetApp-Vmware3 | Non-SSD | 2.50 TB |
| Promise_spin_0_0 | Non-SSD | 2.00 TB |
| Promise_spin_0_1 | Non-SSD | 2.00 TB |
| Promise_spin_0_2 | Non-SSD | 2.37 TB |
| Promise_spin_2_0 | Non-SSD | 2.00 TB |
| Promise_spin_2_1 | Non-SSD | 745.75 GB |
| Promise_SSD_0_0 | Non-SSD | 1.36 TB |

| Network | Type |
|---|---|
| iSCSI Network | Standard port group |
| IGLOOLAB-VLAN6... | Standard port group |
| Production | Standard port group |

**Fault Tolerance**

| | |
|---|---|
| Fault Tolerance Version: | 4.0.0-4.0.0-4.0.0 |

Refresh Virtual Machine Counts

| | |
|---|---|
| Total Primary VMs: | 0 |
| Powered On Primary VMs: | 0 |
| Total Secondary VMs: | 0 |
| Powered On Secondary VMs: | 0 |

**Commands**

- ⬚ New Virtual Machine
- ⬚ Enter Maintenance Mode
- ⬚ Reboot
- ⬚ Shutdown

**Host Management**

This host is currently managed by vCenter Server 192.168.10.154.

Reconnect vSphere Client to this vCenter Server...

Disassociate host from vCenter Server...

The option for direct-to-host restore is available in the VDP configuration interface under the **Emergency Restore** tab:

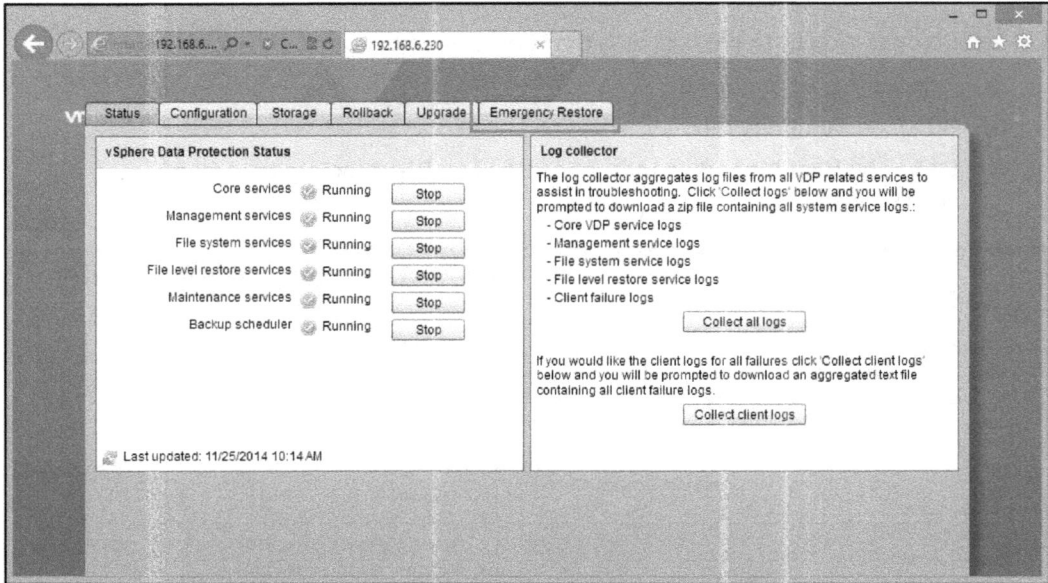

To perform a restore, execute the following steps:

1. Log in to the VDP configuration interface and go to the **Emergency Restore** tab.

2. Expand a VM that has to be restored.

3. Select a restore point.

4. Click on the **Restore** button.

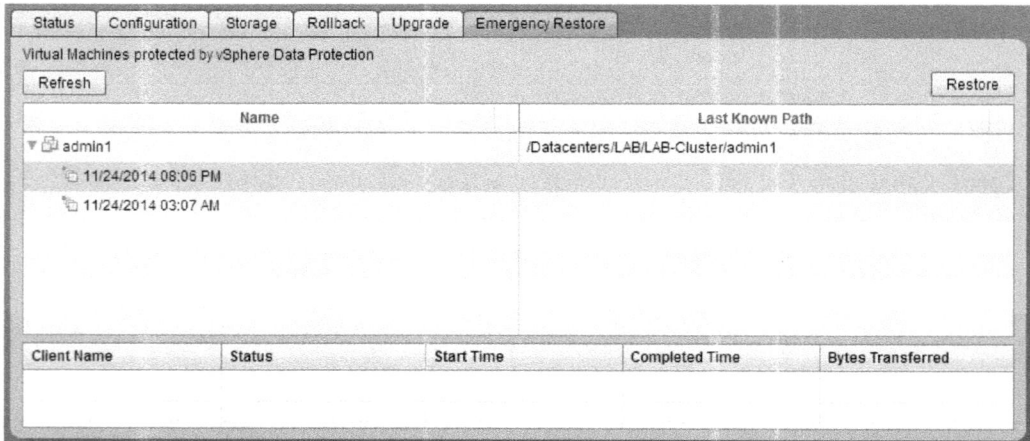

5. You will be prompted for ESXi server address and credentials:

**Host Credentials**

Enter information about the ESX host on which this VDP resides.

ESX hostname or IP: `192.168.10.34`

Port number: `443`

Username: `root`

Password: `**********`

Cancel    OK

> The restored VM can only be placed on the same host, where the VDP appliance is running.

Restore progress can be monitored under the same **Emergency Restore** tab.

Remember that:

► VM is always restored as a new VM
► The restored VM will be placed in the root of the vCenter inventory
► The restored VM will be in the power off state

# Configuring the backup retention policy

VDP offers a few ways to define the retention policy, which are as follows:

► Forever
► For a certain number of days, weeks, months, or years
► Till the specified date
► Custom schedule

Custom schedule includes:

► Daily for a certain number of days, weeks, months, or years
► Weekly for certain number of days, weeks, months, or years

> ▸ Monthly for a certain number of days, weeks, months, or years

> ▸ Yearly for a certain number of days, weeks, months ,or years

The difference between keeping backups for 60 days and doing daily retention for 60 days is that in the first case, backups older than 60 days will be deleted during the next backup job, while daily schedule will check and delete old backups daily.

## How to do it...

To set the retention policy settings when a backup job is being created, edit the existing backup job by following these steps:

1. Select the job in the list.

2. Expand **Backup Job Actions** and choose **Edit**.

3. Click on **Retention Policy** on the left.

# Protecting the vCenter VM

As your environment grows, vCenter becomes a critical management tool, which raises the requirement for it to be highly available.

When vCenter is not available, the environment doesn't go down because all the core functionality is still there. All VMs will still be running; HA and FT will continue to function.

> Also, it's important that all hosts and guests continue to function only for 14 days. After this grace period, critical functionality, such as powering on ESXi hosts or starting VMs, will cease to operate.

What will be lost is the ability to perform a lot of administrative tasks that are not available without vCenter such as:

- ► vMotion and Storage vMotion
- ► HA and FT configuration
- ► DRS manual tasks
- ► DRS recommendation generation
- ► Deploying VMs from a template
- ► Resource availability information updates for HA
- ► Issuing new licenses to hosts

## How to do it...

As you can see, these are important administrative tasks, which, in case of any issues with your environment, may become critical as troubleshooting abilities will depend on them.

The following options are available to protect vCenter Server availability.

### Virtualizing vCenter

This is probably the most obvious and easiest solution. With the existing clustered environment, you will be able to take advantage of all the available virtualization benefits, such as vMotion and HA.

For most environments, using HA and having a brief downtime while vCenter reboots will be enough.

For situations when HA fails to restart vCenter VM, it is recommended to disable DRS for this VM and keep it on the same host unless it needs to be vMotioned for maintenance purposes. This way, if vCenter VM hasn't been restarted, the administrator can always connect directly to the host and power the VM back on.

When the vCenter database is on a separate server, make sure the vCenter VM restart priority is lower than the vCenter database server restart priority. The same is valid for any other services vCenter depends on such as Active Directory and DNS. Often, these services will have a higher priority because they are needed for the whole environment.

Unfortunately, FT is not an option yet for most environments. Its requirement for one vCPU contradicts vCenter requirements to have at least two CPUs.

To summarize this, here is a list of the pros and cons:

| Pros | Cons |
|------|------|
| ▸ Easy to implement | ▸ FT is not yet available |
| ▸ Low cost as no physical server is needed | ▸ Need for manual actions in certain cases |
| ▸ Quick automatic service restore | |
| ▸ Short downtime in case of failure | |

## Clustering the database

Database cluster is a general term for a set of servers or instances connected to the same database. In many cases, it's referred to two or more database servers that share the same storage. It can also be used to describe a number of replicated database servers. In any case, a database cluster increases redundancy, availability, or both at the same time.

This can be a good option if you are not running the database on the same server as vCenter.

There is no additional cost in doing this if you already have a database cluster in your environment. At the same time, it can be expensive if you don't have one yet, mostly because of licensing.

Also, there are additional skills required to maintain such an environment. This should also be considered as there may be additional cost involved.

To summarize this, here is a list of the pros and cons:

| Pros | Cons |
|------|------|
| ▸ No additional cost for existing clusters | ▸ Costly for new implementations |
| ▸ Highest database availability | ▸ Administration skills required |

## Third-party solutions

There are a few clustering solutions available from other vendors, which can be helpful in protecting the vCenter Server availability. Among the most known are the following:

- ▸ **Microsoft Cluster Services** (**MSCS**), which can protect the whole vCenter Server
- ▸ Microsoft SQL Server 2012 AlwaysOn, which takes care of the vCenter database
- ▸ **Veritas Cluster Services** (**VCS**), similar to MSCS, protects the whole server

VMware introduced MSCS support in vSphere 5.5. MSCS has been supported starting from vSphere 3. In fact, vSphere 5.5 introduced some enhancements in MSCS support:

- Native iSCSI and FCoE support
- Round Robin policy support for disks engaged in clustering
- Clustering on a single host (CIB) and across hosts (CAB) as well as N+1 virtual machines.

Other third-party solutions are not certified but VMware's commitment is best effort support. VMware KB 1024051 on the VMware Knowledge Base website `http://kb.vmware.com` gives additional information on vCenter high availability options support.

To summarize this, here is a list of the pros and cons:

| Pros | Cons |
| --- | --- |
| ▸ Ability to provide high uptime<br>▸ No impact in case of OS maintenance | ▸ Licensing cost<br>▸ Administration skills required<br>▸ Possible downtime due to software issues |

# 3
# Increasing Environment Scalability

In this chapter, we will cover the following recipes:

- ▶ Delivering new VMs faster with templates
- ▶ Delivering new VMs faster with customizations
- ▶ Troubleshooting customizations
- ▶ Keeping templates up to date
- ▶ Utilizing host local storage
- ▶ Automating VM deployments
- ▶ Deploying new hosts faster with scripted installation
- ▶ Deploying new hosts faster with autodeploy
- ▶ Keeping host configuration consistent
- ▶ Increasing a VM's RAM and CPU online

## Introduction

In this chapter, we will review some options and features available in vCenter to improve an administrator's efficiency. Templates, customizations, host profiles and other solutions designed to automate and simplify VM, host deployment, and configuration at the end of the day allow faster time to market, which is expected by many businesses nowadays.

# Delivering new VMs faster with templates

Often, when new virtual servers are deployed, there is a set of tasks that are the same for all of them. These tasks are usually OS installation, OS updates, VMware tools installation, and so on.

With vCenter, you can perform these tasks once and create a template. With this template, you can deploy as many servers as you need and only perform tasks that are different on each of them.

So templates make deployment of new virtual machines faster. There are also less chances for a mistake to happen or a step to be missed.

An example of a workflow with and without templates is shown in the following picture:

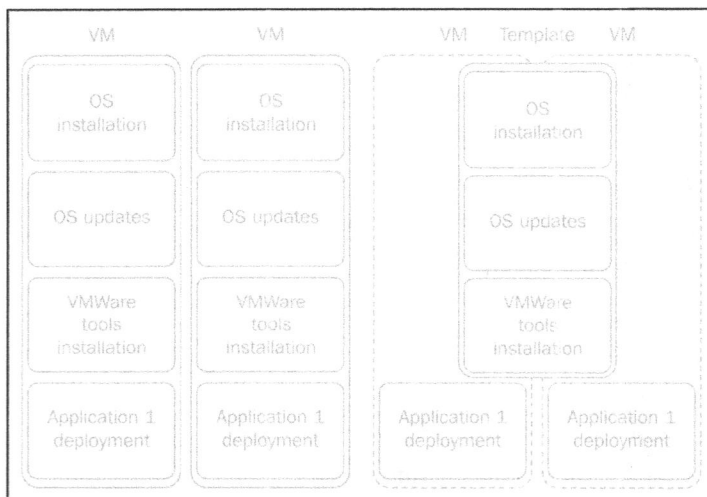

## How to do it...

To create a template:

1.  Create a new VM and perform configuration tasks that have to be repeated for each VM such as OS installation, OS updates, VMware tools installation, and so on.
2.  Shut down the VM and right-click on it.
3.  Go to **Template**.

4. Click on **Convert to Template** as shown in the following screenshot:

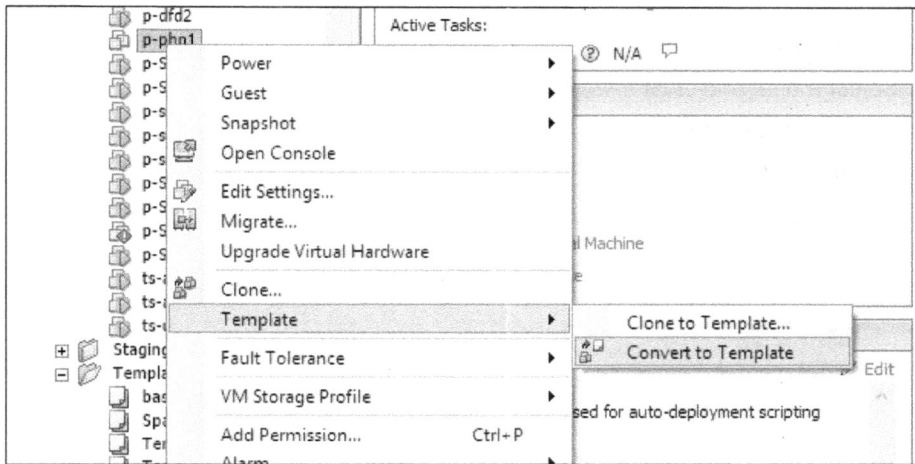

The virtual machine will be converted to a template.

In the Web Client:

1. Right-click on a virtual machine.
2. Go to **All vCenter actions**.
3. Select **Convert to Template**.

To deploy a new VM from a template:

1. Go to the **VMs and Templates** view.
2. Right-click on the template.
3. Choose **Deploy Virtual Machine from this Template...**, as shown in the following screenshot:

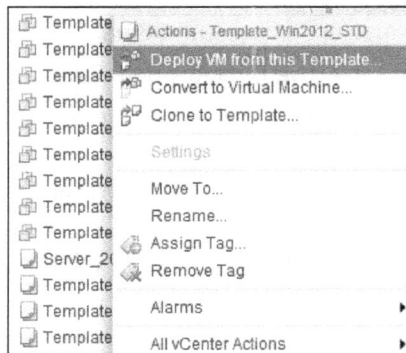

This will open the **Deploy Template** wizard as shown in the following screenshot where you will be required to:

1. Choose a VM name and its location in the inventory
2. Select a host and cluster where it will reside
3. Select a resource pool
4. Choose a datastore
5. Choose the customization

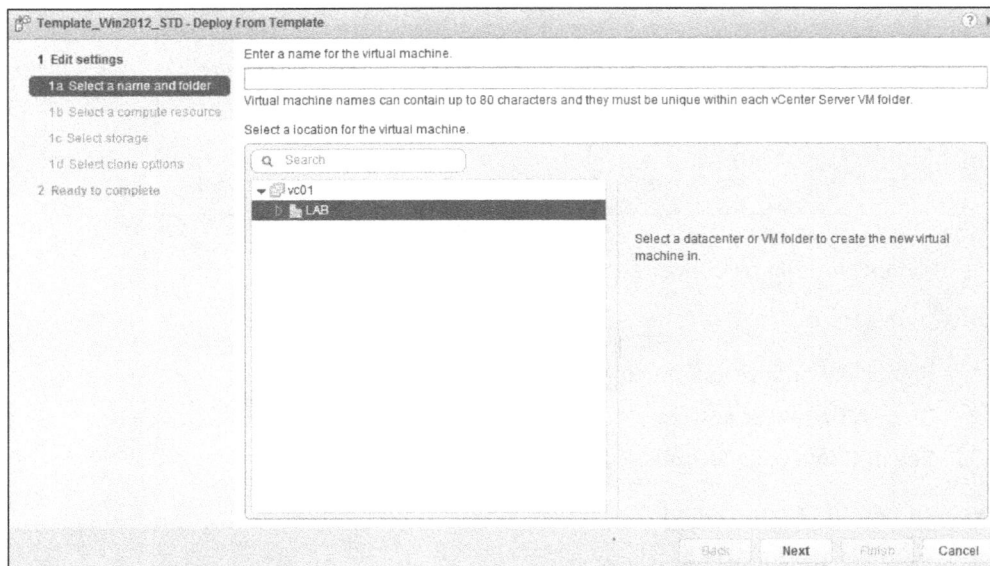

## There's more...

There are a few things that need to be considered when using templates:

▸ Try to keep your templates up to date with OS patches, updates, and so on.

▸ Don't join templates to the Active Directory domain.

▸ Make sure it doesn't have an IP address configured or that this IP address is not used anywhere else to avoid any conflicts.

▸ Give templates meaningful names and use the **Notes** field to add additional information about the template.

▸ Install VMware tools and keep them updated as you update hosts.

# Delivering new VMs faster with customizations

**Customizations** allow the automating of post-deployment tasks such as:

▶ Changing the local administrator password

▶ Changing the computer name

▶ Changing the Windows product key

▶ Configuring IP, DNS, and other network settings

▶ Joining a domain

▶ Changing the time zone

▶ Running custom bat, PowerShell, or bash scripts

## How to do it...

To create a customization:

1. Go to the Home view.
2. Click on **Customization Specifications Manager**.
3. Click on **New**, which will open vSphere Client Windows Guest Customization.

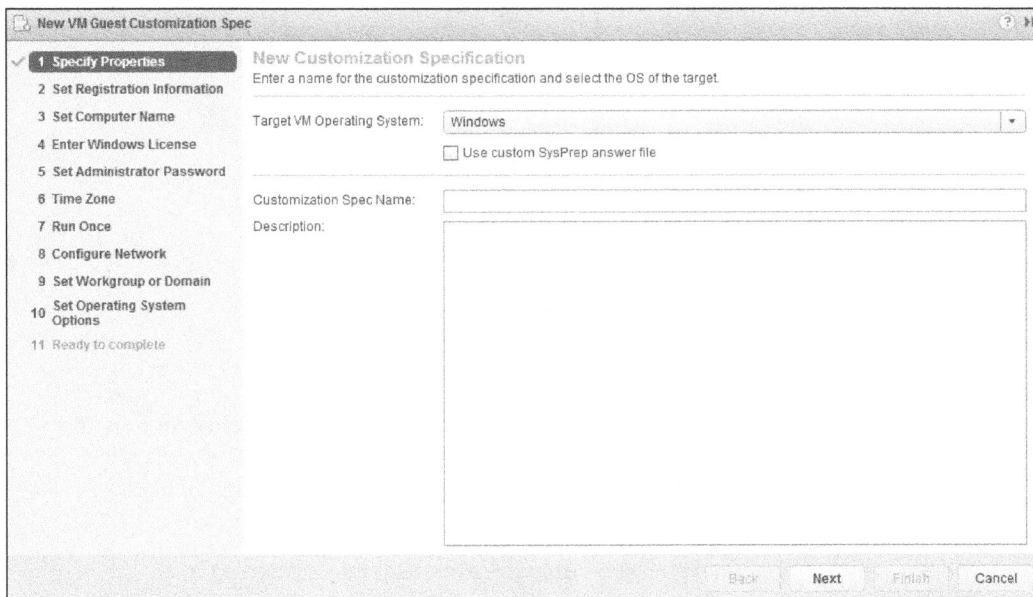

The wizard will ask you a series of questions related to post-deployment tasks that need to be performed:

- ▶ Registration information: owner's name and organization
- ▶ Computer name
- ▶ Windows license key
- ▶ Local administrator password
- ▶ Time zone
- ▶ Network settings
- ▶ Workgroup or domain name
- ▶ Whether a new SID has to be generated
- ▶ Whether there are any commands that need to be run once after deployment

## Using customization

If you are deploying a VM from a template, customization options are available on the last step of the **Deploy Template** wizard:

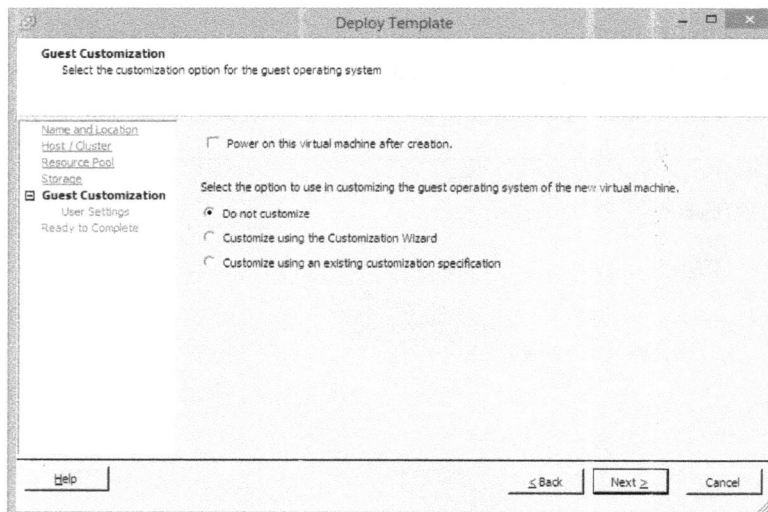

If you already have a customization, choose the last option: **Customize using an existing customization specification**. The second option—**Customize using the Customization Wizard**—will open vSphere Client Guest Customization, the same wizard that's used to create a new customization.

If this option has been chosen, you will be able to save this configuration as a new customization.

When deploying VMs in Web Client, this last step is called **1d Select clone options**.

The first option, **Customize the operating system**, when checked will show the list of existing customizations in the next step:

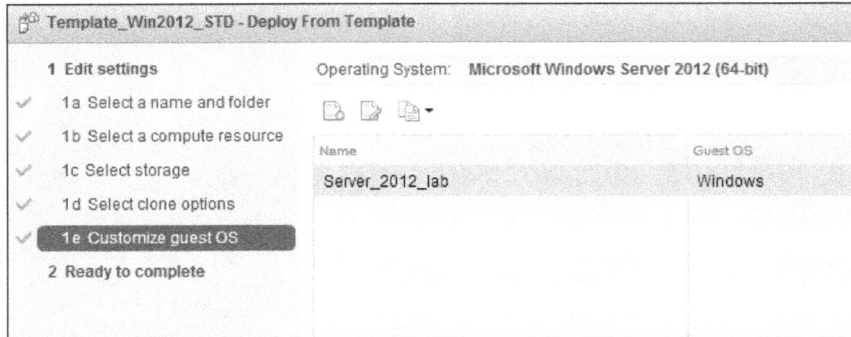

Template_Win2012_STD - Deploy From Template

| | |
|---|---|
| 1 Edit settings | Operating System: Microsoft Windows Server 2012 (64-bit) |
| ✓ 1a Select a name and folder | |
| ✓ 1b Select a compute resource | |
| ✓ 1c Select storage | Name | Guest OS |
| ✓ 1d Select clone options | Server_2012_lab | Windows |
| ✓ 1e Customize guest OS | |
| 2 Ready to complete | |

# Troubleshooting customizations

Customization will run once a VM has been deployed and powered on.

## How to do it...

To track the process, select the VM and go to the **Tasks & Events** tab. Here, under the **Tasks** view, you will be able to see whether customization has started and when it's finished.

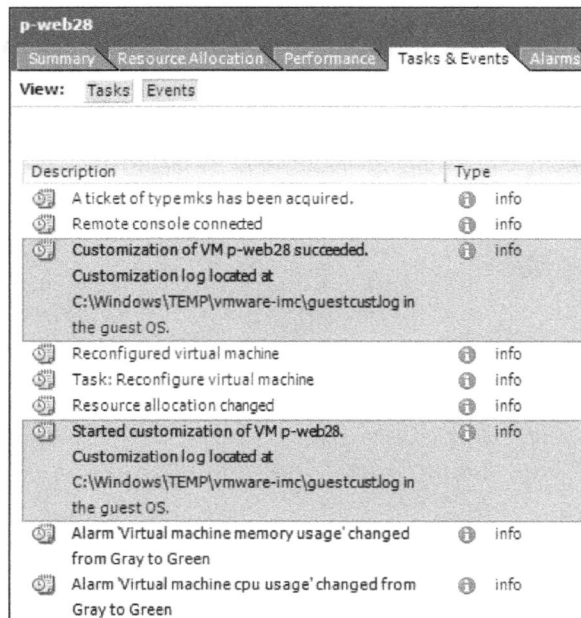

p-web28

Summary | Resource Allocation | Performance | Tasks & Events | Alarms

View: Tasks Events

| Description | Type | |
|---|---|---|
| A ticket of type mks has been acquired. | ℹ | info |
| Remote console connected | ℹ | info |
| Customization of VM p-web28 succeeded. Customization log located at C:\Windows\TEMP\vmware-imc\guestcust.log in the guest OS. | ℹ | info |
| Reconfigured virtual machine | ℹ | info |
| Task: Reconfigure virtual machine | ℹ | info |
| Resource allocation changed | ℹ | info |
| Started customization of VM p-web28. Customization log located at C:\Windows\TEMP\vmware-imc\guestcust.log in the guest OS. | ℹ | info |
| Alarm 'Virtual machine memory usage' changed from Gray to Green | ℹ | info |
| Alarm 'Virtual machine cpu usage' changed from Gray to Green | ℹ | info |

If customization starts but never finishes or fails, review the following log files, which may give you a clue as to what went wrong:

- ▸ `%SYSTEMROOT%\Temp\VMware-cust-nativeapp.log`
- ▸ Log files in the `%SYSTEMROOT%\Temp\vmware-imc\` folder

Once you have the actual error message, search VMware Knowledge Base available at `http://kb.vmware.com` for a solution.

If customization fails to add a new VM to a domain, make sure you use a fully qualified domain name for the domain and username with the following details:

- ▸ Username: `user@domain.local`
- ▸ Domain: `domain.local`

## There's more...

Customization success very much depends on the health of the template or source VM that's being cloned. Customization may fail when:

- ▸ Sysprep runs on the template more than three times
- ▸ The Microsoft Windows Software Licensing Rearm program has run more than three times
- ▸ Third-party software is installed

More details about these issues and how to fix them can be found in the following VMware Knowledge Base `http://kb.vmware.com` articles:

- ▸ The KB article 2014140 can be found at `http://kb.vmware.com/kb/2014140`
- ▸ The KB article 1006025 can be found at `http://kb.vmware.com/kb/1006025`

Also, it can be found in the Microsoft Knowledge Base article at `http://support.microsoft.com/kb/929828`

# Keeping templates up to date

It is a good idea to keep templates up to date with OS patches and VMware tools updates. Also, the same procedure applies to making any changes to an existing template.

## How to do it...

To make changes to an existing template:

1. Go to the **VMs and Templates** view.

2. Right-click on the template.

3. Choose **Convert to Virtual Machine**.

4. The **Convert Template to Virtual Machine** wizard will prompt for cluster or specific host as well as the resource pool future VMs should be put to, as shown in the following screenshot:

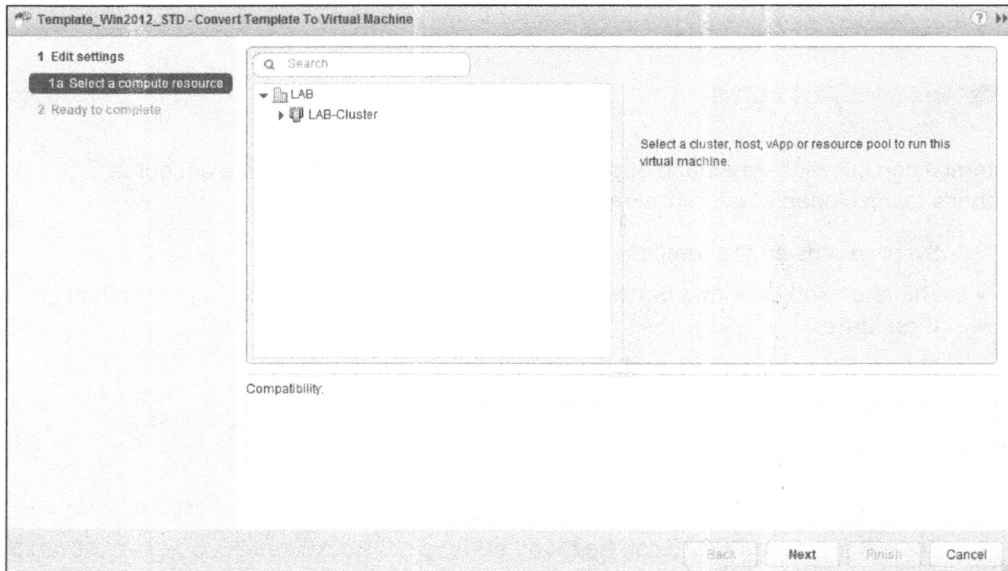

5. Click on **Finish** to start the conversion.

6. Once the conversion has been completed, you can power the VM up and perform the necessary changes and updates.

7. The last step is to convert it back to a template as described in the *Delivering new VMs faster with templates* recipe of this chapter.

If you have an IP address assigned to this VM or you are not sure whether there is anything configured, consider disabling the network card in VM settings before turning it on to avoid any conflicts with running servers.

# Utilizing host local storage

vSphere 5.5 introduced a new feature called **Virtual SAN** (**vSAN**). This feature allows utilizing a host's local storage to create a shared distributed storage for VM placement.

vSAN is a software-based solution built into ESXi; it's scalable and easy to configure and manage.

## Getting ready

vSAN requires a license separate from vSphere and vCenter. The feature is licensed on a per-CPU basis.

The minimum infrastructure requirements for vSAN are:

- ► Each host that is a part of the vSAN cluster has to have at least one **Solid State Disk** (**SSD**) and one **Hard Disk Drive** (**HDD**).
- ► At least three hosts with local storage are required.
- ► At least 1 Gbps network ports are required.

Also, it is recommended to:

- ► Use 10 Gbps NICs.
- ► Have a VMkernel vSAN adapter on every physical NIC.
- ► Have a 1:10 ratio between SSD and HDD capacity.
- ► Hardware RAID is not required and it's better to have just a bunch of disks without any hardware RAID configured.
- ► Create more disk groups of a smaller size rather than less larger groups. Smaller groups mean smaller failure domains and better performance.

▶ Keep the host configuration in the vSAN cluster similar. Refer to the *Keeping host configuration consistent* recipe in this chapter for more details.

▶ Store ESXi logs externally. See the *Configuring remote logging* recipe for more details.

▶ Make sure the HA isolation response is set to power-off, which allows VMs residing on isolated hosts to be restarted.

▶ Avoid using the flash read cache reservation for your storage. Let vSAN take care of that.

Currently, vSAN doesn't support:
  ▶ FT
  ▶ DPM
  ▶ Storage DRS
  ▶ Storage I/O control
  ▶ Virtual disks larger than 2 TB
  ▶ More than 32 hosts
  ▶ More than 100 VMs per host
  ▶ More than 7 HDDs in a disk group
Consider this when planning changes.

# How to do it...

The process of configuring vSAN includes the following steps and is outlined in:

1. Create VMkernel NIC for vSAN.
2. Enable vSAN on the cluster level.
3. Create vSAN disk groups.
4. Create the storage policy (optional).

## Create VMkernel NIC for vSAN

This has to be done on each host participating in the vSAN cluster:

1. Select a host.
2. Go to **Manage | Networking | VMkernel adapters**.
3. Click on the **Add Networking** icon.
4. Select **VMkernel Network Adapter** and click on **Next**.

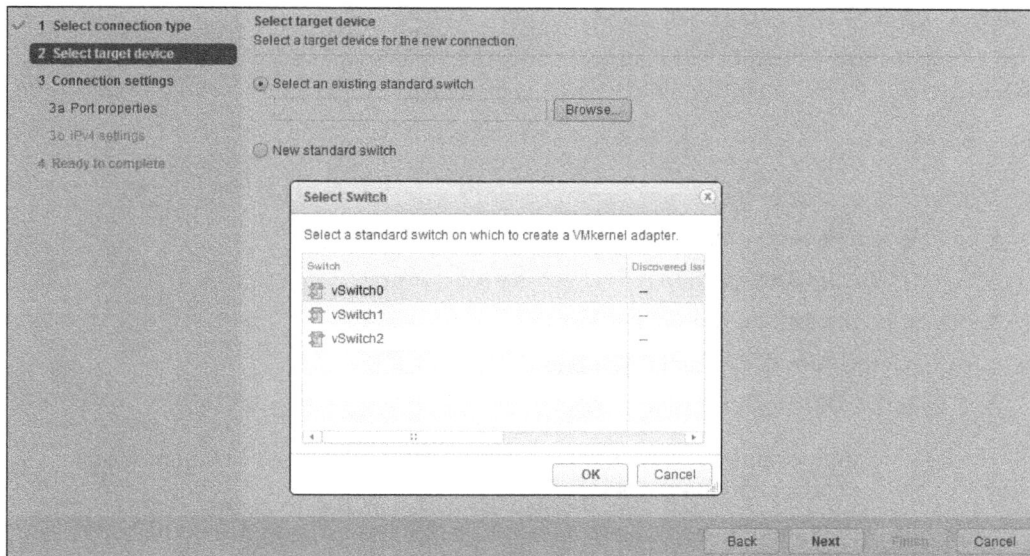

5. Click on **Browse**, select the distributed port group, and click on **Next**.

6. Check **Virtual SAN traffic** under the **Enable services** section and click on **Next**.

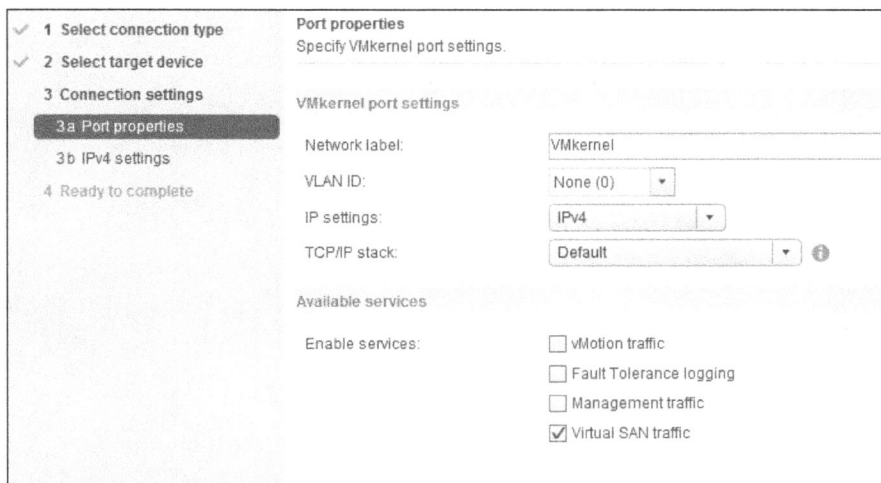

7. Leave the network setting at DHCP or provide static settings and click on **Next**.

8. Click on **Finish**.

## Enable vSAN on cluster level

Once all hosts have VMkernel NIC adapters configured, vSAN can be enabled on the cluster. Before enabling vSAN, make sure vSphere HA is disabled. Disable it temporarily if necessary.

To enable vSAN:

1.  Select the cluster these hosts are part of.
2.  Go to the **Manage** tab.
3.  In the **Virtual SAN section** on the left, select **General**.
4.  Click on the **Edit** button on the right.
5.  Check the **Turn ON Virtual SAN** option.
6.  Select vSAN mode and click on **OK**.

    ❑ In **Automatic** mode, every empty storage on the host will automatically be added to the vSAN storage.

    ❑ In **Manual** mode, the administrator selects the disks that will be used for vSAN manually.

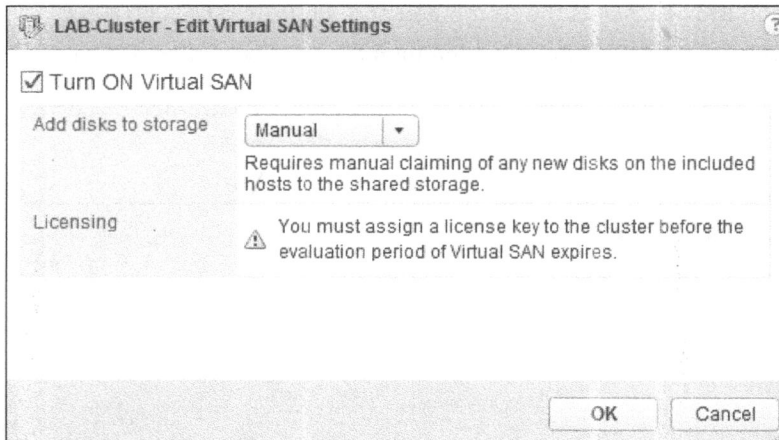

## Create vSAN disk groups

A disk group is a local storage that hosts provide to vSAN. To create a disk group:

1.  Select a cluster.
2.  Go to **Manage | Settings | Disk Management**.
3.  Select a host in the list.
4.  Click on the **Create Disk Group** icon.

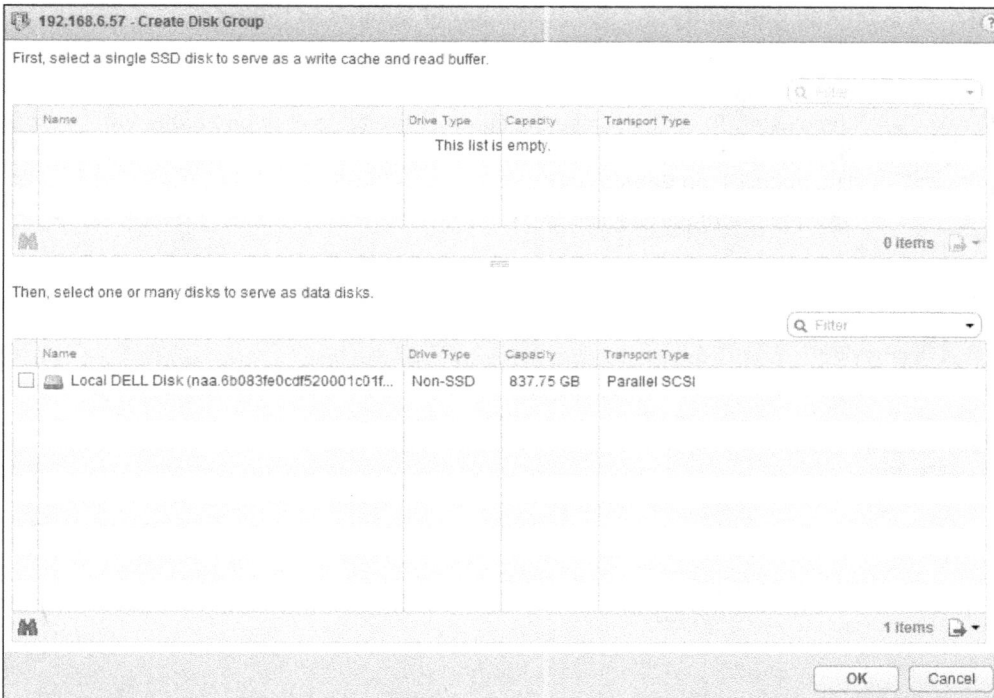

At least one SSD and one spinning disk must be selected. A single disc group can contain up to six spinning disks.

5. Repeat the last step for all hosts participating in vSAN.

There must be at least three hosts in vSAN.

## Creating a storage policy

By default, the newly created vSAN cluster will be able to tolerate one host failure. In general, to tolerate *n* failures, the environment requires 2N + 1 hosts.

If the requirement is to tolerate more host failures, do the following:

1. Under **Home** in Web Client, open **VM Storage Policies**.

2. Click on the **New VM Storage Policy** icon.

3. Give it a name and click on **Next**.

4. Click on **Add Capability** and select **Number of failures to tolerate**.

> If this option is not available, you may need to enable storage policies for the cluster. To do that, close the current dialog and click on **Enable VM Storage policies per compute resource** icon, select a cluster from the list, and click on **Enable**.
>
> This feature requires a license.

5. Set the required value and click on **Next**.

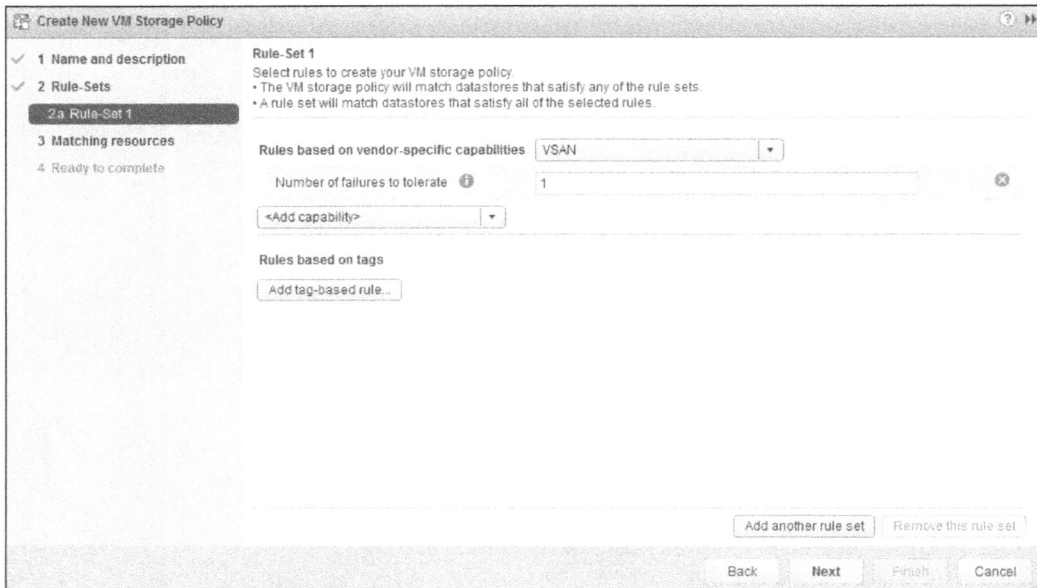

6. Click on **Next** and then on **Finish**.

> Be careful when creating a profile with other settings without specifying the number of failures to tolerate. The default value in this case will be 0.

Once a new profile has been created, it can be applied to a virtual machine. To do this:

1. Right-click on a VM.

2. Select **All vCenter Actions**.

3. Choose **VM Storage Policies**.

4. Click on **Manage VM Storage Policies**.

5. Select the policy and click on the **Apply to disks** button.

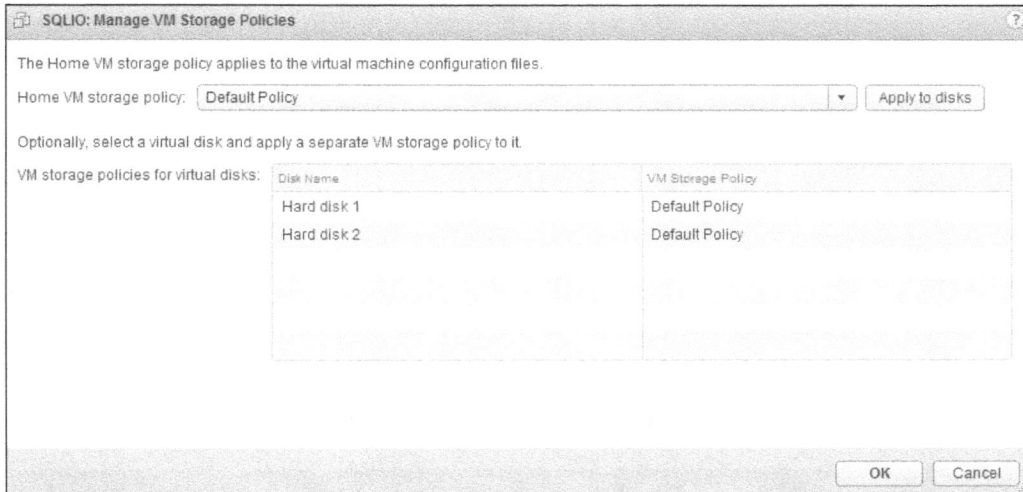

| SQLIO: Manage VM Storage Policies | | ⑦ |
|---|---|---|

The Home VM storage policy applies to the virtual machine configuration files.

Home VM storage policy: [ Default Policy ▾ ] [ Apply to disks ]

Optionally, select a virtual disk and apply a separate VM storage policy to it.

VM storage policies for virtual disks:

| Disk Name | VM Storage Policy |
|---|---|
| Hard disk 1 | Default Policy |
| Hard disk 2 | Default Policy |

[ OK ] [ Cancel ]

6. Click on **OK**.

## How it works...

Each piece of data is written at least twice, that is, there are at least two replicas for each data object on vSAN. Replicas are written to different disks on different hosts. This is to ensure that in the case of a host failure, this data is available on the other host.

Additional replicas will be used to protect against multiple host failures. vSAN will create enough replicas depending on the chosen amount of host failures to tolerate. The number of nodes in a cluster also dictates the maximum number of host failures to tolerate. For example, three node clusters can tolerate only one host failure.

The requirement to have a third host in the vSAN cluster comes from the need of a so called witness host. A witness host doesn't store any replicas. Instead, it stores metadata that helps to keep track of replica placement to ensure at least one replica is always available.

The witness host also plays an important role in a split-brain situation, when two or more hosts are running but are not able to connect to each other. In this situation, the witness host helps to choose the host that will be serving data.

The following diagram shows this architecture for three hosts:

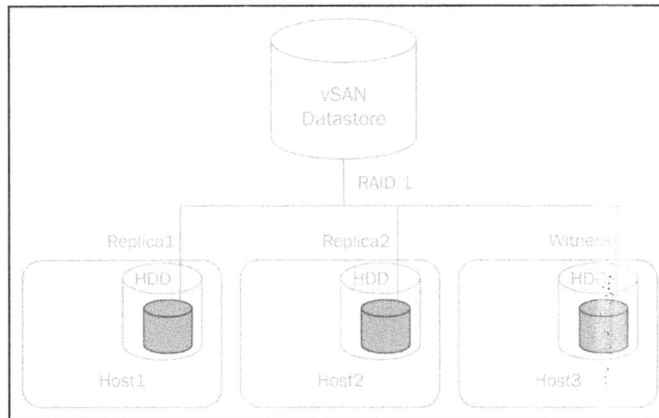

The failure of a witness host doesn't cause any data loss as there is still a full set of data available. If the witness host is not available for more than 60 minutes, it is automatically rebuilt.

# Automating VM deployments

In situations when there is a requirement to deploy many VMs in a short period of time, the process can be automated using **PowerCLI** scripts.

> PowerCLI is not the only way to automate deployments in vSphere. VMware provides an **Application Program Interface** (**API**) and **Software Development Kit** (**SDK**), which can be used in conjunction with several languages to automate a broad range of tasks in vSphere. More information is available at https://www.vmware.com/support/developer/vc-sdk/.

PowerCLI is a snap-in for Windows PowerShell to manage the vSphere environment. It allows administrators to automate any management tasks, including tasks related to guest OS and storage. The tool comes with over 300 cmdlets as well as documentation and examples. PowerCLI is free and can be downloaded from http://my.vmware.com.

> Make sure the version being installed is compatible with the vSphere and PowerShell versions in the environment.

## Getting ready

Before creating and testing a VM deployment script described further, make sure the following is ready:

- ▸ A template to be used
- ▸ Customization to be applied.
- ▸ A list of server names and IP addresses new VMs have to be configured with
- ▸ PowerCLI installed on the machine where the deployment script will be executed

## How to do it...

VM deployment with PowerCLI involves the following:

1. Creating a deployment script
2. Connecting to vCenter and running the script

### Creating a deployment script

In PowerCLI, a new VM can be created with the `New-VM` command. It takes over 30 arguments such as:

- ▸ Target host
- ▸ VM name
- ▸ Template
- ▸ Target datastore
- ▸ Customization

The typical command that can be used is as follows:

```
New-VM -vmhost <Target Host> -Name <VM Name> -Template <Template
name> -Datastore <Datastore name> -OSCustomizationSpec <Customization
name> -Location <Folder name> -Description <VM description>
```

All parameters can be set as variables at the beginning of the script. This way they can be changed if necessary in one place instead of searching for them in the code:

```
$targetHost = "esxi6"
New-VM -vmhost $targetHost ...
```

When the existing customization doesn't include certain settings, it can be modified in the script. For example, to add new VMs to the Windows domain, modify the customization in the following way:

```
Get-OSCustomizationSpec -Name <Existing customization> | New-
OSCustomizationSpec -Name <Temporary customization> -Type Persistent
```

```
Get-OSCustomizationSpec -Name <Temporary customization> | set-
OSCustomizationSpec -Domain <domain> -DomainUsername <Domain user> -
DomainPassword <Domain admin password>
```

> This doesn't change the existing customization in vCenter. The domain user must have permission to add computers to the Active Directory domain.

The `Set-NetworkAdapter` command can be used to assign a VM's NIC to the correct port group. For example, execute the following command:

```
Get-NetworkAdapter -VM <VM name> | Set-NetworkAdapter -NetworkName
<Port group name>
```

Finally, use `Start-VM` to power on a new virtual machine:

```
Start-VM -VM <VM name>
```

More information about all the commands mentioned earlier can be obtained by typing `get-help <command>` in PowerCLI.

## Running a deployment script

A deployment script has to be run against vCenter where VMs will be deployed:

1.  Open PowerCLI.
2.  Type `Connect-VIServer` to connect to vCenter.
3.  You will be prompted for the vCenter FQDN or IP address.

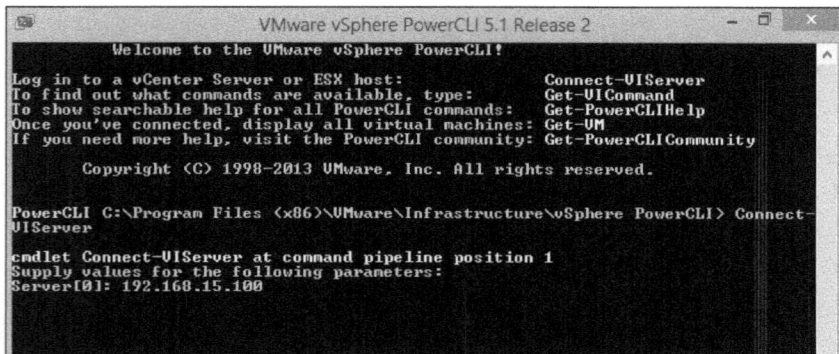

4.  Once connected, you will be prompted for credentials to log in.

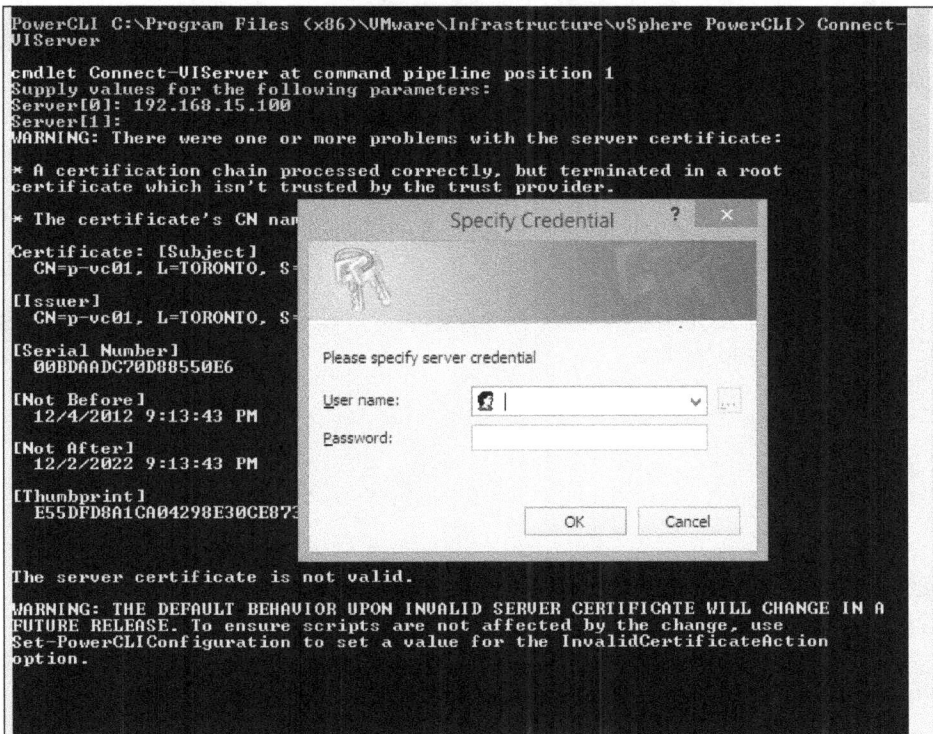

```
PowerCLI C:\Program Files (x86)\VMware\Infrastructure\vSphere PowerCLI> Connect-
VIServer

cmdlet Connect-VIServer at command pipeline position 1
Supply values for the following parameters:
Server[0]: 192.168.15.100
Server[1]:
WARNING: There were one or more problems with the server certificate:

* A certification chain processed correctly, but terminated in a root
certificate which isn't trusted by the trust provider.

* The certificate's CN nam
                                         Specify Credential       ?   ×
Certificate: [Subject]
  CN=p-vc01, L=TORONTO, S=

[[Issuer]
  CN=p-vc01, L=TORONTO, S=
                                    Please specify server credential
[Serial Number]
  00BDAADC70D88550E6
                                    User name:        🔲 |                  ∨  ...
[Not Before]
  12/4/2012 9:13:43 PM              Password:

[Not After]
  12/2/2022 9:13:43 PM
                                                         OK         Cancel
[Thumbprint]
  E55DFD8A1CA04298E30CE87

The server certificate is not valid.

WARNING: THE DEFAULT BEHAVIOR UPON INVALID SERVER CERTIFICATE WILL CHANGE IN A
FUTURE RELEASE. To ensure scripts are not affected by the change, use
Set-PowerCLIConfiguration to set a value for the InvalidCertificateAction
option.
```

5.  You will get the PowerCLI command prompt after a successful connection.

6.  Switch to the folder with the deployment script:

    `cd <path>`

7.  Run the following script:

    `.\<script filename>`

```
Name                        Port  User
192.168.15.100              443   kkuminsky


PowerCLI C:\Program Files (x86)\VMware\Infrastructure\vSphere PowerCLI>
PowerCLI C:\Program Files (x86)\VMware\Infrastructure\vSphere PowerCLI> cd C:\Sc
ripts
PowerCLI C:\Scripts> .\new-vms.ps1
```

# Deploying new hosts faster with scripted installation

Scripted installation is an alternative way to deploy ESXi hosts. It can be used when several hosts need to be deployed or upgraded.

> To deploy a large number of hosts, the Auto Deploy feature described in the *Deploying new hosts faster with auto deploy* recipe in this chapter may be more suitable.

The installation script contains ESXi settings and can be accessed by a host during the ESXi boot from the following locations:

- ► FTP
- ► HTTP or HTTPS
- ► NFS
- ► USB flash drive or CD-ROM

## How to do it...

The following sections describe the process of creating an installation script and using it to boot the ESXi host.

### Creating an installation script

An installation script contains installation options for ESXi. It's a text file with the `.cfg` extension.

The best way to create an installation script is to use the default script supplied with the ESXi installer and modify it. The default script is located in the `/etc/vmware/weasel/` folder location and is called `ks.cfg`.

Commands that can be modified include, but are not limited to:

- ► The `install`, `installorupgrade`, or `upgrade` commands define the ESXi disk—location, where the installation or upgrade will be installed. The available options are:
  - ❑ `--disk`: This option is the disk name which can be specified as path (`/vmfs/devices/disks/vmhbaX:X:X`), VML name (`vml.xxxxxxxx`) or as LUN UID (`vmkLUM_UID`)
  - ❑ `-overwritevmfs`: This option wipes the existing datastore.
  - ❑ `--preservevmfs`: This option keeps the existing datastore.
  - ❑ `--novmfsondisk`: This option prevents a new partition from being created.

▸ The `Network` command, which specifies the network settings. Most of the available options are self-explanatory:

    ❑ `--bootproto=[dhcp|static]`

    ❑ `--device`: MAC address of NIC to use

    ❑ `--ip`

    ❑ `--gateway`

    ❑ `--nameserver`

    ❑ `--netmask`

    ❑ `--hostname`

    ❑ `--vlanid`

A full list of installation and upgrade commands can be found in the vSphere5 documentation on the VMware website at `https://www.vmware.com/support/pubs/`.

## Use the installation script to configure ESXi

In order to use the installation script, you will need to use additional ESXi boot options.

1. Boot a host from the ESXi installation disk.
2. When the ESXi installer screen appears, press *Shift + O* to provide additional boot options.
3. In the command prompt, type the following:

```
ks=<location of the script> <additional boot options>
```

The valid locations are as follows:

▸ `ks=cdrom:/path`

▸ `ks=file://path`

▸ `ks=protocol://path`

▸ `ks=usb:/path`

The additional options available are as follows:

▸ `gateway`: This option is the default gateway

▸ `ip`: This option is the IP address

▸ `nameserver`: This option is the DNS server

▸ `netmask`: This option is the subnet mask

▸ `vlanid`: This option is the VLAN ID

▸ `netdevice`: This option is the MAC address of NIC to use

▸ `bootif`: This option is the MAC address of NIC to use in PXELINUX format

For example, for the HTTP location, the command will look like this:

```
ks=http://XX.XX.XX.XX/scripts/ks-v1.cfg nameserver=XX.XX.XX.XX
ip=XX.XX.XX.XX netmask=255.255.255.0 gateway=XX.XX.XX.XX
```

# Deploying new hosts faster with auto deploy

**vSphere Auto Deploy** is VMware's solution to simplify the deployment of large numbers of ESXi hosts. It is one of the available options for ESXi deployment along with an interactive and scripted installation.

The main difference of Auto Deploy compared to other deployment options is that the ESXi configuration is not stored on the host's disk. Instead, it's managed with image and host profiles by the Auto Deploy server.

## Getting ready

Before using Auto Deploy, confirm the following:

► The Auto Deploy server is installed and registered with vCenter.

> It can be installed as a standalone server or as part of the vCenter installation.

► The DHCP server exists in the environment.

► The DHCP server is configured to point to the TFTP server for PXE boot (option 66) with the boot filename `undionly.kpxe.vmw-hardwired`.

► The TFTP server that will be used for PXE boot exists and is configured properly.

► The machine where Auto Deploy cmdlets will run has the following installed:

   ❑ Microsoft .NET 2.0 or later

   ❑ PowerShell 2.0 or later

   ❑ PowerCLI including Auto Deploy cmdlets

► New hosts that will be provisioned with Auto Deploy must:

   ❑ Meet the hardware requirements for ESXi 5

   ❑ Have network connectivity to vCenter, preferably 1 Gbps or higher

   ❑ Have PXE boot enabled

## How to do it...

Once prerequisites are met, the following steps are required to start deploying hosts.

### Configuring the TFTP server

In order to configure the TFTP server with the correct boot image for ESXi, execute the following steps:

1. In vCenter, go to **Home | Auto Deploy**.
2. Switch to the **Administration** tab.
3. From the Auto Deploy page, click on **Download TFTP Boot ZIP**.
4. Download the file and unzip it to the appropriate folder on the TFTP server.

### Creating an image profile

Image profiles are created using Image Builder PowerCLI cmdlets. Image Builder requires PowerCLI and can be installed on a machine that's used to run administrative tasks. It doesn't have to be a vCenter Server or Auto Deploy server and the only requirement for this machine is that it must have access to the software depot—a file server that stores image profiles.

Image profiles can be created from scratch or by cloning an existing profile. The following steps outline the process of creating an image profile by cloning. The steps assume that:

▶ The Image Builder has been installed.

▶ The appropriate software depot has been downloaded from the VMware website by going to `http://www.vmware.com/downloads` and searching for the software depot.

Cloning an existing profile included in the depot is the easiest way to create a new profile. The steps to do so are as follows:

1. Add a depot with the image profile to be cloned:

   ```
   Add-EsxSoftwareDepot -DepotUrl <Path to softwaredepot>
   ```

2. Find the name of the profile to be cloned using `Get-ESXImageProfile`.

3. Clone the profile:

   ```
   New-EsxImageProfile -CloneProfile <Existing profile name> -
   Name <New profile name>
   ```

4.  Add a software package to the new image profile:

```
Add-EsxSoftwarePackage -ImageProfile <New profile name> -
SoftwarePackage <Package>
```

At this point, the software package will be validated and in case of errors, or if there are any dependencies that need to be resolved, an appropriate message will be displayed.

## Assigning an image profile to hosts

To create a rule that assigns an image profile to a host, execute the following steps:

1.  Connect to vCenter with PowerCLI:

```
Connect-VIServer <vCenter IP or FQDN>
```

2.  Add the software depot with the correct image profile to the PowerCLI session:

```
Add-EsxSoftwareDepot <depot URL>
```

3.  Locate the image profile using the Get-EsxImageProfile cmdlet.

4.  Define a rule that assigns hosts with certain attributes to an image profile. For example, for hosts with IP addresses for a range, run the following command:

```
New-DeployRule -Name <Rule name> -Item <Profile name> -Pattern
"ipv4=192.168.1.10-192.168.1.20"
```

```
Add-DeployRule <Rule name>
```

## Assigning a host profile to hosts

Optionally, the existing host profile can be assigned to hosts. To accomplish this, execute the following steps:

1.  Connect to vCenter with PowerCLI:

```
Connect-VIServer <vCenter IP or FQDN>
```

2.  Locate the host profile name using the Get-VMhostProfile command.

3.  Define a rule that assigns hosts with certain attributes to a host profile. For example, for hosts with IP addresses for a range, run the following command:

```
New-DeployRule -Name <Rule name> -Item <Profile name> -Pattern
"ipv4=192.168.1.10-192.168.1.20"
```

```
Add-DeployRule <Rule name>
```

Please see the *Keeping host configuration consistent* recipe of this chapter for steps on how to create a new host profile.

# Assigning a host to a folder or cluster in vCenter

To make sure a host is placed in a certain folder or cluster once it boots, do the following:

1.  Connect to vCenter with PowerCLI:

    ```
    Connect-VIServer <vCenter IP or FQDN>
    ```

2.  Define a rule that assigns hosts with certain attributes to a folder or cluster. For example, for hosts with IP addresses for a range, run the following command:

    ```
    New-DeployRule -Name <Rule name> -Item <Folder name> -Pattern
    "ipv4=192.168.1.10-192.168.1.20"

    Add-DeployRule <Rule name>
    ```

> If a host is assigned to a cluster it inherits that cluster's host profile.

## How it works...

Auto Deploy utilizes the PXE boot to connect to the Auto Deploy server and get an image profile, vCenter location, and optionally, host profiles. The detailed process is as follows:

▸   The host gets gPXE executable and gPXE configuration files from the PXE TFTP server.

▸   As gPXE executes, it uses instructions from the configuration file to query the Auto Deploy server for specific information.

▸   The Auto Deploy server returns the requested information specified in the image and host profiles.

▸   The host boots using this information.

▸   Auto Deploy adds a host to the specified vCenter Server.

▸   The host is placed in maintenance mode when additional information such as IP address is required from the administrator.

▸   To exit maintenance mode, the administrator will need to provide this information and reapply the host profile.

When a new host boots for the first time, vCenter creates a new object and stores it together with the host and image profiles in the database. For any subsequent reboots, the existing object is used to get the correct host profile and any changes that have been made.

More details can be found in the vSphere 5 documentation on the VMware website at `https://www.vmware.com/support/pubs/`.

# Keeping host configuration consistent

When managing clusters with many ESXi hosts, administrators usually want these hosts to have the same configuration. Such consistency ensures the required redundancy and lets administrators automate many processes such as DRS or DPM.

As hosts have many settings, it can be a difficult task to keep their configuration consistent across the cluster. vCenter offers a feature called **host profiles**. Profiles store the host's configuration and can be used to configure new hosts and validate the configuration for the existing hosts.

## Getting ready

Host profiles are supported starting from vSphere 4. This is a licensed feature that comes with the Enterprise Plus edition.

## How to do it...

The profile workflow is as follows:

1. Configure one host.
2. Create a profile using this host.
3. Add more hosts or clusters to this profile.
4. Check a host's compliance.
5. Apply a profile to hosts that are not compliant if necessary.

### Creating a profile using a reference host

To create a new profile, execute the following steps:

1. Go to **Home | Management view**.
2. Open **Host Profiles**.
3. Click on the **Create Profile** link at the top of the view.

4. Select **Create Profile from existing host** and click on **Next**.

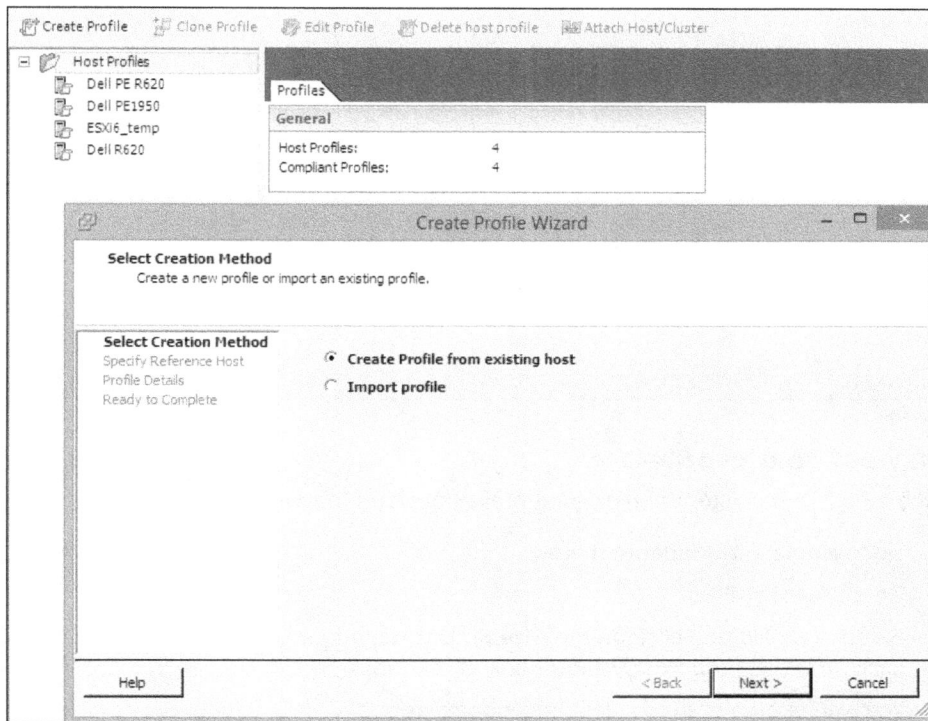

5. Select a host, which has the correct configuration that needs to be replicated and click on **Next**.

6. Choose the name for this profile, click on **Next** and then **Finish**. A new profile will be created.

In the Web Client:

1. Go to **Home | Management view**.

2. Open **Host Profiles**.

3. Click on the plus sign to extract a profile from a host.

4. You will be prompted to choose a host and give a name to the new profile.

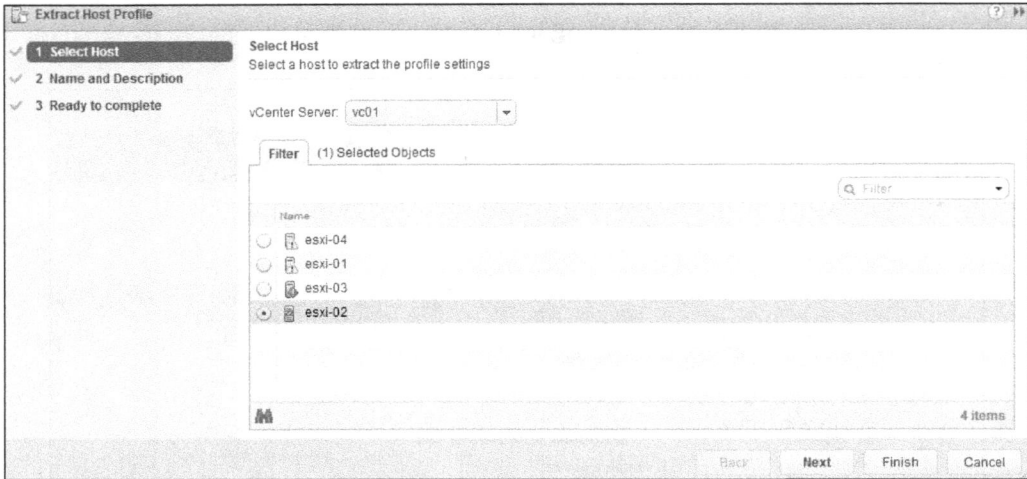

## Add a host to a profile

To attach a host or a cluster to an existing profile, perform the following steps:

1. Go to **Home | Management view**.

2. Open **Host Profiles**.

3. Select a profile and click on the **Attach/Detach** button (in vSphere Client, click on the **Attach Host/Cluster** link at the top).

4. You will be prompted to select hosts or clusters.

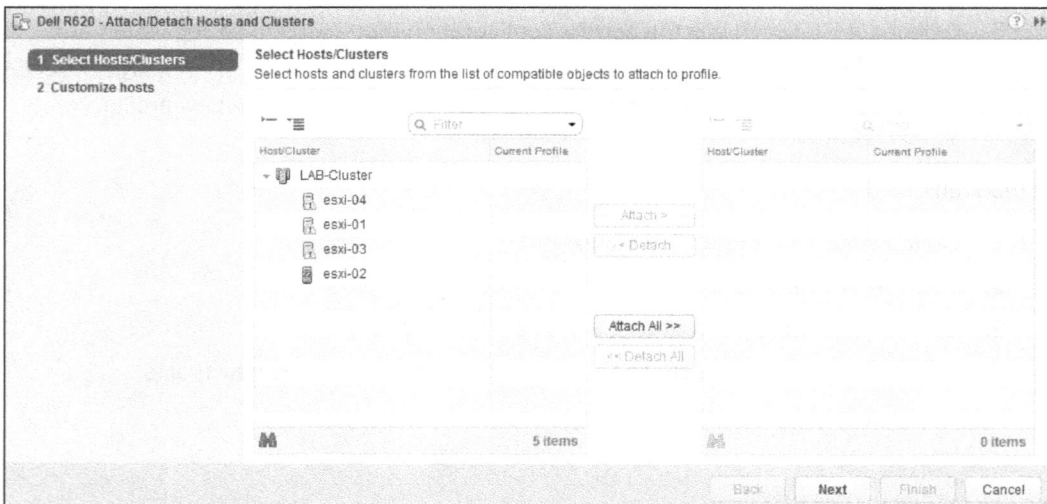

# Check a host's compliance

To check a host's compliance after a profile has been attached, execute the following steps:

1. Go to **Home | Host Profile**.
2. Select a profile that has to be checked.
3. Go to the **Hosts and Cluster** tab.
4. Select a host and click on **Check Compliance**.

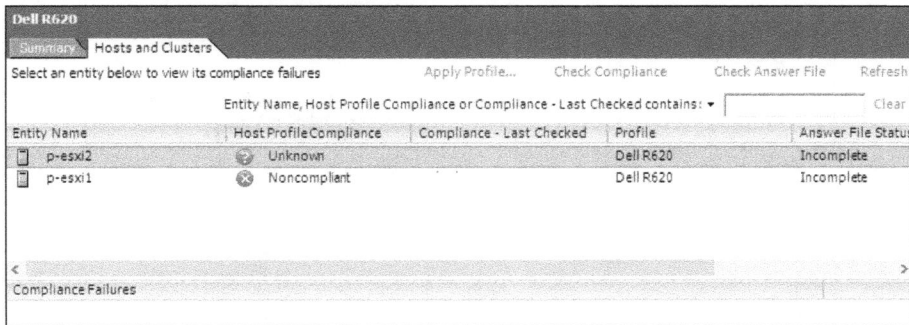

If a host is not compliant, failures will be listed under the host list.

The steps are similar in the Web Client:

1. Go to **Home | Host Profile**.
2. Select a profile that has to be checked.
3. Go to **Monitor | Compliance** to view the compliance status for the attached hosts.

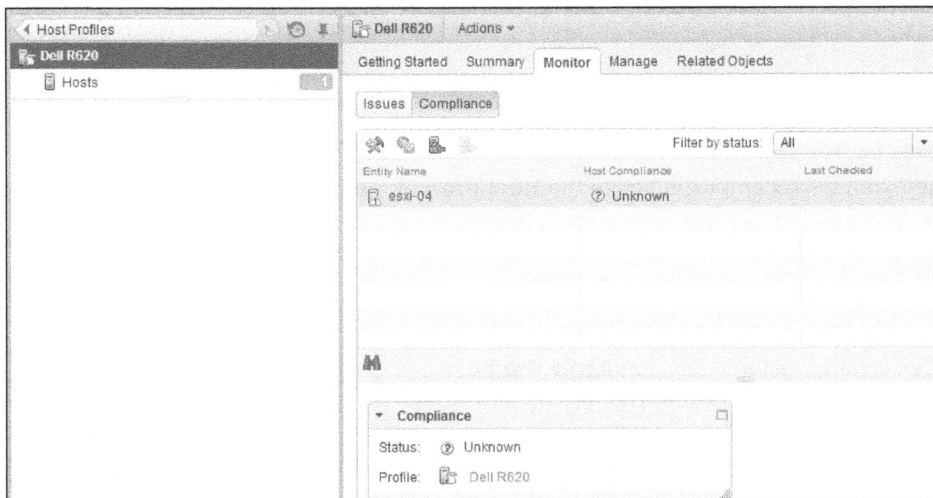

## Applying a profile to a host

To apply a profile to a host, follow these steps:

1. Confirm that the host has a profile attached.
2. Go to the **Hosts and Clusters** view.
3. Right-click on the host.
4. Go to **Host Profile | Apply Profile**.

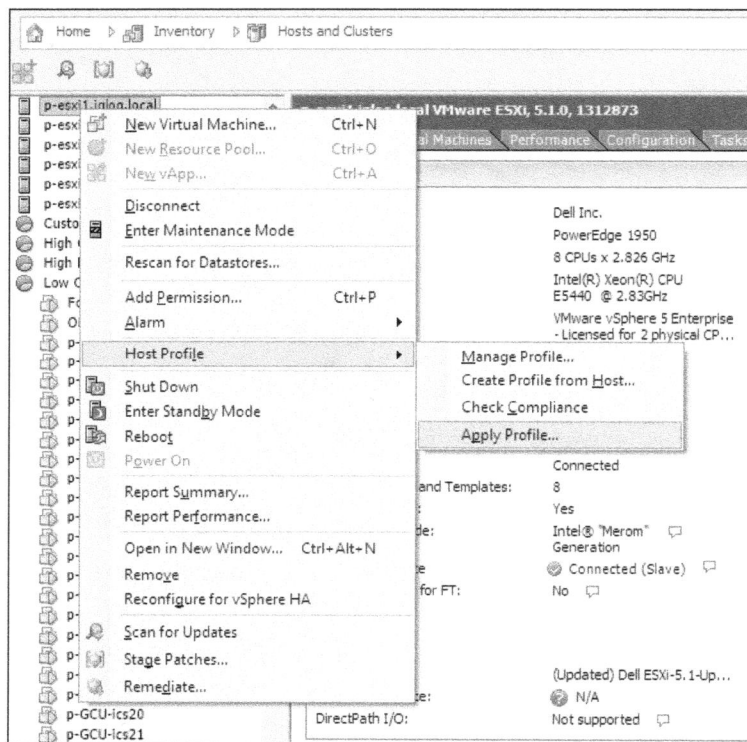

The same can be accomplished from the **Host Profiles** view:

1. Go to **Home | Host Profile**.
2. Select a profile that has to be applied.
3. Go to the **Hosts and Cluster** tab.
4. Select a host and click on **Apply Profile**.

In the Web Client, this option is called **Remediate** and is available under **All vCenter Actions** by right-clicking on the host, or in **Host Profiles** after selecting a profile and an appropriate host from the list:

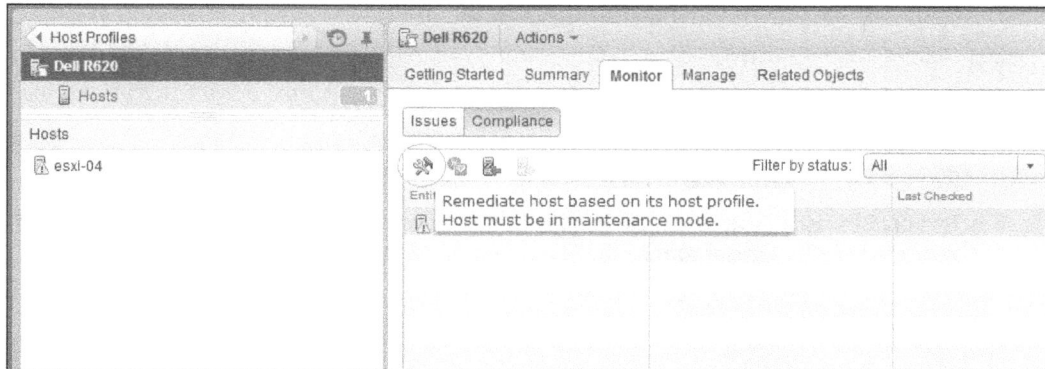

# Increasing a VM's RAM and CPU online

vSphere allows us to increase the amount of memory and vCPUs assigned to a virtual machine online without turning this virtual machine off. This feature is called **Hot Add** and has to be enabled per virtual machine.

## Getting ready

Once the memory or number of processors has been changed, it depends on the guest OS whether it will be able to see changes without a reboot. Operating systems that support Hot Add of CPUs and RAM are as follows:

- Windows Server:
    - Memory Hot Add—starting from Server 2003 Enterprise.
    - CPU Hot Add—64 bit versions starting from Server 2008.
- Linux:
    - Memory Hot Add—Ubuntu starting from v14, Red Hat starting from v5, CentOS starting from 5.0, and Debian starting from v7.
    - CPU Hot Add—Ubuntu starting from v10, Red Hat starting from v5.1, CentOS starting from 5.1, and Debian starting from v7.

## How to do it...

To enable HotPlug or verify the settings, execute the following steps:

1. Shut down a VM if you are changing the settings.

2. Right-click on the VM.

3. Go to **Edit Settings**.

4. Go to the **Options** tab and select **Memory/CPU Hotplug**.

5. Switch **Memory Hot Add** to **Enable**.

6. Switch **CPU Hot Plug** to either **Enable CPU hot add only** or **Enable CPU hot add and remove for this virtual machine** depending on which option is available.

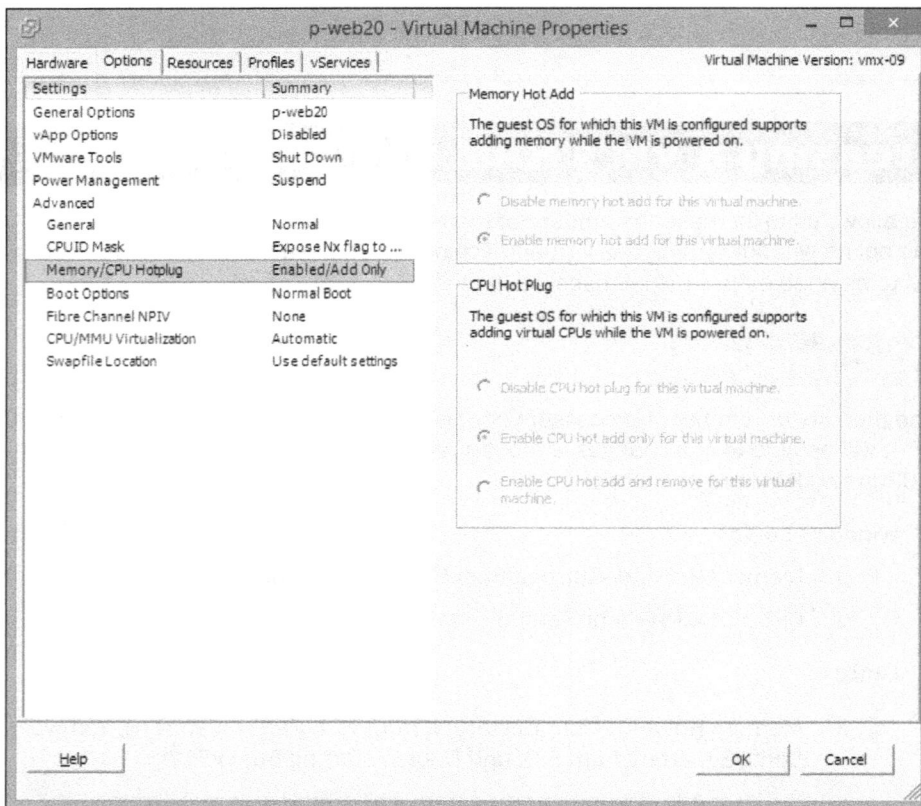

In the Web Client:

1. Select a VM.
2. Go to the **VM Hardware** panel.
3. Click on **Edit Settings**.
4. Go to **Virtual Hardware**.
5. Expand **\*CPU** options.
6. Select **Enable CPU Hot Add**.

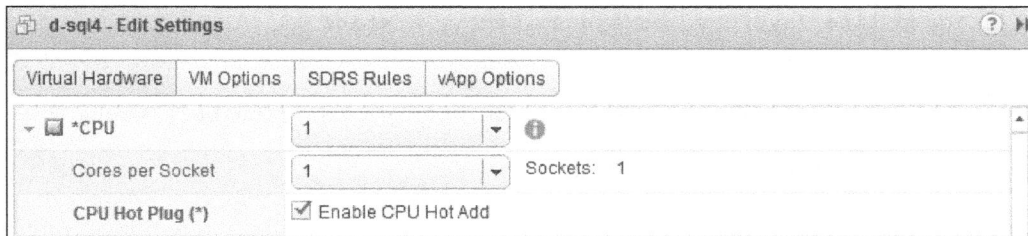

| d-sql4 - Edit Settings | | | | ? ▶▶ |
|---|---|---|---|---|
| Virtual Hardware | VM Options | SDRS Rules | vApp Options | |
| ⌄ 🖥 *CPU | 1 ⌄ ❶ | | | |
| Cores per Socket | 1 ⌄ | Sockets: 1 | | |
| CPU Hot Plug (*) | ☑ Enable CPU Hot Add | | | |

7. Expand **\*Memory** options.
8. Select **Memory Hot Plug** and click on **OK**.

| d-sql4 - Edit Settings | | | ? ▶▶ |
|---|---|---|---|
| Virtual Hardware | VM Options | SDRS Rules | vApp Options |
| ▸ 🖥 *CPU | 1 ⌄ ❶ | | |
| ⌄ 🧠 *Memory | | | |
| RAM | 2048 ⌄ | MB ⌄ | |
| Reservation | 0 ⌄ | MB ⌄ | |
| | ☐ Reserve all guest memory (All locked) | | |
| Limit | Unlimited ⌄ | MB ⌄ | |
| Shares | Normal ⌄ | 20480 ⌄ | |
| Memory Hot Plug (*) | ☑ Enable | | |

Once HotPlug is enabled even if VM is running, perform the following steps:

1. Right-click on the VM.
2. Go to **Edit Settings.**
3. In the **Hardware** tab, select **Memory** or **CPU** and increase them as required.
4. Click on **OK**.

> [ Note that, unfortunately, decreasing the assigned memory requires VM to be off. ]

## There's more...

Some Linux OSes require additional memory to be set manually online. To do this, follow the ensuing examples:

- Verify which memory is offline:

```
grep line /sys/devices/system/memory/*/state
```

- Set the memory online:

```
echo online > /sys/devices/system/memory/memory[number]/state
```

- Verify the results with the following command:

```
free -m
```

# 4
# Improving Environment Efficiency

In this chapter, we will cover the following recipes:

- ▶ Meeting higher I/O needs with the VMware Paravirtual controller
- ▶ Improving network performance with the VMXNET 3 network adapter
- ▶ Using new virtual hardware
- ▶ Controlling storage space used by virtual disks
- ▶ Managing space used by snapshots
- ▶ Improving host productivity with Flash Read Cache
- ▶ Speeding up VMs with Flash Read Cache
- ▶ Optimizing host power consumption
- ▶ Considering NUMA when configuring RAM
- ▶ vCPU versus pCPU and time slots

## Introduction

This chapter describes some features and enhancements offered by vCenter, along with vSphere 5, designed to increase environment efficiency. This includes new virtual hardware, a SCSI controller and network card, efficient space utilization, power consumption, and the utilization of flash memory to make hosts and VMs faster.

# Meeting higher I/O needs with the VMware Paravirtual controller

Virtual machine hardware Version 7 introduced a new **VMware Paravirtual storage adapter (PVSCSI)**. It is considered a high-performance storage adapter recommended for VMs with high I/O usage. PVSCSI can handle high I/O with higher storage throughput while keeping CPU utilization low.

> In ESXi 4, the LSI Logic adapter performs better than PVSCSI for VMs doing less than 2,000 IOPS.

More details are available in the VMware KB 1017652 article at `http://kb.vmware.com/kb/1017652`.

The following operating systems support PVSCSI:

► Windows Server 2003

► Windows Server 2008

► Windows Server 2008 R2

► Windows Server 2012

► Windows Server 2012 R2

► Windows 8

► Red Hat Linux 5

These operating systems don't include drivers for PVSCSI by default and the drivers have to be loaded before the virtual disk is recognized during OS installation.

## How to do it...

The best option is to choose the Paravirtual SCSI controller during VM creation. New virtual drives using PVSCSI can be added later even if the boot drive does not use PVSCSI. Additional steps are required to change the SCSI controller for the existing drives if they are bootable.

# PVSCSI for a new VM

When a new virtual machine requires the Paravirtual SCSI controller, perform the following steps:

1.  Choose the **Custom** configuration in the first step of the **Create New Virtual Machine** wizard.

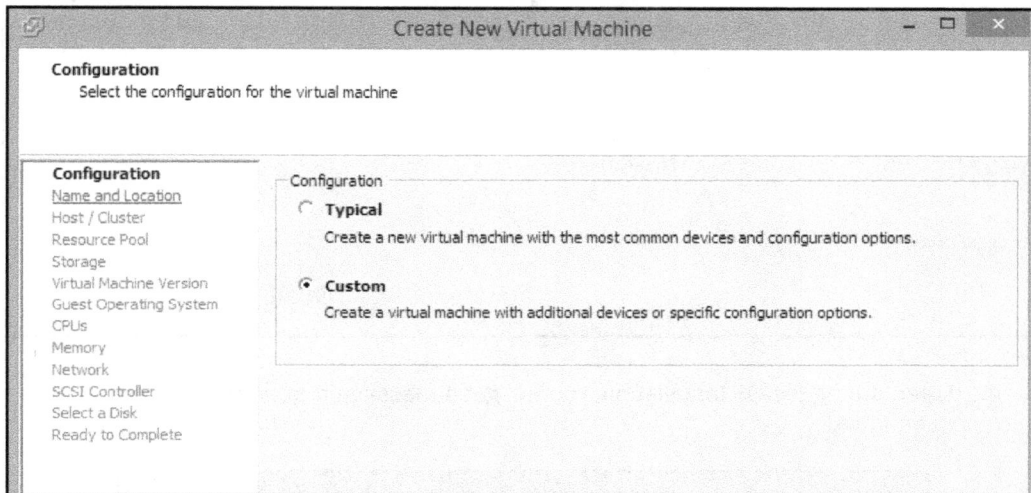

2.  In the **Virtual Machine Version** step of the wizard, select **Virtual Machine Version: 7** or later.

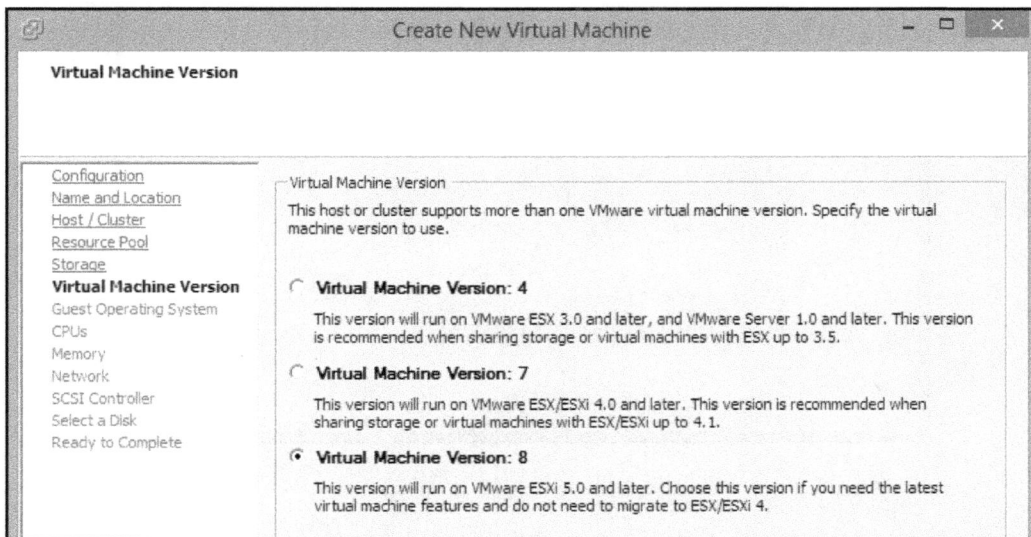

3. In the **SCSI Controller** step, select **VMware Paravirtual**.

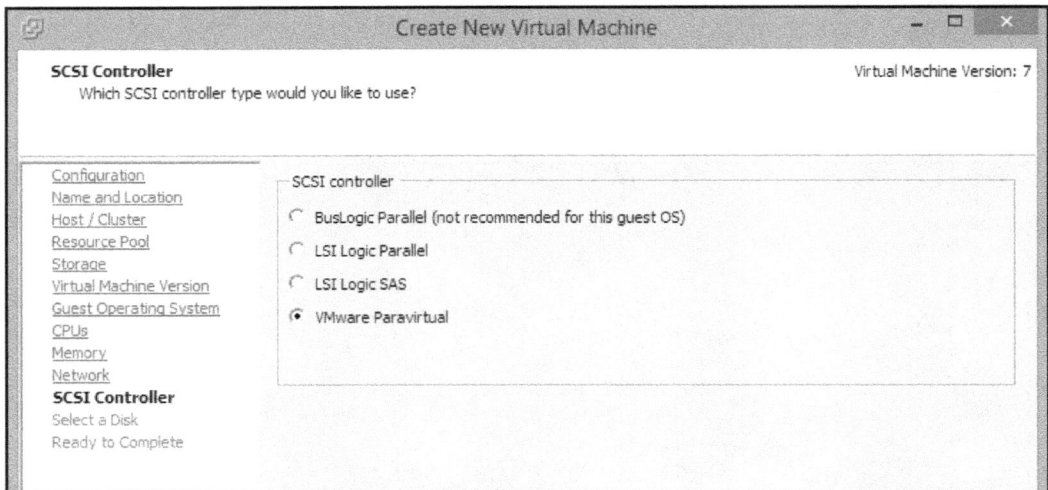

4. Later, during the OS installation, you will get a message that no drives have been found.

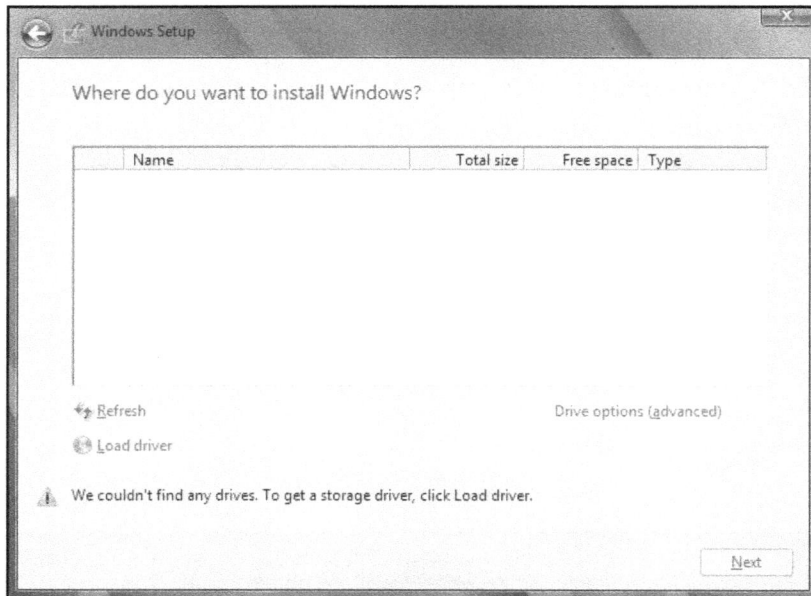

5.  Click on the **Connect/Disconnect the Floppy Devices of the Virtual Machine** button on the VM toolbar and select **Connect to floppy image on a datastore....**

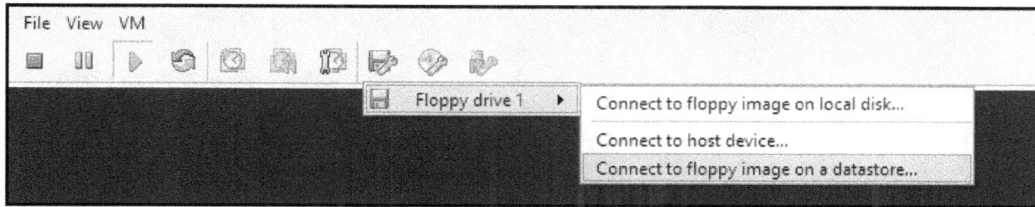

6.  In the **Browse Datastores** dialog, go to the `vmimages\floppies` folder, select the `vmscsi.flp` image, and click on **OK**.

> These images exist on datastores by default. For Windows 2012 installation, use the Windows 2008 image.

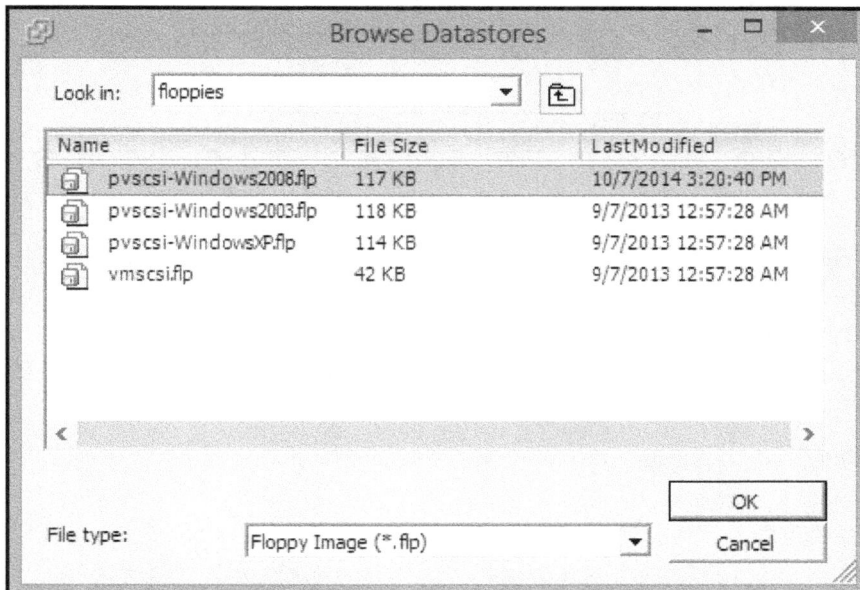

7.  Once the floppy image is connected, click on the **Load Driver** link in the Windows Setup dialog and then click on **Browse**.

8. Expand **Floppy Disk Drive (A:)** in the list, select an appropriate folder, and click on **OK**.

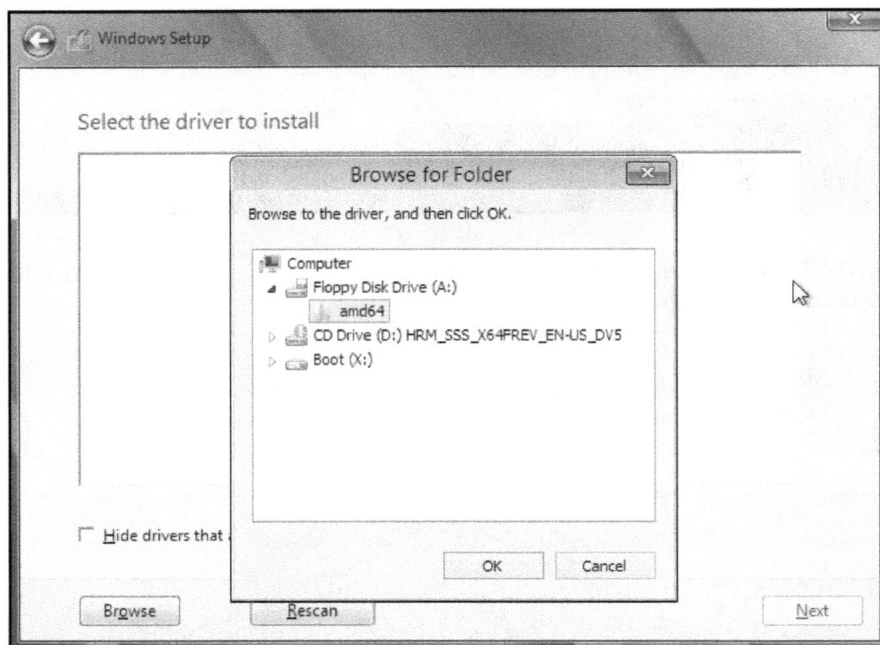

9. Select the driver in the list and click on **Next**.
10. Once it's done, you will see the drives listed. Proceed with the OS installation.

## PVSCSI for new virtual drives

To add a new virtual drive using PVSCSI to an existing VM that has been built with a different SCSI adapter, execute the following steps:

1. Shut down the virtual machine.
2. Go to VM settings.

3. Click on the **Add** button and select **Hard Disk** from the list. Click on **Next**.

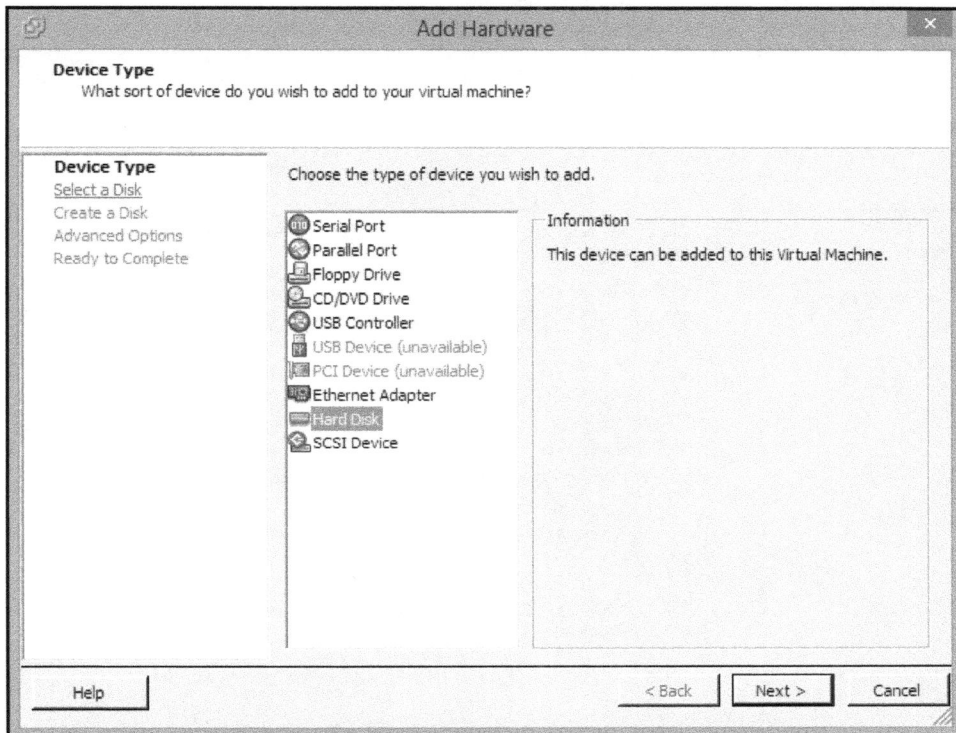

4. In the next step, select **Create a new virtual disk** and click on **Next**.
5. Choose a virtual drive size, provisioning, and location, and click on **Next**.

6.  In the next step, select the new SCSI node. In most cases, VMs have one SCSI adapter, and SCSI (1:0) will be the choice.

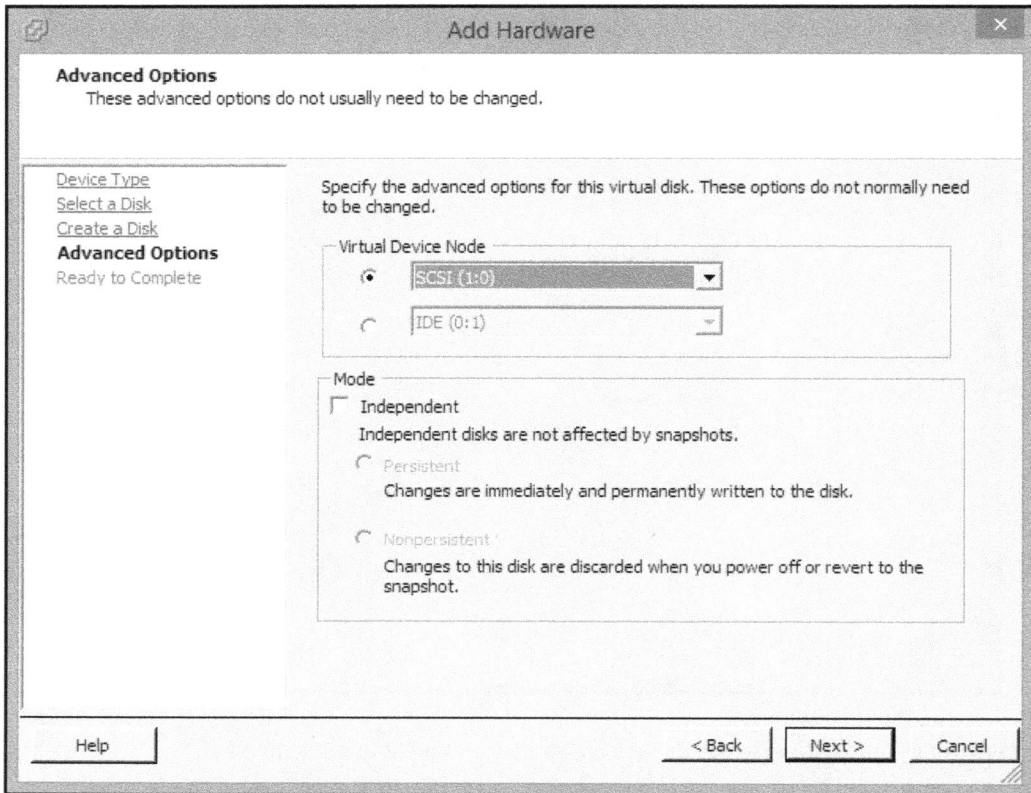

7.  Click on **Next** and then on **Finish**.
8.  In the list of hardware, you will see a new hard disk and one more SCSI controller.
9.  Select the new SCSI controller from the list and click on **Change Type...**.

10. Choose **VMware Paravirtual** from the list, click on **OK**, and then on **OK** again.

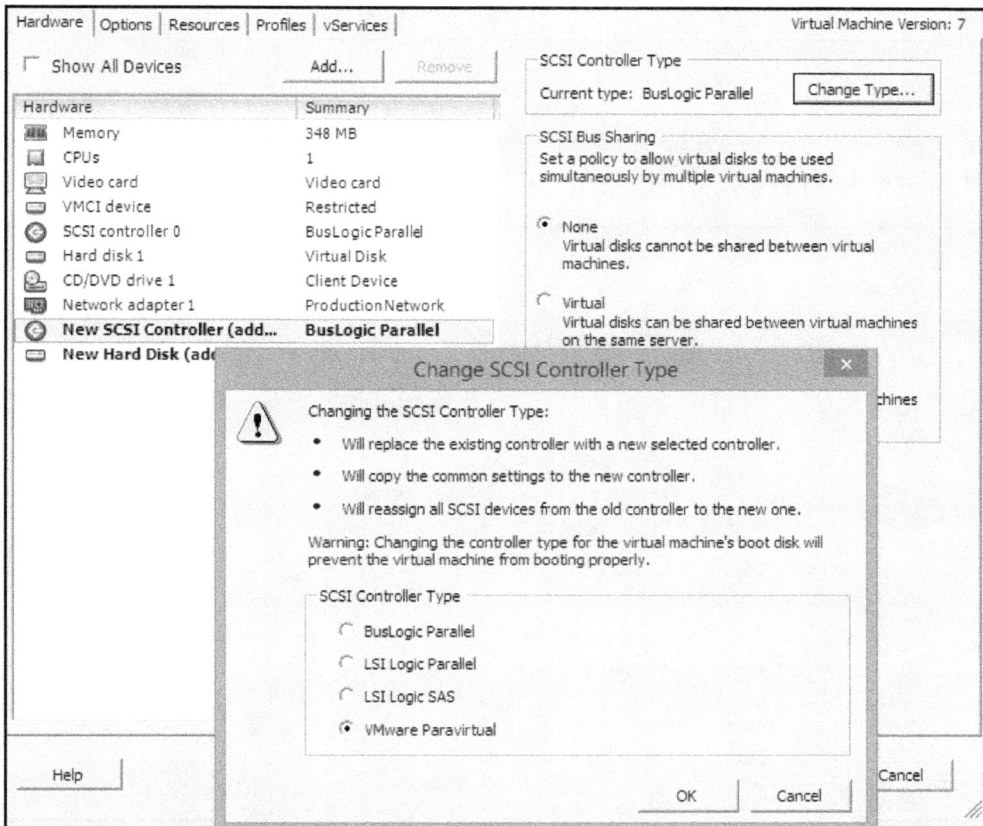

11. Once the changes have been applied, start the VM. Windows will install the required drivers automatically and you will be able to configure the new drive.

## PVSCSI for existing OS virtual drives

To switch the existing virtual drives to PVSCSI, perform the following steps:

1. Shut down the VM.
2. Go to VM settings.
3. Select the SCSI controller, click on **Change Type**, and select **VMware Paravirtual**.
4. Click on **OK** twice.

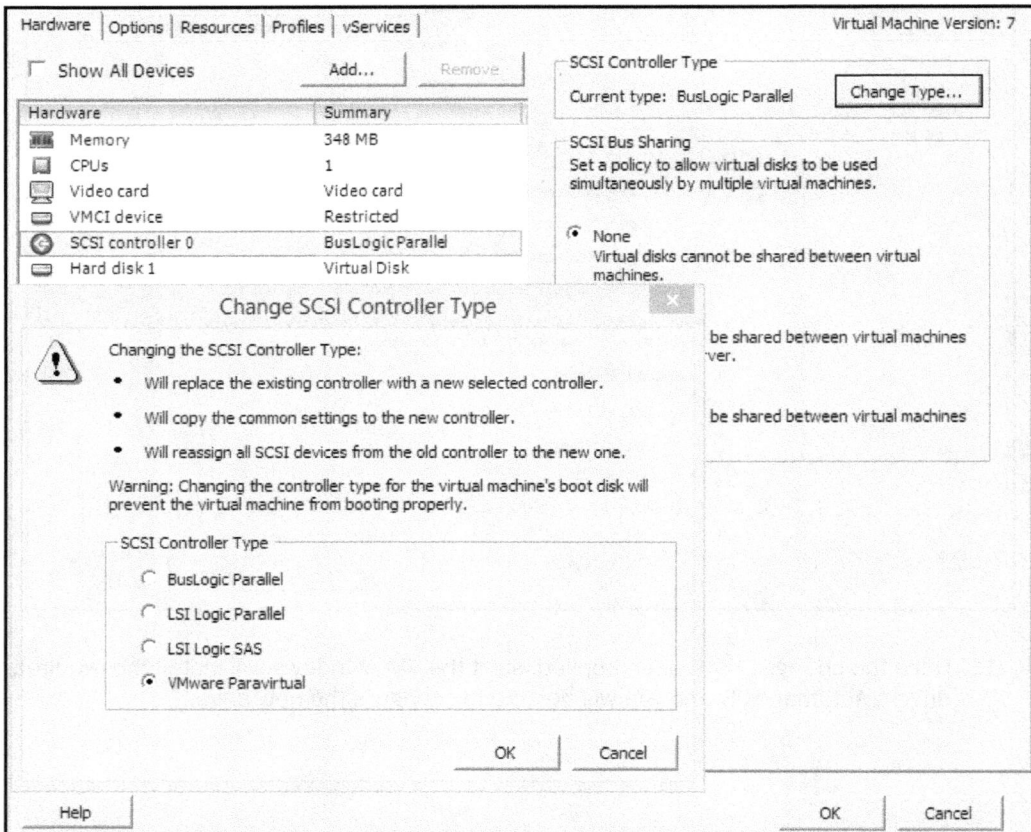

Switching the existing SCSI adapter to Paravirtual may prevent the installed operating system from booting when it's installed on a virtual drive that's using this SCSI adapter. In order to switch the existing bootable virtual drives to use PVSCSI, follow the ensuing steps:

1. Go through the steps outlined in the previous section, PVSCSI, for new virtual drives to install the required drivers.

2. Shut down the VM.

3. Go to VM settings.

4. Select the first SCSI controller and change its type to **Paravirtual**.

5. Remove the added second virtual drive. The second SCSI adapter will be removed automatically.

6. Start the VM and confirm the guest OS boots.

# Improving network performance with the VMXNET 3 network adapter

The VMXNET 3 new generation high performance network adapter, in addition to features supported by its predecessors, also includes support for Receive Side Scaling, MSI/MSI-X interrupt delivery, and IPv6 offloads.

VMXNET 3 is supported in virtual hardware Version 7 or later.

The following operating systems support VMXNET 3:

- Windows XP or later (32 bit and 64 bit)
- Windows Server 2003 or later (32 bit and 64 bit)
- Red Hat Linux 5 or later
- SUSE Linux 10 and later
- Debian 4 and later
- Ubuntu 7.04 and later

Drivers for VMXNET 3 are not included by default in the preceding operating systems and VMware tools, which contain the driver, have to be installed first before this network adapter is recognized by the OS.

## How to do it...

The network adapter type has to be chosen during VM creation. It can't be changed later, and in order to use a different adapter type, the existing NIC has to be removed and a new one has to be created.

The VMXNET 3 adapter type can be chosen in the **Create New Virtual Machine** wizard:

1.  In the **Virtual Machine Version** screen of the wizard, choose **Virtual Machine Version: 7** or later.

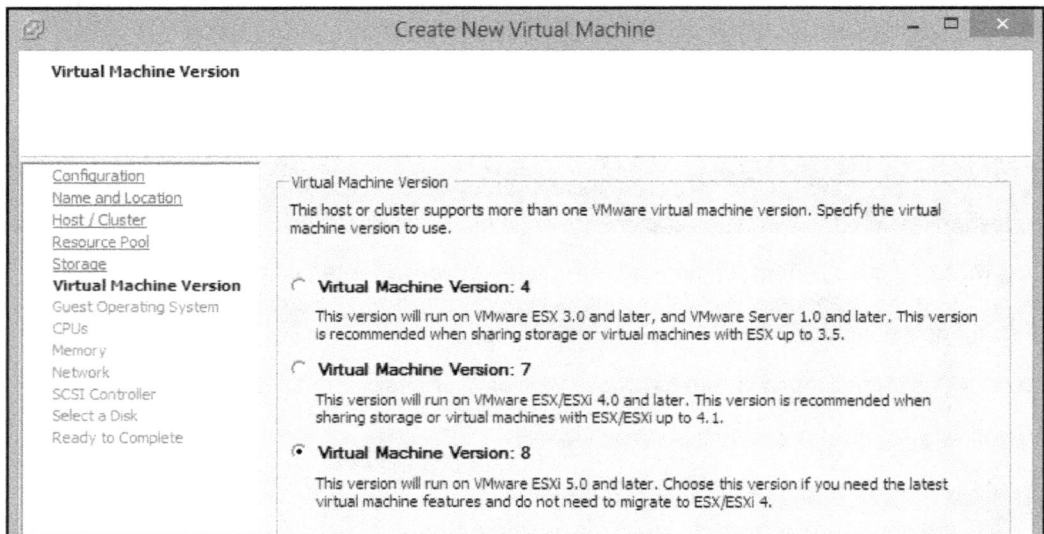

2. In the **Network** step, select **VMXNET 3** in the **Adapter** drop-down box for each NIC that requires it.

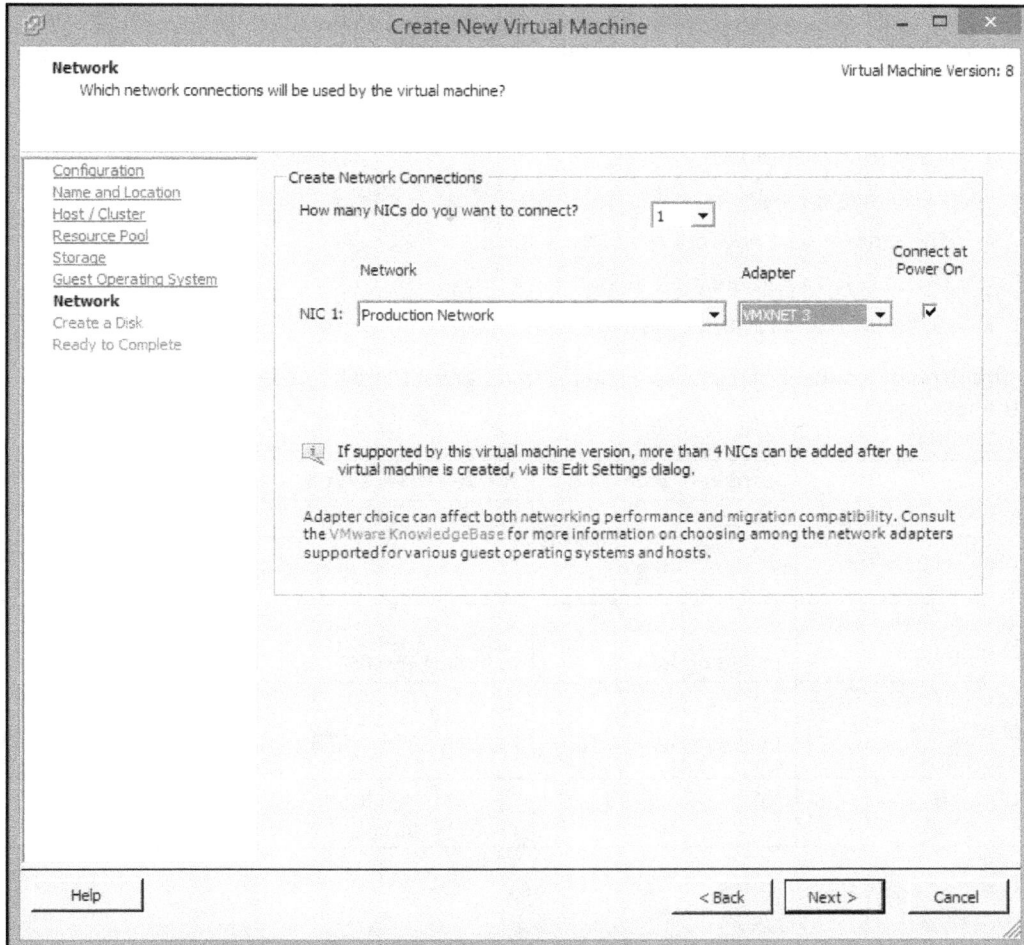

3. Finish the wizard to create a new VM.

4. After the OS is deployed, install VMware tools to make sure the network adapter is recognized by the OS.

# Using new virtual hardware

The virtual machine hardware version is a set of hardware features. In most cases, it's the host's physical hardware used for virtual features, including PCI slots, EFI, CPUs, and so on.

The hardware version defines the following:

▶ Memory limits for VMs

▶ CPU limits for VMs

▶ The storage and network adapters available

▶ Guest OSes available for a VM

▶ Other virtual hardware capabilities

Comparison of a subset of features available in different hardware versions is outlined in the following table:

| | Hardware version 8 | Hardware version 9 | Hardware version 10 |
|---|---|---|---|
| Memory limit, GB | 1011 | 1011 | 1011 |
| Maximum number of CPUs | 32 | 64 | 64 |
| Maximum number of storage adapters | 4<br>Including PVSCSI | 4<br>Including PVSCSI | 4<br>Including PVSCSI |
| Maximum number of network adapters | 10<br>Including VMXNET3 | 10<br>Including VMXNET3 | 10<br>Including VMXNET3 |
| USB 3.0 | No | Pass-through from client PC to VM | Pass-through from client PC to VM |

## How to do it...

The hardware version is chosen during VM creation. By default, VM's hardware version corresponds to the ESXi version of the host where this VM is being created:

▶ ESXi 5.0—hardware version 8

▶ ESXi 5.1—hardware version 9

▶ ESXi 5.5—hardware version 10

The administrator can leave the default version or choose an earlier version.

# Choosing a virtual hardware version

The hardware version can be chosen during VM creation. In vCenter Client:

1.  Right-click on a host, folder, or cluster, and select **New Virtual Machine**.
2.  In the **Virtual Machine Version** step of the **Create New Virtual Machine** wizard, choose the required hardware version.

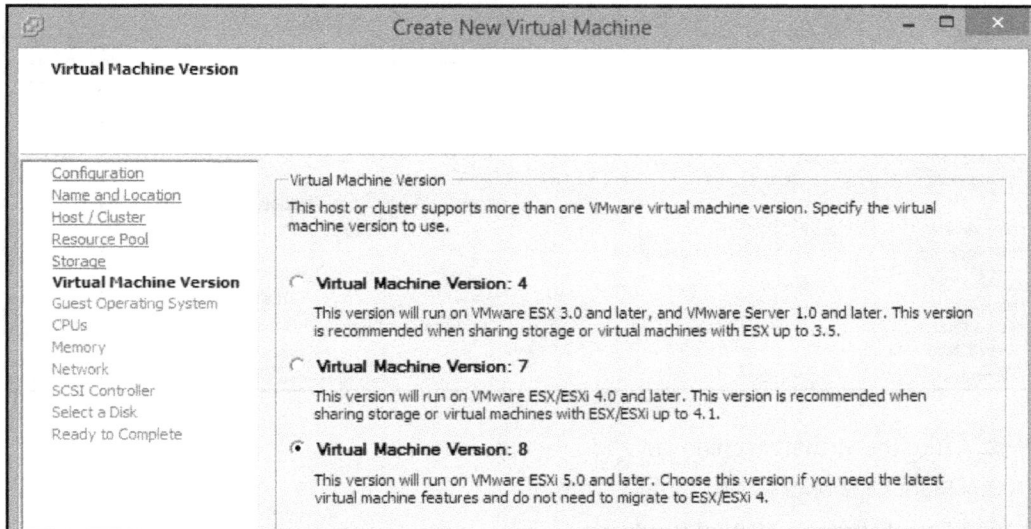

In Web Client, perform the following steps:

1.  Right click on a host, folder, or cluster, go to **All vCenter Actions**, and select **New Virtual Machine**.
2.  In step **2d Select compatibility**, choose the ESX version that corresponds to the required hardware version.

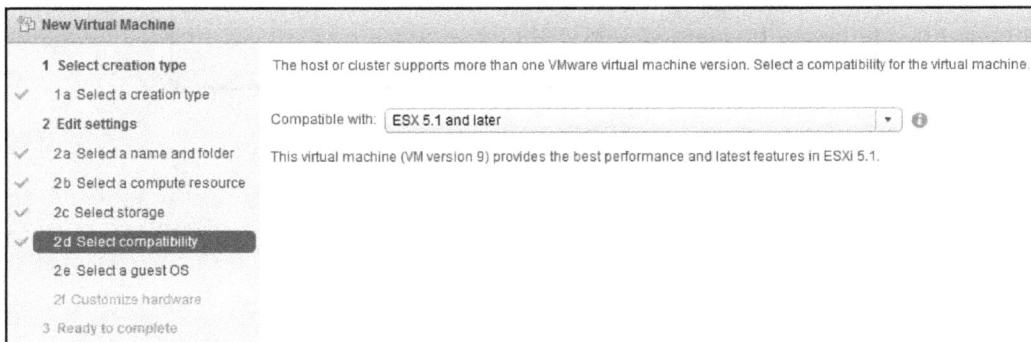

## Upgrading the virtual hardware

1. Check whether the latest version of VMware tools is installed by opening the VM **Summary** tab. VMware tools should have a green check mark and the word **Current** in brackets.

| Summary | Resource Allocation | Performance | Tasks & Events | Alarms | Console | Permissions | Maps | Storage Views | Update Mana |

**General**

| | |
|---|---|
| Guest OS: | CentOS 4/5/6 (64-bit) |
| VM Version: | 7 |
| CPU: | 1 vCPU |
| Memory: | 4096 MB |
| Memory Overhead: | 43.43 MB |
| VMware Tools: | ⊚ Running (Current) |
| IP Addresses: | 192.168.15.51      View all |
| DNS Name: | p-solr1 |
| EVC Mode: | Intel® "Merom" Generation |
| State: | Powered On |
| Host: | p-esxi4 |
| Active Tasks: | |
| Record/Replay Status: | |
| vSphere HA Protection: | ⊚ Protected |

**Resources**

| | |
|---|---|
| Consumed Host CPU: | 19 MHz |
| Consumed Host Memory: | 3992.00 MB |
| Active Guest Memory: | 819.00 MB |
| | Refresh Storage Usage |
| Provisioned Storage: | 174.09 GB |
| Not-shared Storage: | 174.09 GB |
| Used Storage: | 174.09 GB |

| Storage | Status | Drive Type |
|---|---|---|
| 🗄 P-GRP1-NoSnaps1 | ⊚ Normal | Non-SSD |

| Network | Type | Sta |
|---|---|---|
| 💻 Production Netwo... | Standard port group | ⊚ |

2. Turn the virtual machine off.

3. Right click on the VM.

4. Select **Upgrade Virtual Hardware**.

| | |
|---|---|
| 🗗 Template Win2l | |
| 🗗 Templa | Power ▶ |
| 🗗 Templa | Guest ▶ |
| 🗐 Templa | Snapshot ▶ |
| 🗐 Templa | |
| 🗗 Templa 💻 | Open Console |
| 🗐 Templa 🗗 | Edit Settings... |
| 🗗 Templa 🖳 | Migrate... |
| 🗐 Win201 | |
| ⊟ 📁 TurnedOff | **Upgrade Virtual Hardware** |

You will be asked to confirm the action.

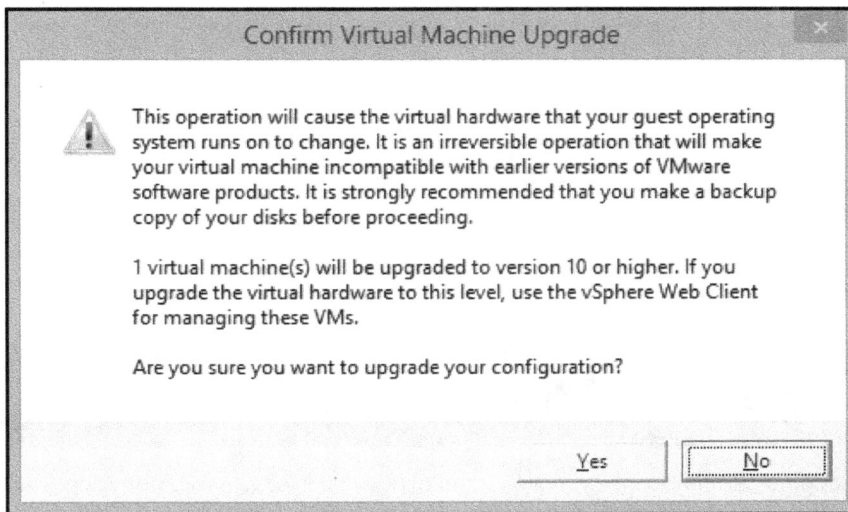

Once you click on **Yes**, VM's virtual hardware will be upgraded to the most recently available version.

In Web Client, this option is available by going to **All vCenter Actions | Compatibility | Upgrade VM Compatibility**:

> It is recommended to take a snapshot of the VM before upgrading its virtual hardware. In case it doesn't boot after the upgrade, revert to the snapshot.
>
> If a snapshot hasn't been taken prior to the upgrade, there are two options available to downgrade the hardware:
>
> ▶ The first option is to create a new VM with the older hardware version and attach a virtual drive from the original VM.
>
> ▶ The second option is to use VMware vCenter Converter Standalone to downgrade the hardware version.
>
> More information is available in the KB 1028019 article at `http://kb.vmware.com/kb/1028019`.

# Controlling storage space used by virtual disks

A virtual machine can have one or more virtual disks assigned to similar physical servers that can have one or more hard drives and volumes.

When a virtual machine is being created, vCenter suggests the size of the virtual disk based on the guest OS selection in the previous steps of the wizard. The administrator can always expand the drive size if necessary.

Each virtual disk has a provisioning setting, which defines how the available storage space is allocated for this virtual disk. VMware supports thick and thin provisioned disks. When a **thick provisioned** disk, which is the default format for new virtual drives, is used, all the required space is allocated in the storage right away. For example, when a 40 GB virtual disk is created, you will have 40 GBs less on your storage right away, even if this disk is not 100 percent used.

The other option is a **thin provisioned** disk, which uses only as much storage space as it actually needs. If only 5 GB is used on a 40 GB disk, then only 5 GB of storage space is used.

Thin provisioning allows overprovisioning of storage space. In other words, with thin provisioning, it's possible to assign more space to virtual machines than is available in the storage.

> Most **Storage Area Networks** (**SAN**) today support thin provisioning. If that is the case, it's better to utilize this capability and avoid using thin provisioned disks for virtual machines.

Thin provisioning may cause issues when one or more virtual drives start using more space. That is why it's essential to have proper monitoring and alerts in place to control the available storage space. Please refer to the *Controlling datastore space utilization* recipe in *Chapter 6, Basic Administrative Tasks*.

## How to do it...

Usually, disk provisioning is chosen during VM creation. Storage vMotion allows converting from thin to thick and the other way around.

### Choosing disk provisioning for new VMs

In vCenter Client, virtual disk settings, including provisioning, are available in the **Create a Disk** step of the **Create New Virtual Machine** wizard.

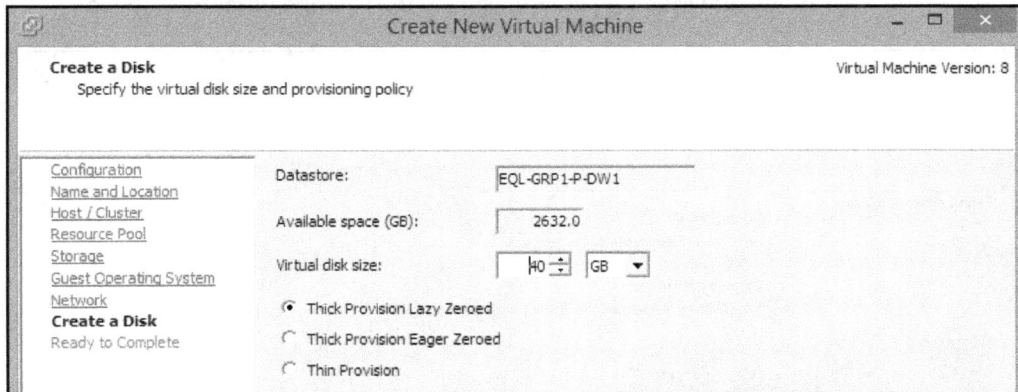

In Web Client, the disk provisioning option is available in step **2f Customize hardware**. Under the **Virtual Hardware** tab, expand the **New Hard disk** section to change the **Disk Provisioning** option.

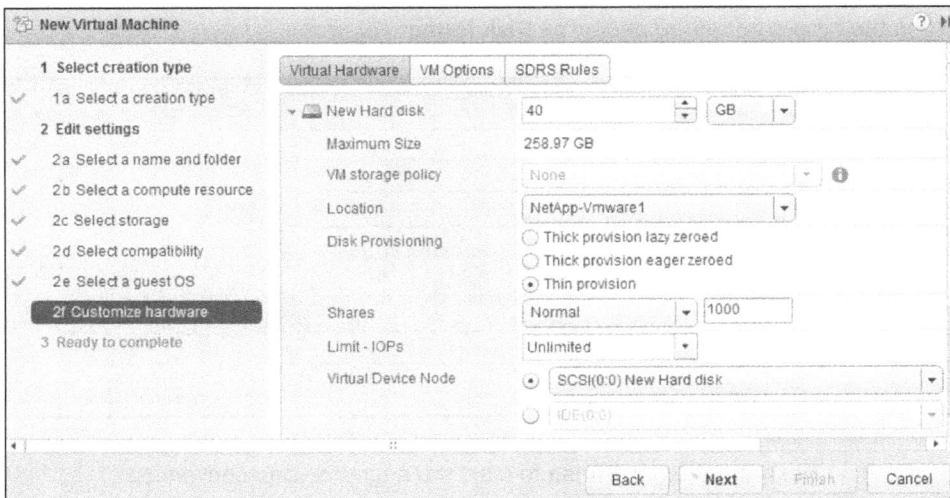

## Converting disk formats

To convert between thin and thick disk provisioning formats, administrators can use Storage vMotion. For storage migration to be possible, the destination datastore must have enough free space to accommodate an additional VM.

In vCenter Client, perform the following steps:

1. Right click on the VM.

2. Select **Migrate**.

3. In the **Migrate Virtual Machine** wizard, choose the **Change datastore** option.

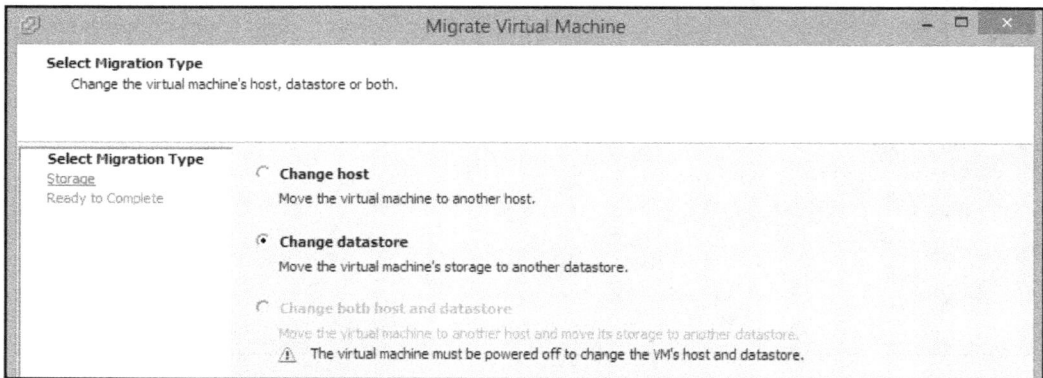

4. Click on **Next**, select **Datastore**, where this VM will be migrated to, and click on **Advanced**.

5. Select the virtual disk that has to be converted and choose the required format in the drop-down menu under the **Disk format** column.

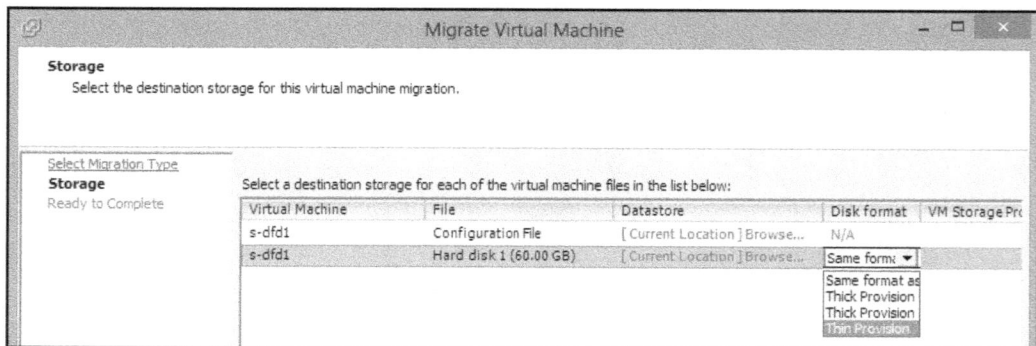

6. Click on **Next** and then on **Finish** to start the migration and conversion.

In Web Client, perform the following steps:

1. Right click on the virtual machine and select **Migrate**.

2. Choose the **Change datastore** option and click on **Next**.

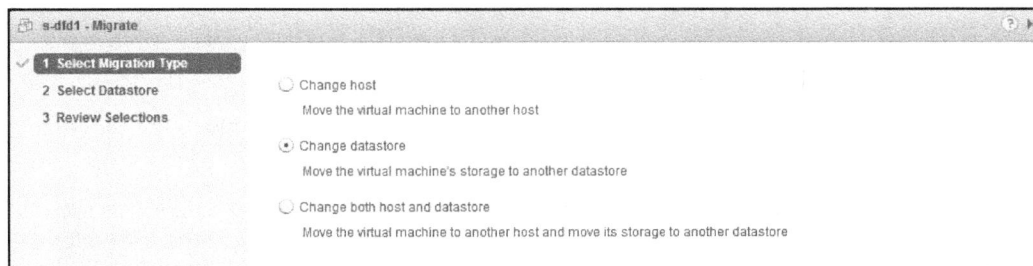

3. Select the datastore where this VM will be migrated and change the disk format option on top to convert all the virtual drives.

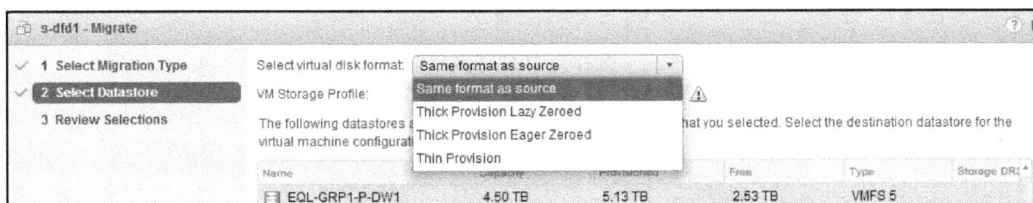

4. For individual disk conversion, click on **Advanced**, select the virtual disk in the list, and change **Disk format** from the drop-down menu.

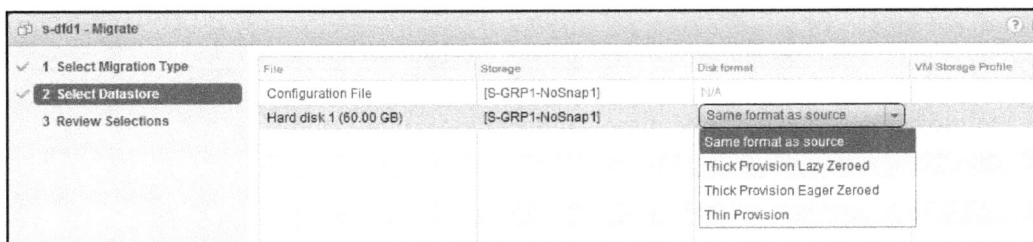

5. Click on **Next** and then on **Finish** to start the migration and conversion.

# Managing the space used by snapshots

**Snapshots** is one of the most useful, and at the same time dangerous, vCenter features. Snapshots allow saving the current VM state for rollback purposes.

At the same time, as changes happen to the virtual machine, a snapshot takes more space, which may potentially lead to a deficit of free space.

More details about snapshots and how to control space usage can be found in the *Controlling space used by snapshots* recipe in *Chapter 6, Basic Administrative Tasks*.

vCenter allows configuring an alarm for VMs with a snapshot larger than the specified size. Such an alarm can be used to locate virtual machines with snapshots. It can be useful for audit or cleaning purposes.

## How to do it...

To create this alarm in vCenter Client, execute the following steps:

1.  Go to the **Datacenter** level, switch to the **Alarms** tab, and then to the **Definitions** view.

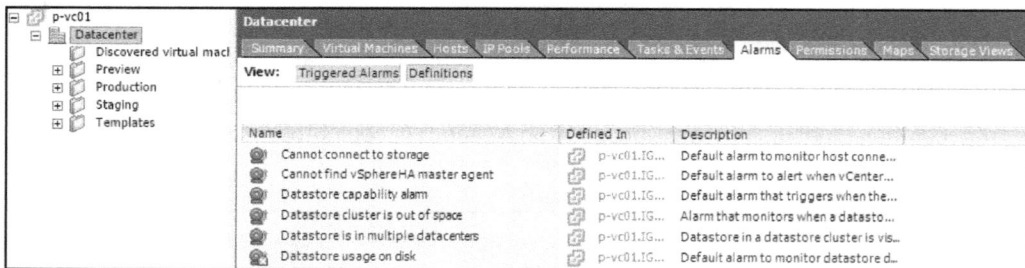

2.  Go to **File | New | Alarm** or press *Ctrl + M*.

3. In the **General** tab of the **Alarm Settings** dialog, give this alarm a name and make sure **Virtual Machines** is selected for **Monitor** under the **Alarm Type** section.

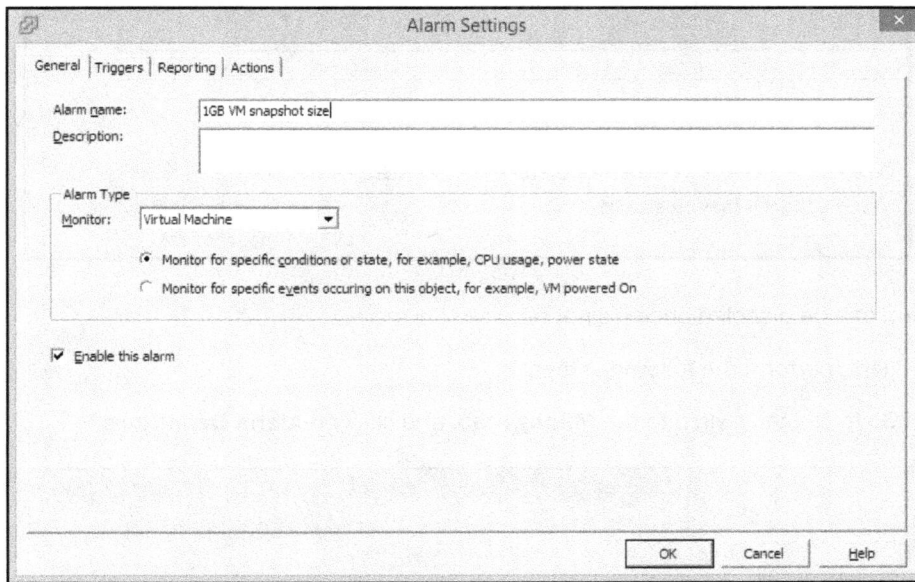

4. In the **Triggers** tab, click on **Add**, select the **VM Snapshot Size (GB)** trigger, and configure the thresholds.

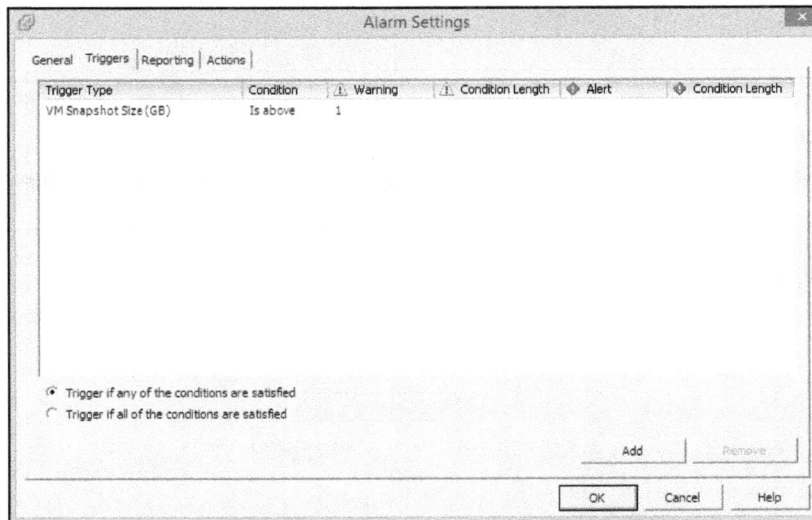

5. Click on **OK**.

Once the alarm is saved, all VMs with a snapshot will get a warning condition. The full list of VMs can be viewed under the **Alarm** tab in the **Triggered Alarms** view on the datacenter level.

The alarm can be disabled once it's not required anymore.

In Web Client, perform the following steps:

1.  Go to cluster, switch to the **Manage** tab, and click on **Alarm Definitions**.

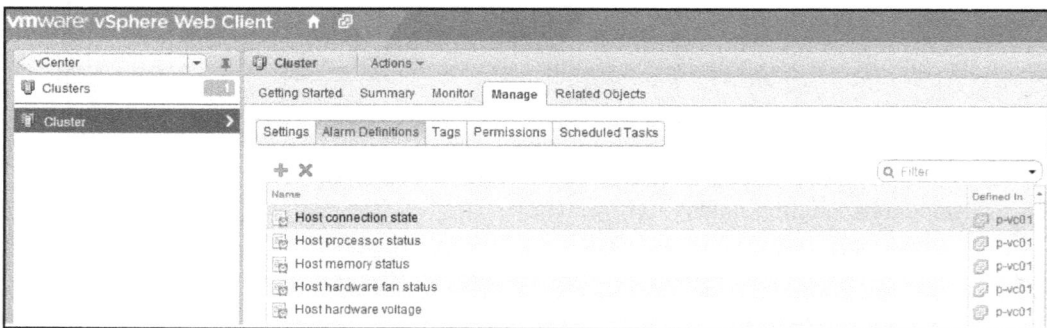

2.  Click on the plus sign to create a new alarm.
3.  Give the new alarm a name and set the **Monitor** value to **Virtual Machines**.

4.  Click on **Next**. Click on the plus sign to add a trigger and select **VM Snapshot Size** in the drop-down menu.

5.  Click on **Finish**.

> Once the alarm is saved, all VMs with a snapshot will get a warning condition. The full list of VMs can be viewed by going to **Monitor | Issues** on the datacenter level. The alarm can be disabled once it's not required anymore.

# Improving host productivity with Flash Read Cache

One of the new features introduced in vSphere 5.5 is **Flash Read Cache**. It allows utilizing the flash memory installed on a host to improve the performance of this host or its virtual machines.

This is achieved by using **Virtual Flash File System (VFFS)**, which is a logical container used by vSphere to group local flash devices into a single resource. VFFS can be used to provide resources to the host and virtual machines simultaneously.

vSphere supports a maximum of **8** flash devices per VFFS, a maximum of **4 TB** per flash device, and a maximum of **32 TB** in total per VFFS.

> The Flash Read Cache feature is available only with the Enterprise Plus license.

## Getting ready

As Flash Read Cache is supported by vSphere 5.5 or later, the participating hosts must be running ESXi 5.5, and vCenter should also be Version 5.5 or later.

All participating hosts must have at least one free SSD drive, which will be used as a flash resource.

The virtual flash resource has to be configured first before Host Swap Cache can be set up. To do this in Web Client, perform the following steps:

1.  Select a host.

2.  Go to **Manage | Settings | Virtual Flash** and Select **Virtual Flash Resource Management**.

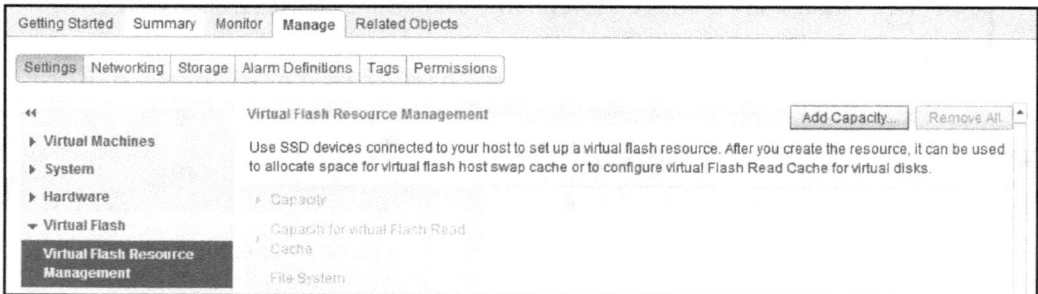

| Getting Started | Summary | Monitor | Manage | Related Objects |

| Settings | Networking | Storage | Alarm Definitions | Tags | Permissions |

Virtual Flash Resource Management    [Add Capacity...]  [Remove All]

Use SSD devices connected to your host to set up a virtual flash resource. After you create the resource, it can be used to allocate space for virtual flash host swap cache or to configure virtual Flash Read Cache for virtual disks.

- Virtual Machines
- System
- Hardware
- Virtual Flash
  - **Virtual Flash Resource Management**
    - Capacity
    - Capacity for virtual Flash Read Cache
    - File System

3.  Click on **Add Capacity**.

4.  Select the SSD drive that will be used for Flash Cache and click on **OK**.

If the SSD drive you want to use is not displayed in the list, refer to the following VMware KB article on how to manually identify a drive as an SSD one: `http://kb.vmware.com/kb/2013188`

## How to do it...

To enable Host Swap Cache for a particular host in Web Client, execute the following steps:

1.  Select a host.

2.  Go to **Manage | Settings | Virtual Flash | Virtual Flash Host Swap Cache**.

3.  Click on **Edit**.

4.  Check **Enable virtual flash host swap cache** and specify the amount of memory allocated to swap this host cache.

5.  Click on **OK**.

Multiple hosts can be configured for Read Cache with the following steps:

1. Select a cluster.
2. Go to the **Hosts** tab and select multiple hosts.
3. Right click on any selected host, go to **All vCenter Actions**, and click on **Add Flash Read Cache Capacity**.
4. Confirm the number of hosts to be configured.
5. Select SSD disks for each host and click on **OK**.

To check Host Swap Cache settings for a particular host, execute the following steps:

1. Select a host.
2. Go to the **Summary** tab.
3. Check **Flash Read Cache Resource** under the **Hardware** section.

# Speeding up VMs with Flash Read Cache

Flash Read Cache is a new feature introduced in vSphere 5.5 which allows accelerating virtual machines by using flash memory installed on the host. In most cases, this will be achieved using SSD disks installed on the hosts. PCI-E devices can also be utilized.

This feature, which is completely transparent for a virtual machine, can increase the read speed. It can also improve the write speed by reducing storage read operations. As a result, it not only accelerates busy virtual machines but also reduces storage I/O load by generating less storage network traffic.

With Flash Read Cache systems, applications considered before to be too I/O intensive can now be virtualized.

Flash Read Cache also supports vMotion, so virtual machines with virtual drives configured to use this feature can be migrated between hosts that are configured with flash resource. There are two settings available for cached content migration: always migrate (copy) and never migrate (drop).

> Snapshots, cloning, and migration preserve the cache.

Unfortunately, at this point, FT is not supported for VMs configured with Flash Cache. Thin provisioning and overprovisioning is also not supported.

The HA feature is supported, and when VM is restarted on another host, its cache will be rebuilt. Remember that a VM will fail to restart on a host that doesn't have flash cache memory available or if the Flash Cache on this host is full.

> The Flash Read Cache feature is available only with the Enterprise Plus license.

## Getting ready

Since Flash Read Cache is supported by vSphere 5.5 or later, make sure the participating hosts in a cluster run ESXi 5.5 and your vCenter is also 5.5.

All participating hosts must have at least one free SSD drive, which will be used as a flash resource.

Virtual machines that will be configured for Flash Cache must use hardware Version 10. Please refer to the *Using new virtual hardware* recipe in this chapter for more details on the hardware version and ways to upgrade the existing VMs.

Virtual Flash Resource has to be configured first before Virtual Flash Read Cache can be set up. To do this in Web Client, execute the following steps:

1. Select a host.

2. Go to **Manage | Settings | Virtual Flash** and select **Virtual Flash Resource Management**.

3. Click on **Add Capacity**.

4. Select the SSD drive and click on **OK**.

If the SSD drive you want to use is not displayed in the list, refer to the following VMware KB article on how to manually identify this drive as an SSD one: `http://kb.vmware.com/kb/2013188`

> Flash Read Cache can be configured only for a virtual drive. There is no way to configure it on virtual machine level for all its virtual drives at the same time.

## How to do it...

Flash Read Cache for a particular virtual machine can be set up in Web Client:

1. Right click on a virtual machine and click on **Edit Settings**.
2. Expand the virtual disk that requires Flash Read Cache to be assigned.
3. Enter the amount of memory you want to assign to this virtual disk and click on **OK**.

Flash Read Cache settings for a virtual machine can be verified under the **Summary** tab if you expand the hard disk under the VM **Hardware** section.

To disable Flash Read Cache for a particular virtual drive, simply set the reservation amount to **0**.

# Optimizing host power consumption

vSphere offers two features that allow reducing the power consumption by hosts during off-peak hours. The first one is **Distributed Power Management** (**DPM**). It allows reducing a cluster's power consumption by placing certain hosts in standby mode. When the current load and resource reservations allow so, DPM migrates virtual machines off of the host and puts the host in standby mode. When more resources are needed, the host will be taken out of standby mode and used to host VMs.

While DPM places the entire host in the reduced power consumption state, the other feature called **Host Power Management** (**HPM**) allows reducing the host power consumption by placing only certain hardware into the low power consumption state. Devices or components in this state are inactive or run at a lower speed.

## Getting ready

For DPM to work properly, ESXi hosts should support at least one of the following protocols so that vSphere is able to bring them back up from standby mode:

- **Wake-on-LAN (WOL)**
- **Intelligent Platform Management Interface (IPMI)**
- Hewlett-Packard **Integrated Lights Out (iLO)**

vSphere's preferred order for these protocols is IPMI, iLO, and then WOL. IPMI and iLO require **Baseboard Management Controller** (**BMC**), which can be enabled by going to **Configuration | Power Management** for each host. If BMC is supported, there will be an option to provide credentials, and IP and MAC addresses used by the network card associated with BMC.

In case BMC is not supported, you can test whether the host supports WOL. To do this:

1. Select the host from the inventory.
2. Go to the **Summary** tab and click on **Enter Standby Mode**.
3. The host should power down.
4. Click on **Power On** and confirm that the host exited from standby mode and is fully operational.

For HPM, it is also recommended to enable all C-states available in BIOS and let vSphere decide on their usage. Refer to the *How it works* section of this recipe, for more details about C-states.

## How to do it...

Both DPM and HPM settings can be configured using vCenter Client or Web Client.

### Configuring DPM

To enable power management for the cluster using vCenter Client, execute the following steps:

1. Right click on the cluster and select **Edit Settings**.
2. Go to **Power Management** under **vSphere DRS**.

3. Configure the **Power management** option and **DPM Threshold**.

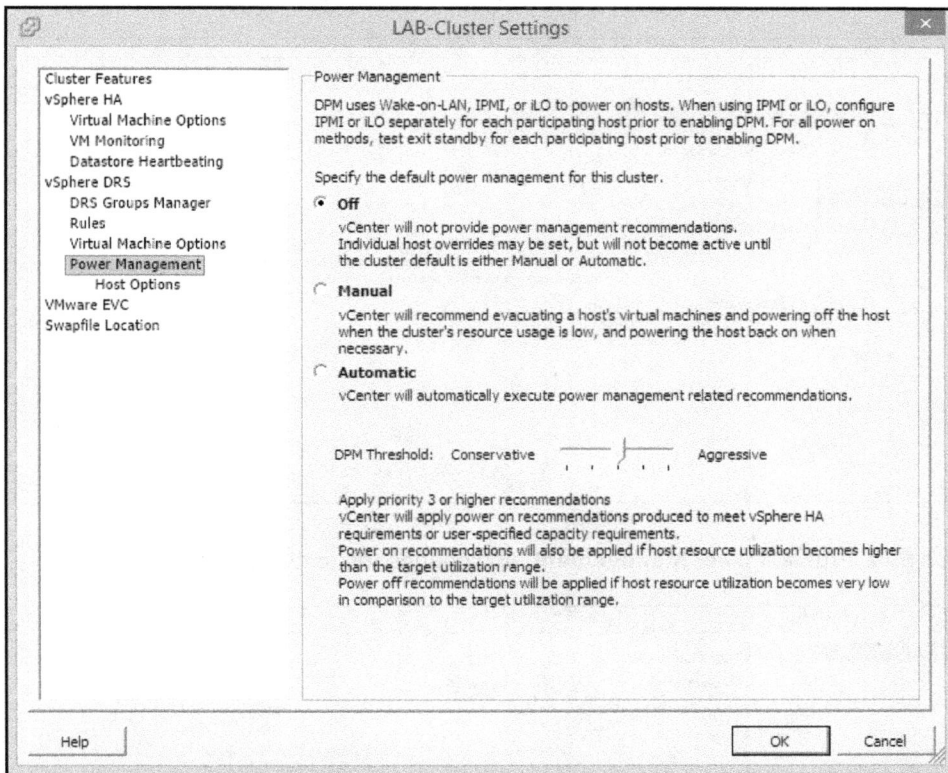

The more aggressive a DPM threshold is, the more priority levels vCenter will use to make a decision.

4. Go to **Host Options** to configure per-host DPM settings if necessary.

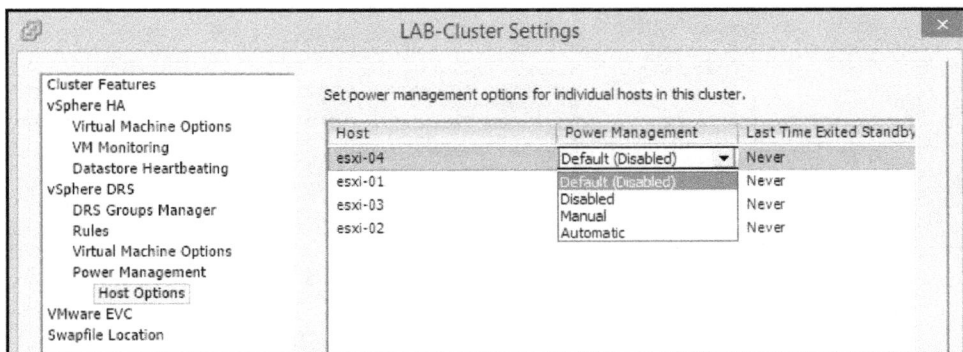

In Web Client, DPM options can be accessed by going to **Manage | Settings | vSphere DRS** screen available when a cluster is selected from the inventory.

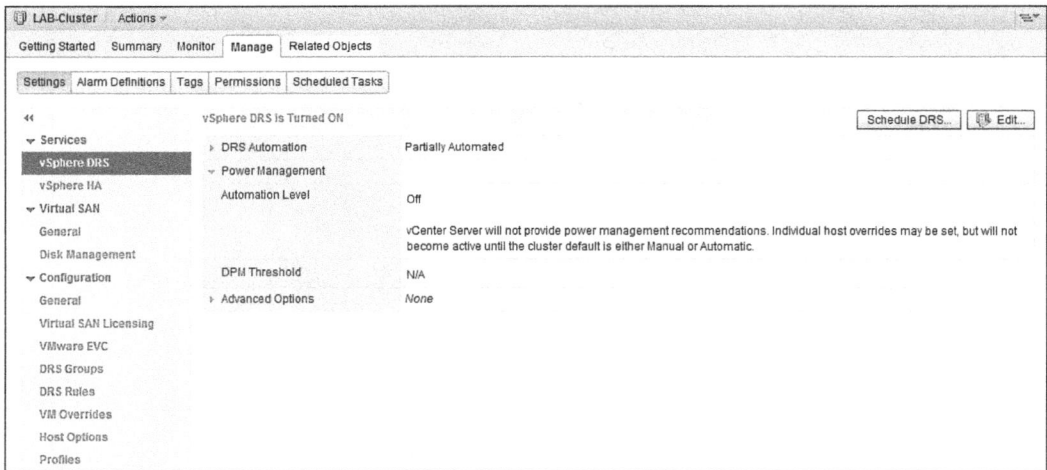

Click on **Edit**, expand **Power Management**, and change the settings as required.

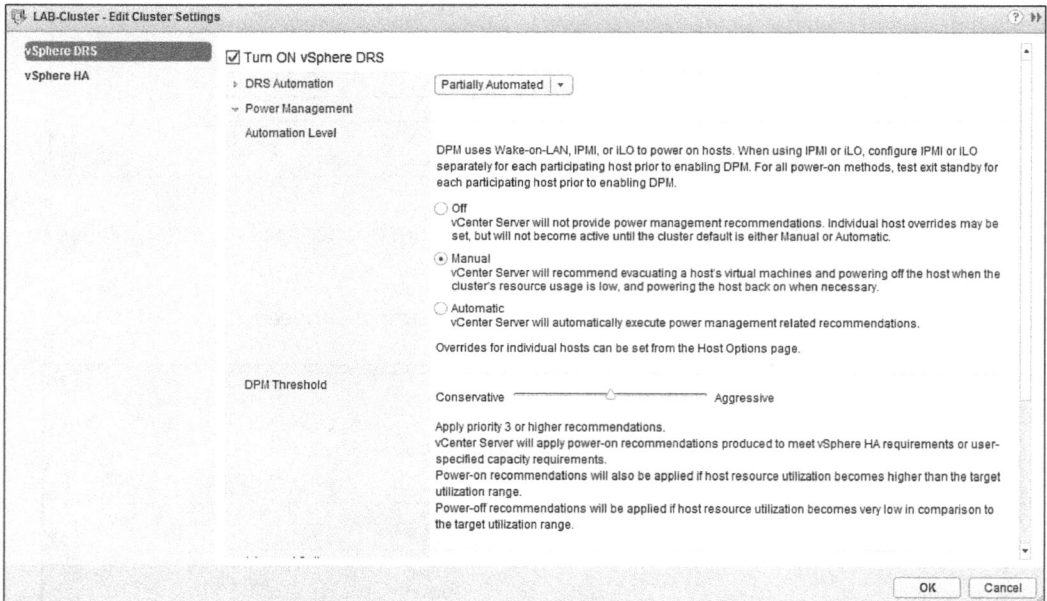

# Configuring HPM

To configure HPM settings for a host in vCenter Client:

1. Select the host in the inventory.
2. Go to the **Configuration** tab and click on **Power Management**.
3. Click on **Properties** on the right side of the screen, select power policy, and click on **OK**.

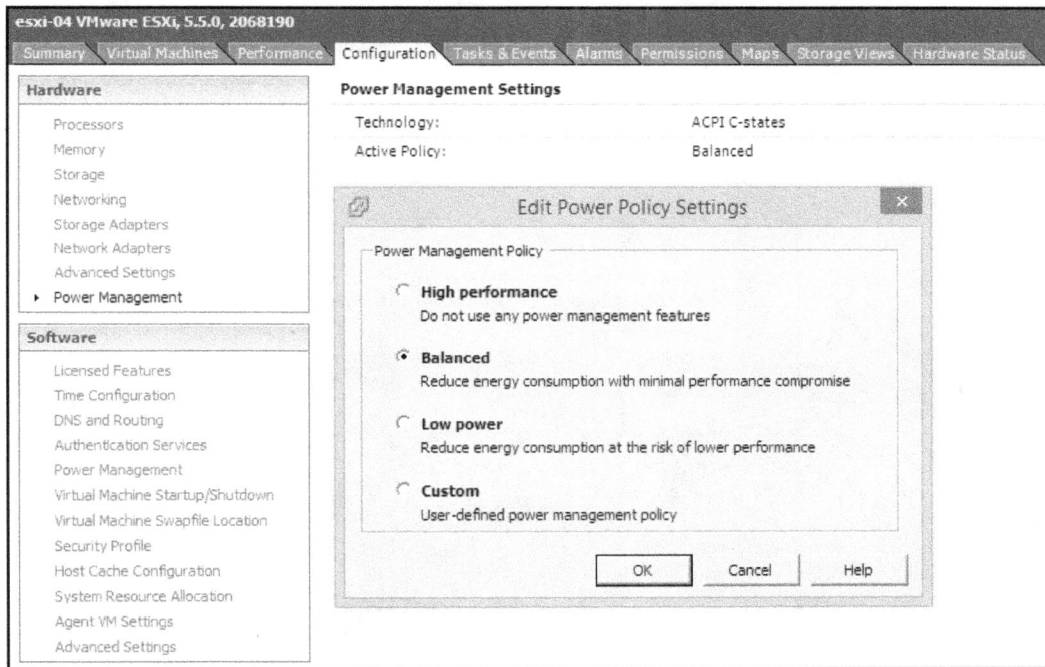

To change host HPM settings in Web Client, perform the following steps:

1. Select host in the inventory.
2. Go to **Manage** | **Settings** | **Power Management**.
3. Click on the **Edit** button on the right.

4. Select power policy and click on **OK**.

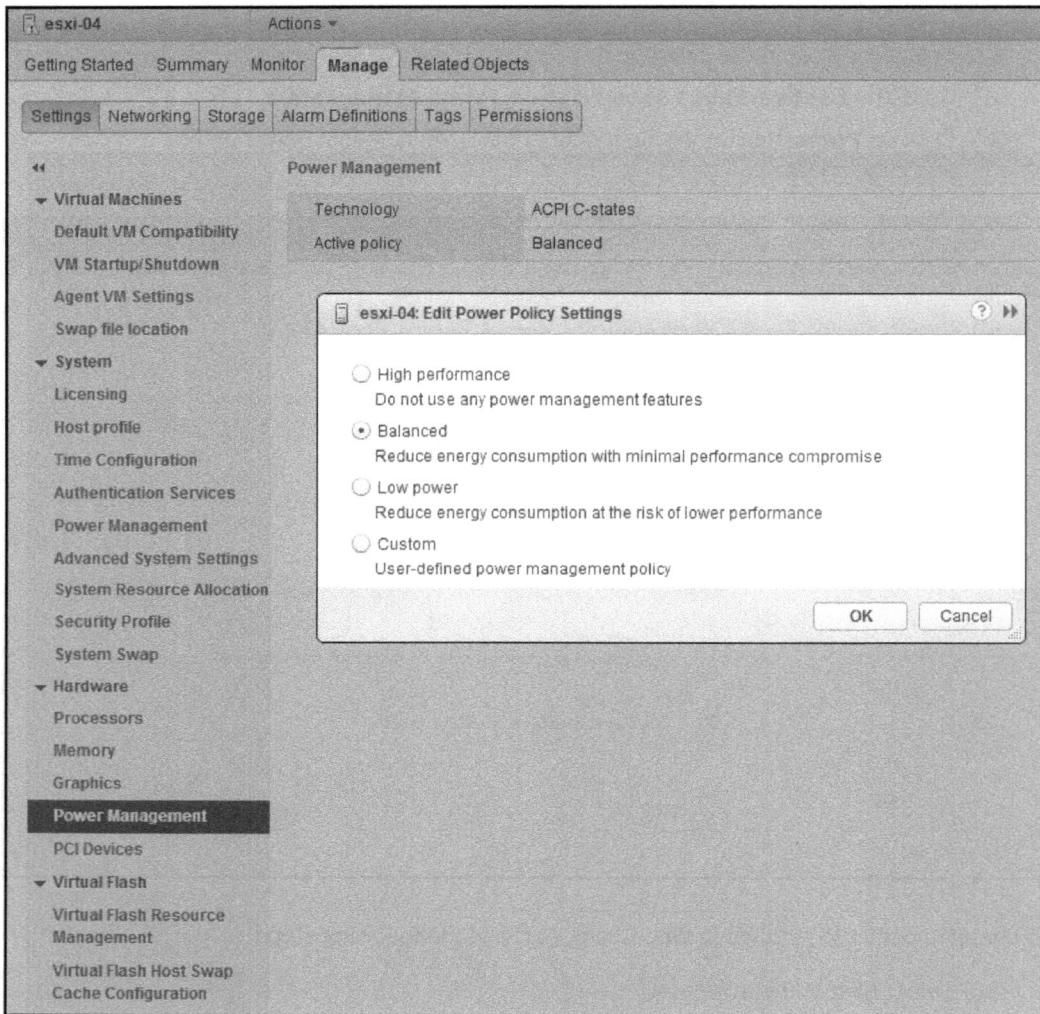

# How it works...

To manage power options, vSphere uses **Advanced Configuration and Power Interface** (**ACPI**). It is an open standard that allows device configuration to be performed by the operating system. ACPI is a set of platform-independent interfaces for power management, hardware configuration, and monitoring.

Processor performance states are defined in ACPI as follows:

-   **C0**: It is defined as the maximum performance and power consumption. A processor in this state can be in one of several power-performance states called P-states. P-states vary from P0, which is the maximum power and frequency, to P(n), which is the lowest performance state supported.

    P-states are implementation-specific. Intel calls it SpeedStep, while AMD calls it PowerNow or Cool'n'Quiet.

-   **C1**: It is defined as the halt state when a processor does not execute instructions. When a processor supports enhanced halt state (C1E), it may be chosen instead of C1. This state allows little performance impact and in certain cases, has no impact or even increases performance for some single-threaded workloads.

-   **C2**: It is defined as the deeper state with lower power consumption. It takes more time for a processor in this state to come back to full performance

-   **C3**: It is defined as the sleep state when a processor doesn't need to keep its cache coherent.

All the preceding states explained allow a better understanding of the available HPM power options:

-   The **high performance** policy uses only C0 and C1/C1E, as well as the highest P-states. This was the default option for ESXi 4.0 and 4.1

-   The **balanced** policy uses P-states to reduce power consumption. It is the default option for ESXi 5.

    ESXi 5.5 provides additional power saving when this policy is chosen by utilizing C-states higher than C1.

-   The **low power** policy aggressively uses deep C-states. There is a risk of degraded VM performance when this policy is chosen.

## There's more...

The **custom** policy for HPM uses advanced configuration parameters available in vSphere Client by going to **Configuration | Advanced Settings** and opening the **Power** dialog box:

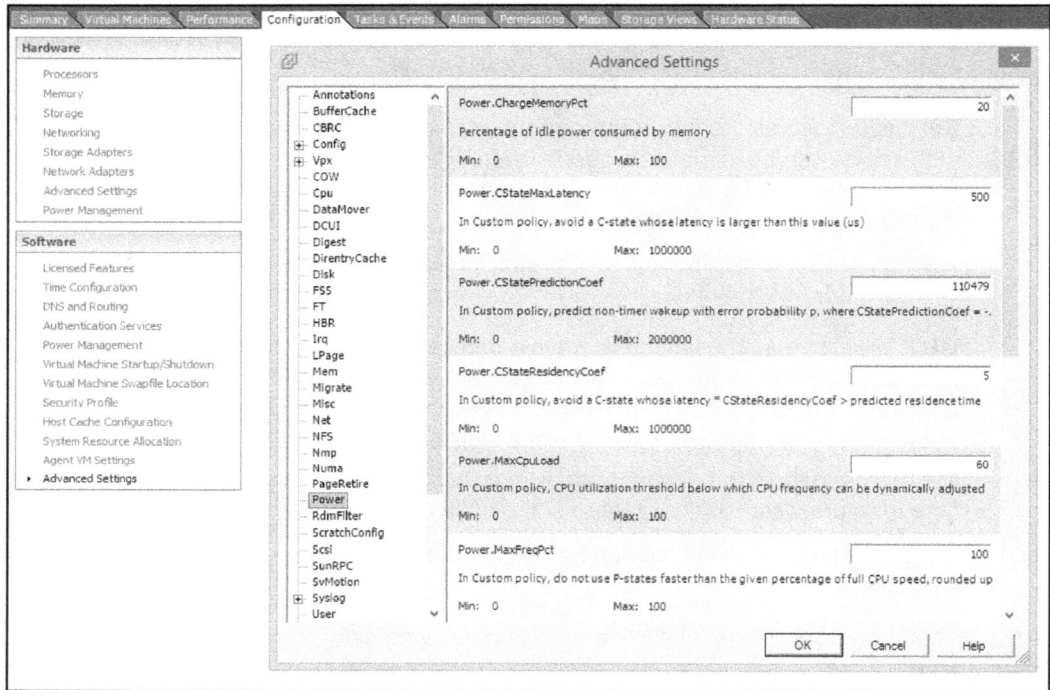

In Web Client, these settings are located by going to **Manage | Settings | Advanced System Settings**. Search for `Custom policy` to filter relevant settings:

| Getting Started | Summary | Monitor | **Manage** | Related Objects |
| --- | --- | --- | --- | --- |

| Settings | Networking | Storage | Alarm Definitions | Tags | Permissions |
| --- | --- | --- | --- | --- | --- |

Advanced System Settings

VM Startup/Shutdown
Agent VM Settings
Swap file location
▼ System
  Licensing
  Host profile
  Time Configuration
  Authentication Services
  Power Management
  **Advanced System Settings**
  System Resource Allocatic
  Security Profile
  System Swap
▼ Hardware
  Processors
  Memory
  Power Management

Q Custom policy

| Name | 1 ▲ Value | Description |
| --- | --- | --- |
| Power.CStateMaxLatency | 500 | In Custom policy, avoid a C-state whose latency is lar... |
| Power.CStatePredictionCoef | 110479 | In Custom policy, predict non-timer wakeup with error... |
| Power.CStateResidencyCoef | 5 | In Custom policy, avoid a C-state whose latency * CS... |
| Power.MaxCpuLoad | 60 | In Custom policy, CPU utilization threshold below whi... |
| Power.MinFreqPct | 0 | In Custom policy, do not use P-states slower than th... |
| Power.PerfBias | 6 | In Custom policy, Performance Energy Bias Hint (Inte... |
| Power.TimerHz | 100 | In Custom policy, dynamic power management timer... |
| Power.UseCStates | 0 | In Custom policy, use ACPI C-states when processor... |
| Power.UsePStates | 1 | In Custom policy, use ACPI P-states to save power w... |
| Power.UseStallCtr | 0 | In Custom policy, use stall cycles performance counter |

10 of 944 items

The Esxtop command-line utility can be used to check host power consumption and other power information. To accomplish this, perform the following steps:

1.  Access a host's command line via SSH or a console. Please refer to the *Accessing hosts via SSH* and *Securing host management access* recipes in *Chapter 1, vCenter Basic Tasks and Features* for more information.

2.  Type `esxtop` and press *Enter*.

3.  Press *P*. An example of what the result will look like is shown in the following screenshot:

```
10:45:14pm up 60 days 21:30, 850 worlds, 46 VMs, 67 vCPUs; CPU load average: 0.21, 0.20, 0.19
Power Usage:   150W, Power Cap:  N/A
PSTATE MHZ:

CPU %USED %UTIL %C0 %C1 %C2
  0  11.3  31.2  30  63   6
  1   7.6  22.8  22  63  15
  2   9.9  26.9  27  61  13
  3   7.3  21.2  21  54  25
  4   8.4  23.1  23  60  18
  5   8.5  23.0  23  47  31
  6   6.7  18.8  18  54  27
  7   8.9  23.5  23  44  33
  8  10.2  25.8  26  47  27
  9   5.5  15.6  15  45  40
 10   5.5  15.2  15  50  35
 11   6.6  17.5  17  37  47
 12   6.9  18.0  18  58  24
 13   6.1  16.0  15  37  48
 14   8.8  22.8  23  59  19
 15   7.7  20.3  20  36  45
```

▶ **Power Usage** is the actual power consumption reported by a sensor on a server's power supply. It can be shown as 0 if the sensor is not present or if ESXi is not able to read the value.

▶ **PSTATE MHZ** shows frequencies of each P-state. According to the preceding screenshot, P-state is not available for the particular server.

▶ **%USED** is the percentage of nominal speed at which each logical CPU currently operates.

▶ **%UTIL** is the percentage of time when each logical CPU is not idle.

When `%USED` is lower than `%UTIL`, the CPU is in a P-state higher than P0. When `%USED` is higher than 100 percent, it means the CPU is in turbo mode.

# Considering NUMA when configuring RAM

**Non-Uniform Memory Access** (**NUMA**) is a modern approach to server memory design. Contemporary multiprocessor servers consist of several isolated one-socket computers joined together on one motherboard. Each processor has its own memory slots and only this processor has access to memory installed in these slots. The same way each processor has its own PCI-E bus where other devices connect.

Processors request each other's devices and memory through a high-speed bus. It connects all the available processors, and access to the CPU's own memory is faster than access to memory that belongs to other processors.

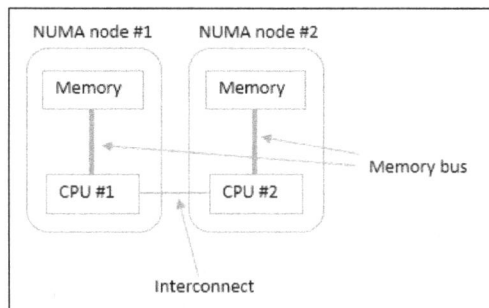

vSphere 5 is NUMA-aware and when possible, it places vCPUs on physical processors that own the VM's memory. It is important to consider NUMA requirements when managing your infrastructure.

## How to do it...

There are a few potential issues administrators may face when considering the NUMA architecture:

1. Server manufacturers often enable NUMA-emulation in BIOS by default. When it's enabled, the server presents itself as a non-NUMA device, which prevents vSphere from using NUMA-related optimization. VMware recommends disabling this option to let vSphere manage VM placement considering NUMA.

2. When creating a VM with more memory than is currently assigned to one processor on a host, it's better to configure this VM with more than one vCPU. This assigned memory will be distributed equally between two physical processors instead of using one physical CPU and accessing the rest of the memory from the other CPU.

For example, on a host with two processors and 32 GB of memory (16 GBs on each socket), a VM that requires 24 GB of memory will be faster with two vCPUs than with one. This way, vSphere will spread two vCPUs between two physical processors and take 12 GB of memory from each physical processor instead of taking 8 GB from the other processor.

3. Be aware of VMs in your environment with a large amount of memory assigned compared to the amount of memory available per slot on your hosts. In such environments, smaller VMs may need more vCPUs as well so that vSphere can fit their memory into the remaining memory in each slot.

   In the previous example, the second VM with 6 GB should have two vCPUs so that its memory is distributed between sockets and each of them takes 3 GB. In this way, the second VM doesn't need to request an additional 2 GB of memory from the other processor.

4. At the same time, a large number of vCPUs should be assigned to VMs with care. vSphere uses processor physical cores to run a VM, which has less or equal number of vCPUs than the number of available physical cores.

   When a VM has more vCPUs than physical cores per processor, vSphere will use **hyper-threading**—a technology that allows addressing two virtual cores per physical core and shares the workload between them if possible. Even at this point, because of hyper-threading, you may lose up to 30 percent of performance.

   If a VM has more vCPUs than the number of processor cores taking into account hyper-threading, vSphere will start using cores from other processors, which means further performance degradation.

# vCPU versus pCPU and time slots

The core of the vSphere system is the so called **hypervisor**—a process that serves running virtual machines. One of the main tasks of a hypervisor is to manage a VM's access to hardware resources in the most efficient way. It does this according to the available resources and configures the importance of running VMs.

All vCPUs assigned to a VM are treated as a chain. Each vCPU is a link in this chain. In vSphere terms, it's called **world**. Each VM has as many worlds as it has vCPUs assigned plus two invisible service worlds. One of these service worlds is responsible for the VM itself; the other one is responsible for its input/output.

All such chains from each VM create a queue, which becomes an input to the hypervisor process. Each VM gets a timeslot—a period of time when a hypervisor gives it access to the actual hardware. During its timeslot, a VM gets access to a host's physical CPU (pCPU). The timeslot is limited to less than 1 millisecond. Once it's over, the scheduler puts this VM back in the queue according to the VM's priority and current load.

If there is only one VM running on a host, it will be able to use the host's hardware during each timeslot. In case there are few VMs running on a host and their total number of worlds is less than the number of available pCPUs or cores on the host, the hypervisor will be able to fit all of these VMs in each time slot.

When VMs use more worlds than pCPUs available, the hypervisor will need more than one timeslot to run all VMs, and it will try to fit them in each timeslot in the most efficient way, taking NUMA into consideration as well.

Performance loss starts when there are a few large VMs running, which use the whole timeslot, along with small VMs, which cannot fill a timeslot. In this case, small VMs will be wasting timeslots.

## How to do it...

Administrators can use the following guidelines to minimize performance penalties related to the size of VMs:

1.  Assign minimum possible resources to VMs. Don't give two vCPUs to a VM that performs fine with one. The administrator can use VMware Operations or third-party performance analysis tools to identify current bottlenecks.

2.  Avoid creating large VMs compared to the host size.

3.  Consider NUMA requirements when assigning resources to VMs.

4.  Use Paravirtual devices to minimize overhead related to the input/output world of a VM. Please refer to the *Meeting higher I/O needs with VMware Paravirtual controller* and *Improving network performance with VMXNET 3 network adapter* recipes in this chapter.

# 5
# Optimizing Resource Usage

In this chapter, we will cover the following recipes:

- ► Prioritizing VMs with shares
- ► Ensuring VMs have enough resources to run
- ► Limiting resources used by VMs
- ► Grouping VMs by resource usage
- ► Balancing loads between hosts
- ► Balancing loads between datastores
- ► Configuring storage load balancing thresholds
- ► Limiting VM storage I/O consumption
- ► Limiting VM network I/O consumption

## Introduction

In this chapter, we will take a look at vSphere features and options available for resource usage optimization. Common strategies in this area include better distribution of load between hosts and datastores, prioritization of resource consumers according to their importance and needs, as well as proper resource usage limitation, including CPU, memory, network, and storage I/O.

# Prioritizing VMs with shares

vSphere allows administrators to prioritize virtual machines by configuring their importance using a feature called **shares**. The more shares a VM has, the more resources it is allowed to consume when competing with other virtual machines. Shares is of relative importance to VMs or pools and they apply within the same parent.

> Shares are usually specified as high, normal, and low, which configures VM priority as 4:2:1 ratio.

This feature is one of the few approaches to resource distribution and performance tuning available to administrators. Shares are taken into account only when there is resource contention. In other words, the feature settings make sense only when two or more virtual machines compete for resources.

The actual number of resources a VM gets may change each time it is powered on. If a host is upgraded with more memory, each virtual machine will get a larger portion of RAM according to the ratio.

> Shares are also helpful in environments where frequent changes to available resources happen, and as a result, VMs compete for resources.

## How to do it...

To change virtual machine shares, execute the following steps:

1. Right-click on a VM.
2. Go to **All vCenter Actions | Edit Resource Settings**.

3. Adjust CPU and memory shares, and click on **OK**.

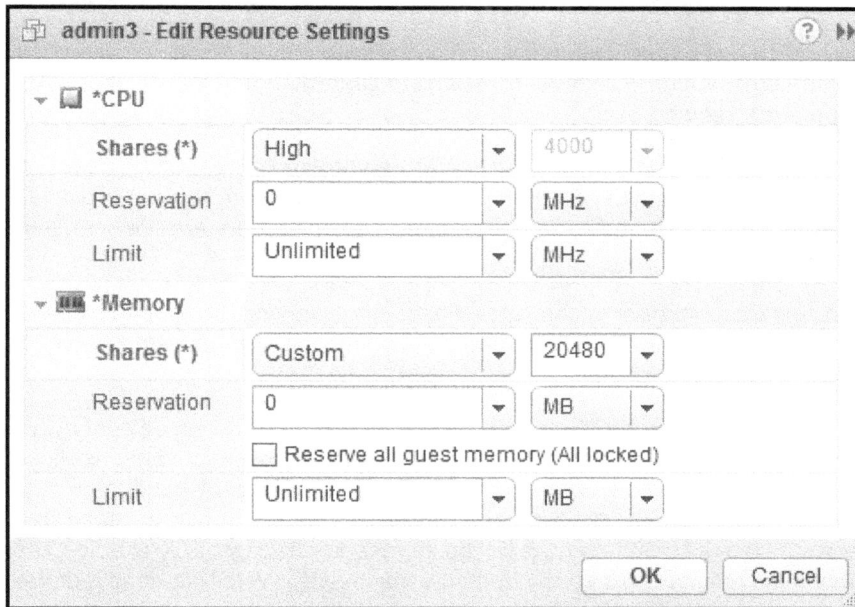

In vCenter Client, perform the following steps:

1. Right-click on a VM.
2. Go to **Edit Settings | Resources**.
3. Adjust CPU and memory reservations by selecting **CPU** and **Memory** from the list.
4. Click on **OK**.

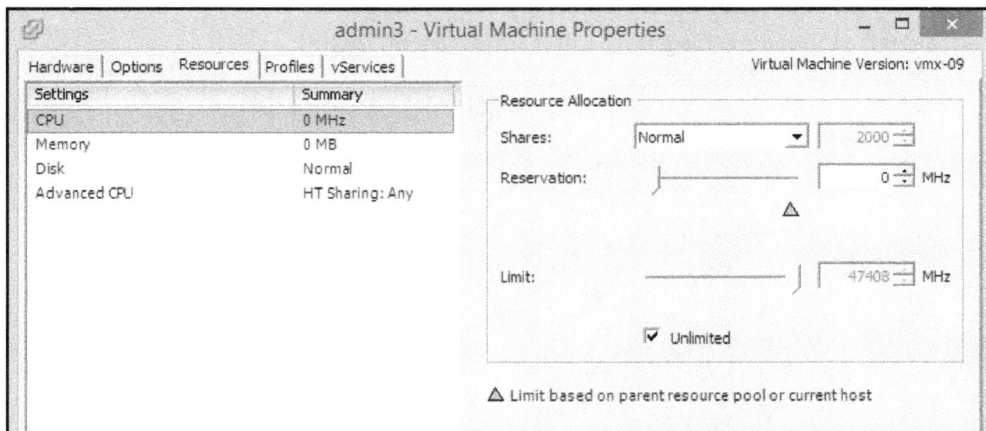

# Ensuring VMs have enough resources to run

Some virtual machines or applications need a certain number of resources allocated and available all the time. vSphere uses **reservations** to guarantee that a particular VM always has the resources it requires.

Reservations are configured as the amount of CPU and memory that will be reserved for a particular virtual machine. vCenter makes sure there are enough resources available to satisfy the required reservation before powering the VM on. If there are not enough resources, the VM will stay off.

vCenter also considers admission control settings when verifying the available resources for the configured reservation. A VM may be denied in being powered on even when it looks like a host or cluster has enough resources.

At the same time, it is better not to allocate all the environment resources right away. VMs get more resources as they need them until the reserved limit is reached. vSphere allows virtual machines to keep the resources once allocated, even if a VM doesn't need them anymore. If all the available cluster resources have been allocated, VMs eventually may take them, which will lead to memory overcommitment. It will be allowed in this case. ESXi is able to handle such situations by transferring memory from idle machines to VMs that need it at the present moment. Such memory reallocation takes more time, which causes performance degradation.

The default value for all resource reservations is 0.

## How to do it...

To change virtual machine resource reservations, perform the following steps:

1. Right-click on a VM.
2. Go to **All vCenter Actions | Edit Resource Settings**.
3. Adjust CPU and memory reservation, and click on **OK**.

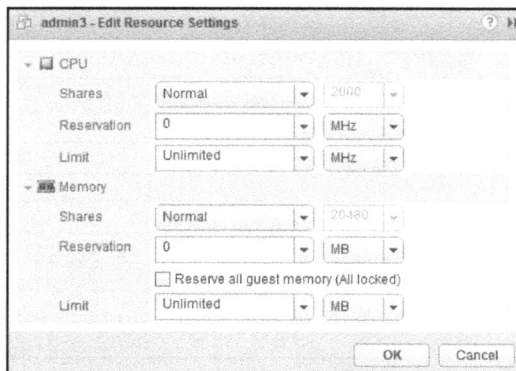

In vCenter Client, perform the following steps:

1. Right-click on a VM.

2. Go to **Edit Settings | Resources**.

3. Adjust CPU and memory reservations by selecting **CPU** and **Memory** in the list.

4. Click on **OK**.

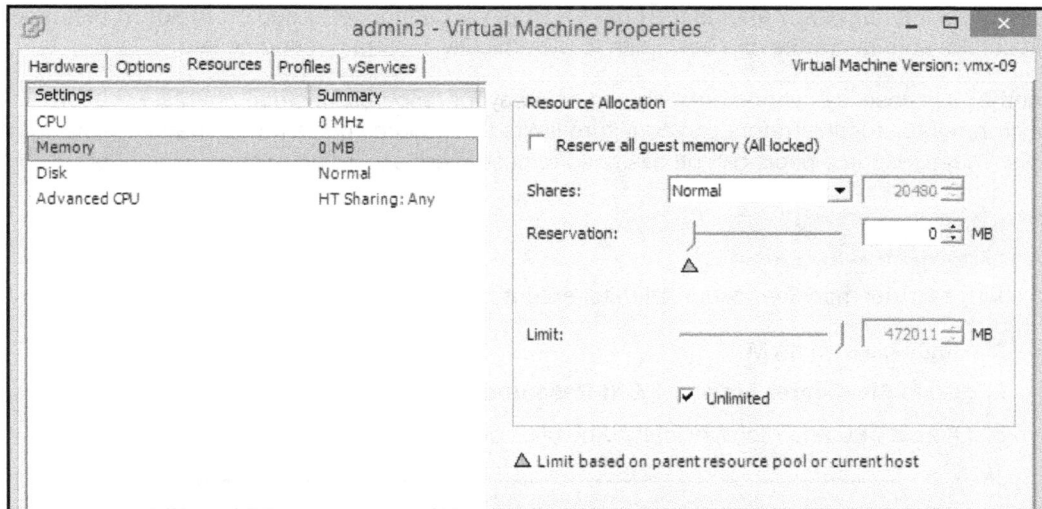

# Limiting resources used by VMs

By default, the configured amount of memory and CPU is the amount a VM can take. In addition to resource allocations, vSphere allows specifying the maximum amount of CPU and memory a particular VM can use by configuring **limits**.

Limits are expressed in MHz for CPU and MB for memory. Administrators can use them to constrain user expectations or to simulate resource shortage.

Limits should be used carefully. When they are lower than the number of assigned resources, a VM is not allowed to use more than the limit. At the same time, the guest OS is not aware of limits; it can see only the allocated resources. Once it hits the limit, vSphere will not allow it to use more resources. In this situation, VMkernel will try to reclaim the memory from the guest OS. Eventually, this may result in excessive swapping, which, in turn, results in performance degradation.

> **Hypervisor swapping** refers to a situation when the hypervisor swaps out the guest physical memory directly into the VM's swap file. This file is created when as VM starts and is stored together with its files. Access to the data stored in a swap file on a disk is slower than access to the host's memory. That's why memory swapping means worse performance.

The most common use case for limits is a situation when a rogue VM consumes excessive resources. If it negatively affects the host and this VM cannot be turned off to adjust resource allocation, administrators can use limits to dynamically constrain resource usage.

Another use case is environments where users pay for resources instead of VMs. For such environments, administrators can configure limits for resource pools rather than for individual VMs. These resource pools can be assigned to customers according to purchased quotas.

## How to do it...

To change virtual machine resource limits, execute the following steps:

1. Right-click on a VM.
2. Go to **All vCenter Actions | Edit Resource Settings**.
3. Adjust CPU and memory limits, and click on **OK**.

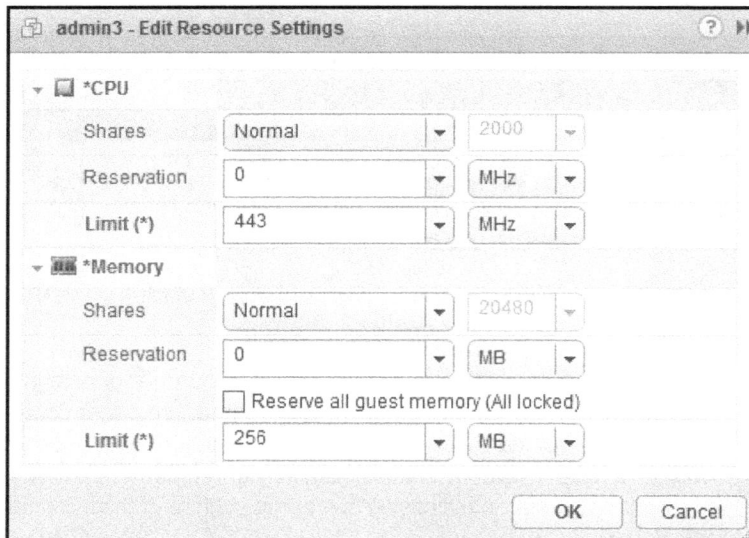

In vCenter Client, perform the following steps:

1. Right-click on a VM.

2. Go to **Edit Settings | Resources**.

3. Adjust CPU and memory limits by selecting **CPU** and **Memory** in the list.

4. Click on **OK**.

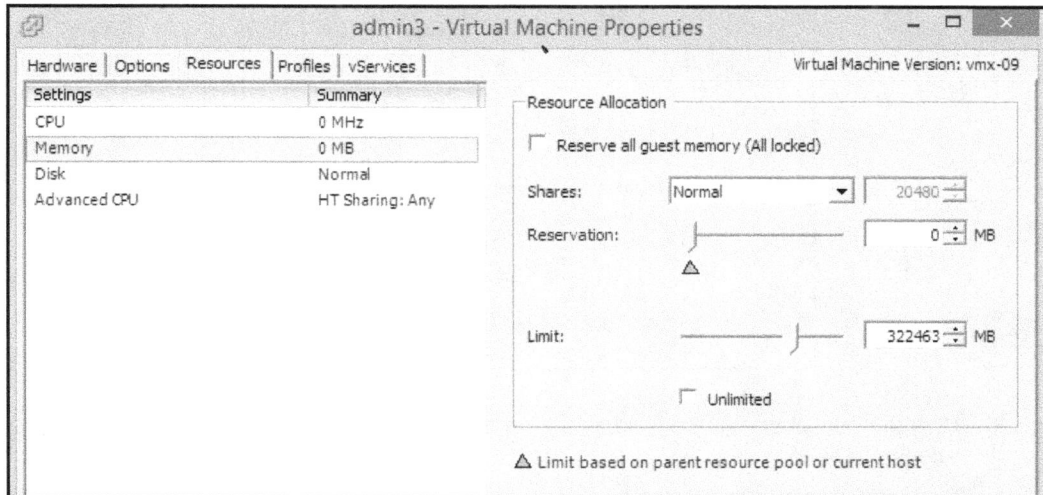

# Grouping VMs by resource usage

vCenter gives administrators an ability to group virtual machines and assign resources to the groups as well as prioritize them. This greatly simplifies administration and can be achieved by creating **resource pools**.

Resource pools are independent from hosts and clusters, and can only be created in vCenter. Once a VM is assigned to a pool, all resource allocations and priorities configured for the pool apply to this virtual machine as well.

Resource pools are indispensable when there is a need to manage virtual machines with different requirements for memory and CPU. VMs with high CPU requirements can be assigned to a pool with higher CPU shares, while secondary VMs can be members of a pool with low CPU and memory priority.

Another application of this feature is control delegation within the vSphere environment. For example, a vCenter administrator can create resource pools for different departments and delegate control of these pools to department-level administrators. They will be able to create and manage virtual machines within the configured boundaries of the delegated resource pools.

## How to do it...

To create a new top-level resource pool, execute the following steps:

1. Navigate to **vCenter** | **Clusters**.

2. Right-click on a cluster and click on **New Resource Pool...**.

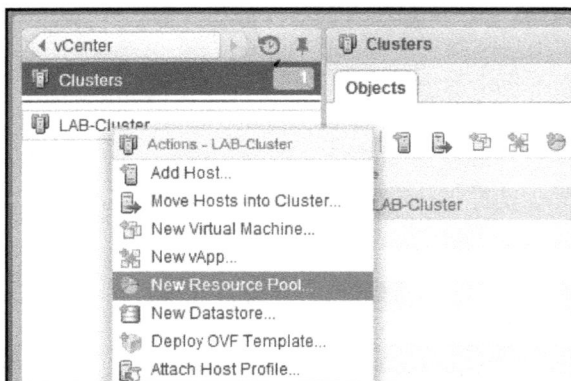

3. Give the new pool a name, and configure the CPU and memory shares, reservations, and limits as required.

4. Click on **OK** to create a new pool.

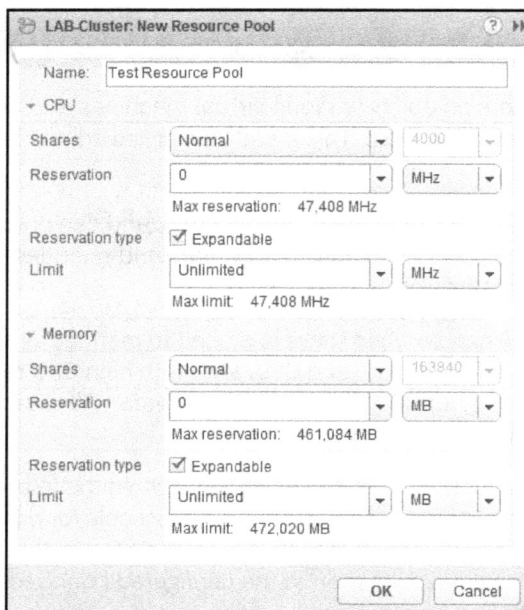

To create a child resource pool, perform the following steps:

1. Navigate to **vCenter | Resource Pools**.

2. Select the parent resource pool from the list.

3. Open the **Actions** menu and select **New Resource Pool...**.

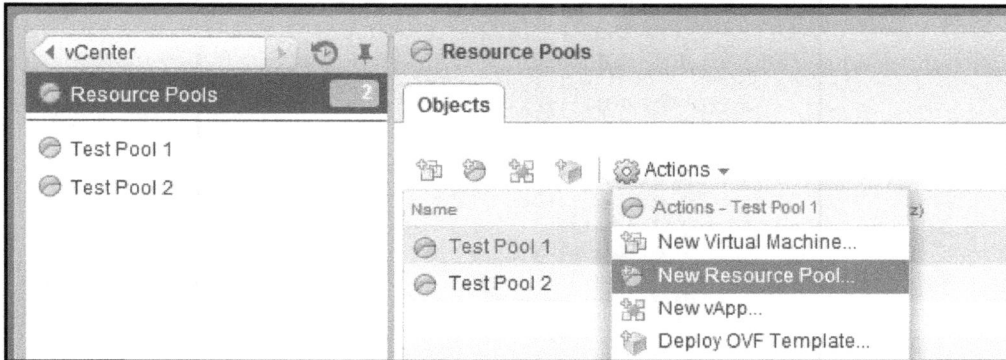

4. Give the new pool a name, and configure the CPU and memory shares, reservations, and limits as required.

5. Click on **OK** to create a new pool.

Pool hierarchy can be verified under the **Hosts and Clusters** view. An example of what the hierarchy may look like is shown in the following screenshot:

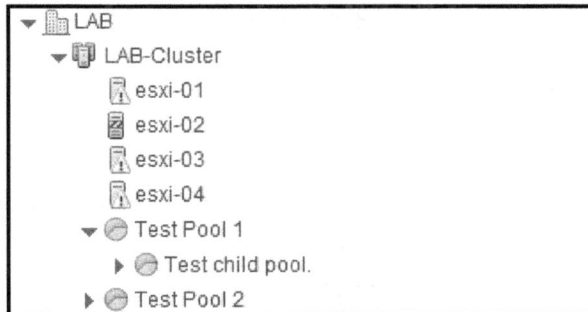

To edit or delete a resource pool, perform the following steps:

1. Navigate to **vCenter | Resource Pools**.

2. Select the resource pool in the list.

3. Open the **Actions** menu and go to **All vCenter Actions**.

4. Select **Edit CPU Settings**, **Edit Memory Settings**, or **Remove from Inventory** as required.

In vCenter Client, the options to create, edit, or delete resource pools are available under the **Hosts and Clusters** view by right-clicking on a pool or cluster:

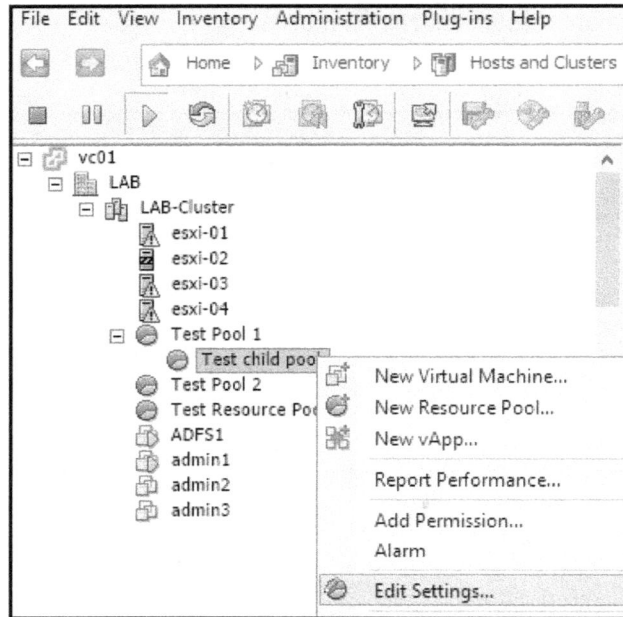

To assign a virtual machine to a pool, drag and drop it into a resource pool object. Another way to assign a VM to a pool is during migration between hosts or clusters. Also, you will be asked to specify the resource pool during VM creation.

## There's more...

Be aware of the following rules that apply when a VM is assigned to a pool:

- ▶  VM share values will change to reflect the total number of shares of the pool.
- ▶  Any custom share values will be maintained.
- ▶  Reservations and limits configured for this VM will not change. When a pool doesn't have enough resources to satisfy VM reservations, vCenter will not allow the VM to move to the pool.

# Balancing loads between hosts

**Distributed Resource Scheduler** (**DRS**) is a feature designed to optimize VM placement between hosts in a cluster. It compares cluster resource utilization to the current demand. Based on that, it generates recommendations on VM placement. If configured to do so, it can perform VM migrations automatically according to these recommendations.

For example, a cluster on the left side of the diagram is not balanced. After applying DRS recommendations, host resources are utilized more efficiently.

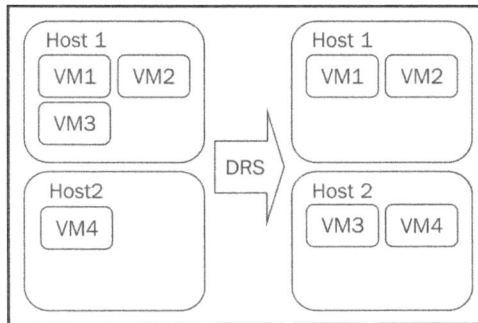

## Getting ready

The following requirements must be met before hosts can be joined to the DRS cluster:

▸ There is a shared storage between all hosts.

▸ All VMs are located on volumes that are shared between all hosts.

▸ All VMs use volume names to specify the location of virtual disks.

▸ If **Raw Device Mapping** (**RDM**) VMFS volumes are being used, they must be in virtual compatibility mode.

▸ There is a gigabit network connecting all hosts.

▸ All hosts have compatible processors. Please refer to the *Using hosts with different CPUs in one cluster* recipe in *Chapter 1, vCenter Basic Tasks and Features* for more details.

## How to do it...

The DRS feature is a cluster-wide setting. It is also possible to change the automation level per virtual machine.

## Creating a DRS cluster

Turning on DRS for a cluster can be accomplished in Web Client with the following steps:

1. Right-click on a cluster.
2. Select **Settings** in the menu.
3. Go to **Manage | Settings | Services | vSphere DRS**.

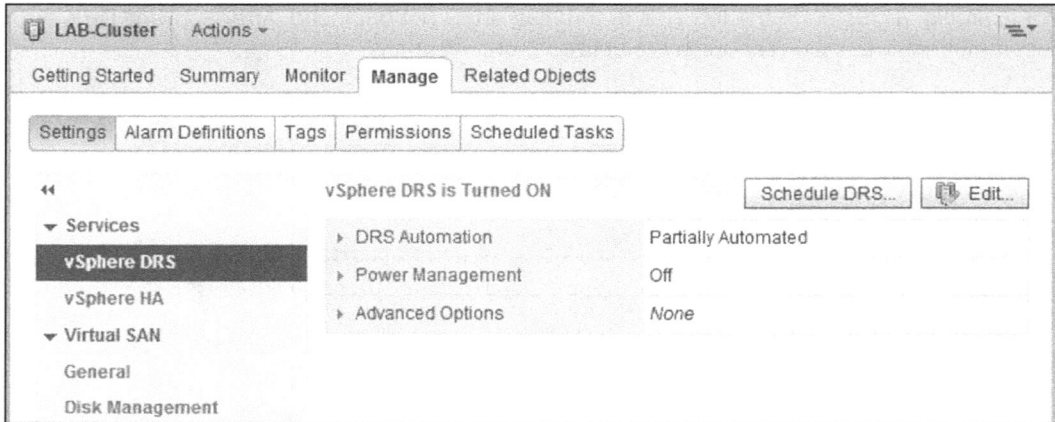

4. Click on the **Edit** button.
5. Check the **Turn ON vSphere DRS** option.
6. Select the **DRS Automation** level and click on **OK**.

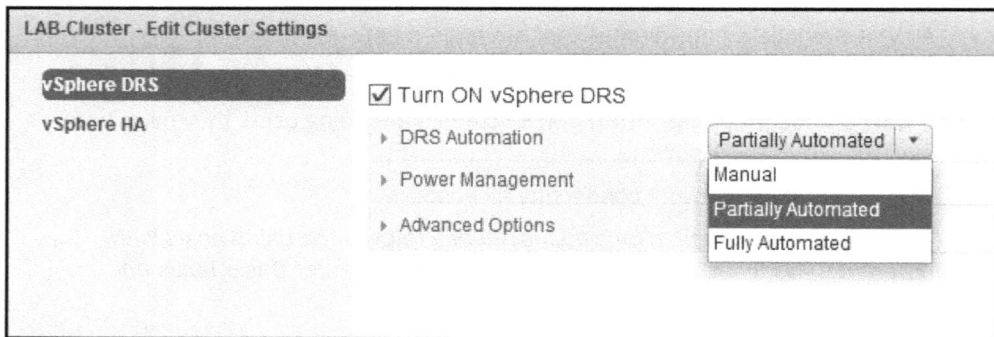

In vCenter Client, perform the following steps:

1. Switch to the **Hosts and Clusters** settings view.
2. Right-click on a cluster and go to **Edit Settings**.

3. Select **vSphere DRS**, choose the automation level, and click on **OK**.

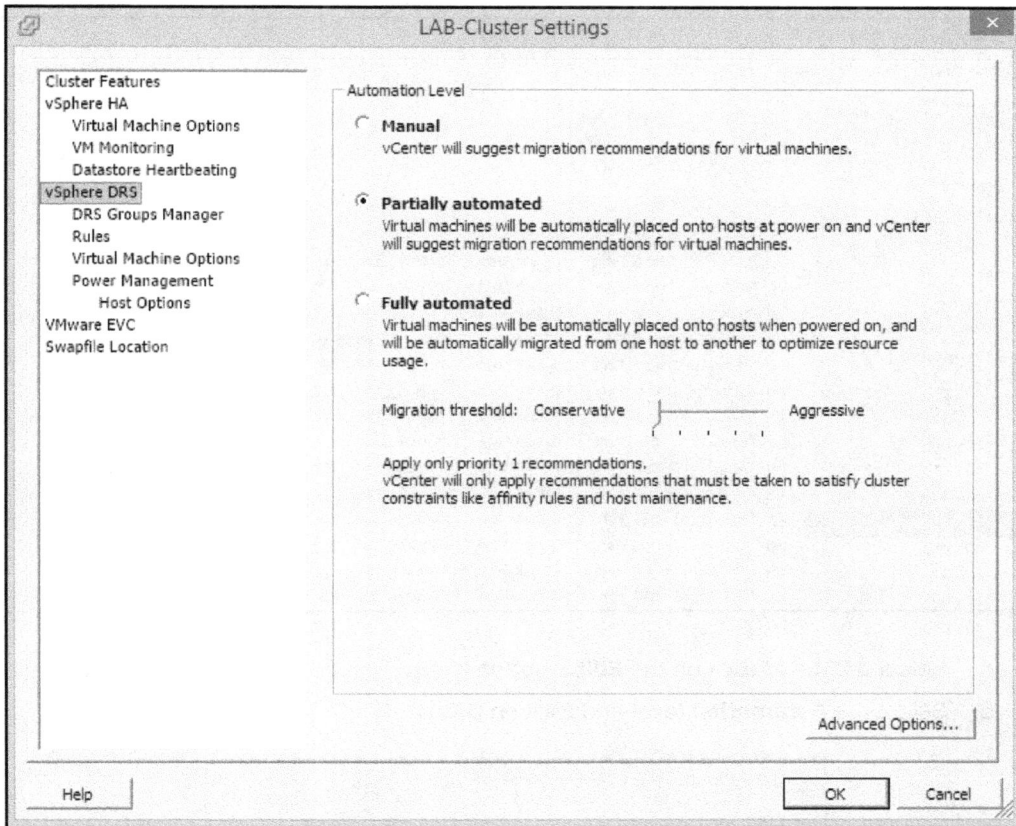

For **Fully automated** mode, it's recommended to avoid setting the **Aggressive** migration threshold. This setting can lead to too many VM migrations and unnecessary overload.

## Configuring VM options

The cluster DRS automation level can be overwritten per virtual machine. To do this in Web Client, perform the following steps:

1. Right-click on a cluster.
2. Select **Settings** in the menu.

3. Go to **Manage | Settings | Services | VM Overrides**.

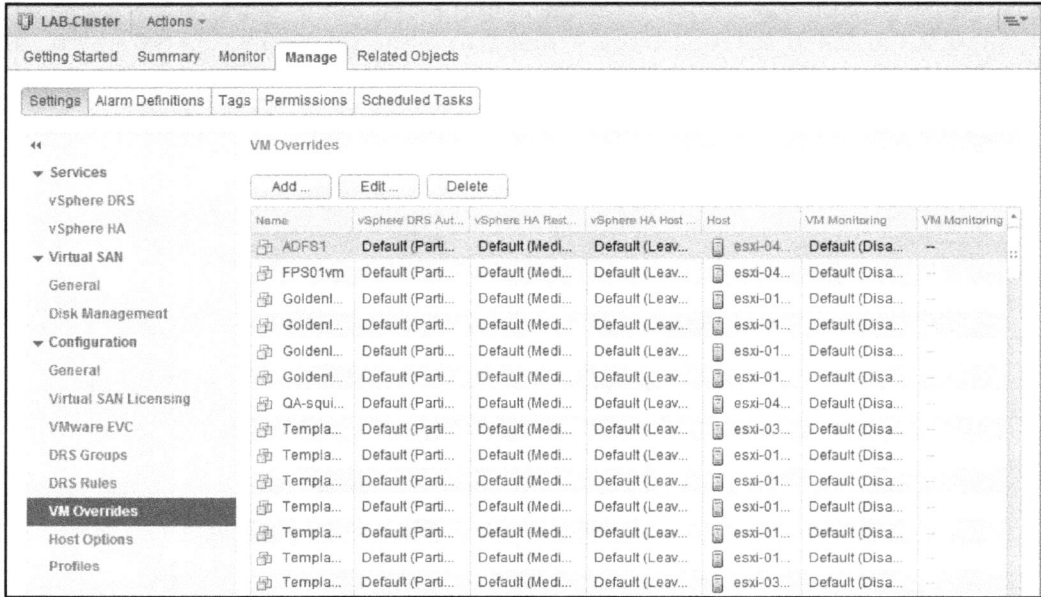

4. Select a VM and click on the **Edit...** button.

5. Select the **Automation level** and click on **OK**.

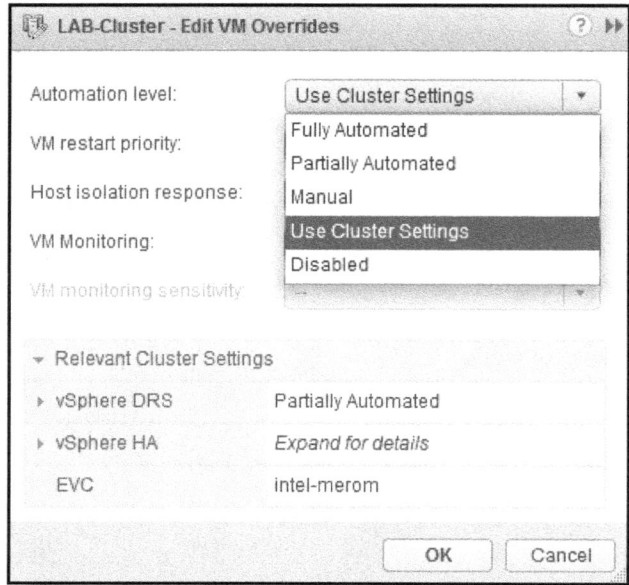

In vCenter Client, perform the following steps:

1. Switch to the **Hosts and Clusters** settings view.

2. Right-click on a cluster and go to **Edit Settings**.

3. Go to **vSphere DRS | Virtual Machine Options**.

4. Select a VM, choose a different automation level, and click on **OK**.

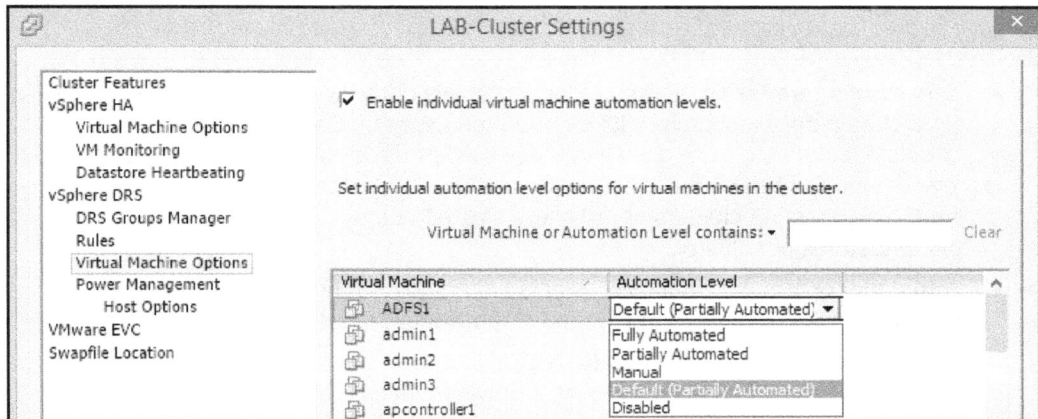

## Disabling DRS

DRS can be turned off from cluster settings. Once it is disabled, resource pool hierarchies and affinity rules will be lost. To avoid this, it is recommended to change the automation level instead of disabling DRS completely.

# Balancing loads between datastores

**Storage Distributed Resource Scheduler** (**SDRS**), which has been introduced in vSphere 5, is one of the most exciting features available in vSphere.

Storage performance has always been one of the pain points for virtual environment administrators. While datastore space utilization is easier to monitor and manage, storage I/O load has always been difficult to keep track of and even more difficult to manage properly. At the same time, I/O congestion can lead to dramatic performance degradation. Furthermore, I/O usage usually changes throughout the day and week, which makes it difficult to fairly balance the I/O load for a long period of time.

SDRS analyses storage space utilization and I/O load over a period of time, and makes recommendations for VM placement to ensure proper load and to prevent future imbalance of I/O usage and latency. If configured, it can also apply recommendations automatically.

SDRS is a solution for storage resource utilization similar to DRS, which is for host resource usage. While DRS balances CPU and memory usage between hosts, SDRS balances space and I/O utilization between datastores. More details about DRS can be found in the *Balancing loads between hosts* recipe in this chapter.

The following are the key features of SDRS:

 ▸ **Resource aggregation** allows grouping multiple datastores in a **datastore cluster**—a pool of datastore resources with shared management. Datastore clusters makes it possible to balance loads between these datastores during VM migrations and initial placement. Current vSphere 5.1 limitations are 32 datastores per datastore cluster and 256 datastore clusters per vSphere cluster. vSphere 5.5 allows up to 64 datastores per cluster.

 ▸ **Initial placement** automatically selects a datastore for new VMs based on the current space utilization and I/O load of individual datastores in a cluster.

 ▸ **Load balancing** is the core feature of SDRS. It monitors storage usage and once configured thresholds are exceeded, it provides recommendations on VM migrations to fairly balance the load. In fully automated mode, it applies recommendations automatically.

 ▸ **Datastore maintenance mode** makes sure all VMs are migrated from a datastore when it is placed in maintenance mode. Migrations can be performed automatically or presented to administrator for validation.

 ▸ **Affinity rules**, which are similar to DRS affinity rules, provide the ability to place virtual disks of the same VM in different datastores or keep them together (this is the default option). More details about affinity rules can be found in the *Automating VM placement with storage affinity* recipe in *Chapter 6, Basic Administrative Tasks*.

SDRS load balancing has a built in mechanism called online device modeling. Its purpose is to determine if two datastores belong to the same physical storage. This is accomplished by injecting random I/O reads into single and multiple datastores and detecting correlations in performance change. The obtained information is used to predict storage utilization after VM migration and generate placement recommendations.

While online device modeling is supposed to avoid moving virtual machines within the same physical SAN, it still makes more sense to group together datastores that belong to different physical storages. Doing otherwise makes achieving true load balancing more difficult. The following image illustrates the idea.

In the following image, datastores located on different SANs are joined to one cluster. Such architecture offers more advantage when balancing loads between datastores within a cluster.

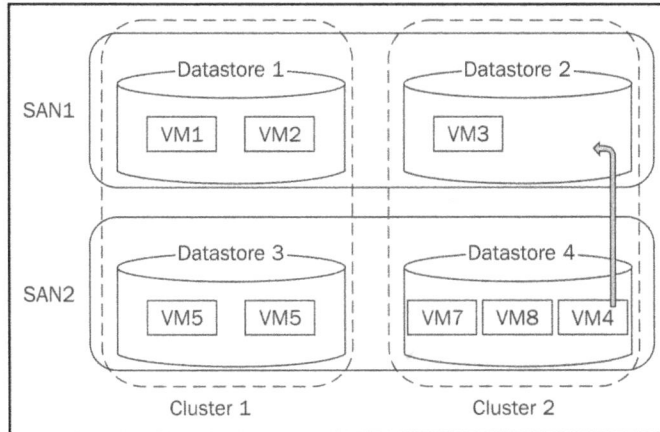

## How to do it...

The resource aggregation feature is utilized by creating datastore clusters; the initial placement is used when a datastore cluster, instead of individual datastore, is chosen during VM creation. Load balancing happens when administrators review and apply migration recommendations.

### Creating a datastore cluster

In Web Client, a new datastore cluster can be created under **Datastore Clusters**:

1.  Click on the **Create a new datastore cluster** button.

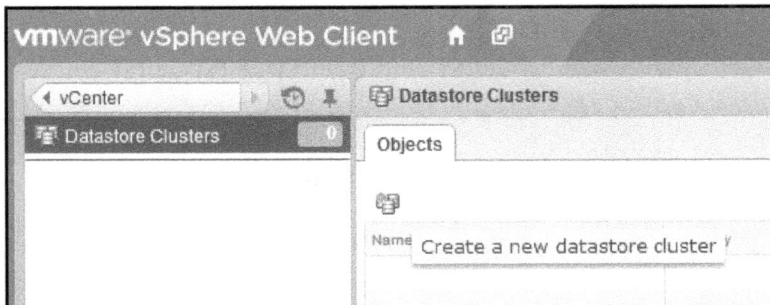

2. Specify a name for the new cluster and select the datacenter where it should be placed. Leave the **Turn ON Storage DRS** option checked as we create a new cluster to take advantage of this feature.

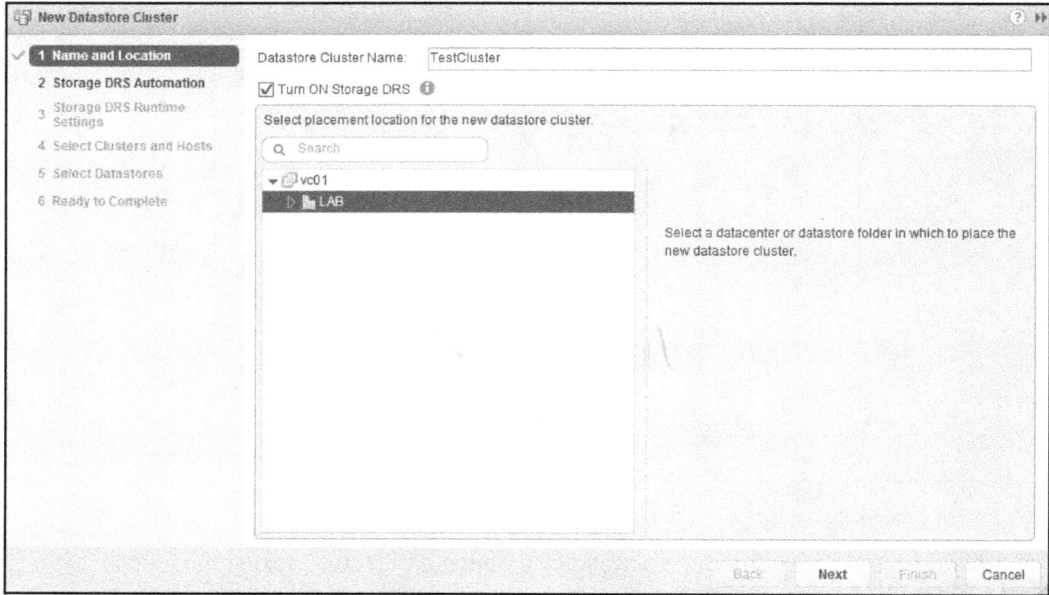

3. Click on **Next**.

4. Select **Automation level** and click on **Next**.

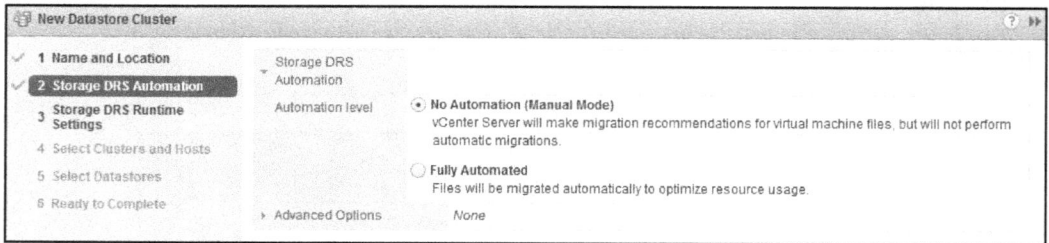

5. Adjust **Storage DRS Thresholds** if necessary and click on **Next**.

6. Select clusters or standalone hosts that will use this datastore cluster and click on **Next**.

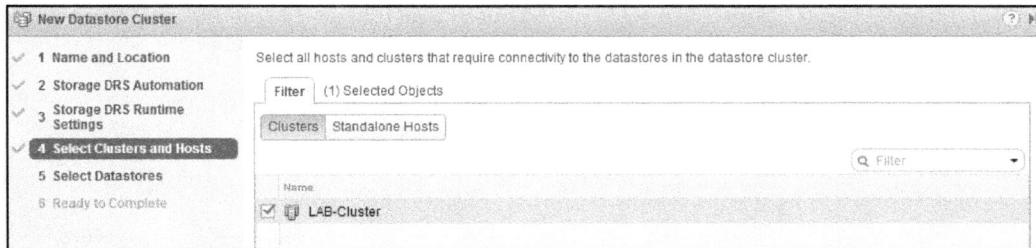

7. Choose datastores that need to be joined to the cluster and click on **Next**.

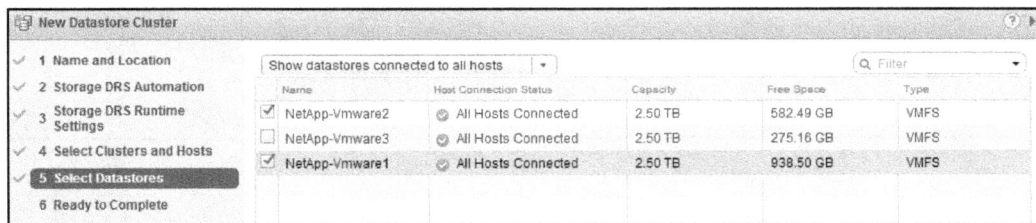

8. Review the configuration and click on **Finish**.

In vCenter Client, perform the following steps:

1. Switch to the **Datastore and Datastore Clusters** view.

2. Right-click on the datacentre object and select **New Datastore Cluster**.

3. Provide a cluster name, leave the **Turn on Storage DRS** option checked and click on **Next**.

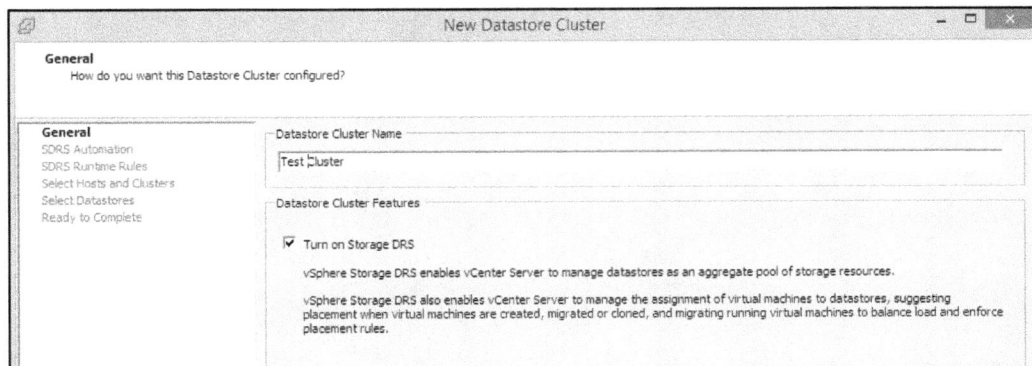

4. Choose automation mode and click on **Next**.

5. Adjust **Storage DRS Thresholds** and disable **I/O Metric Inclusion** if necessary.

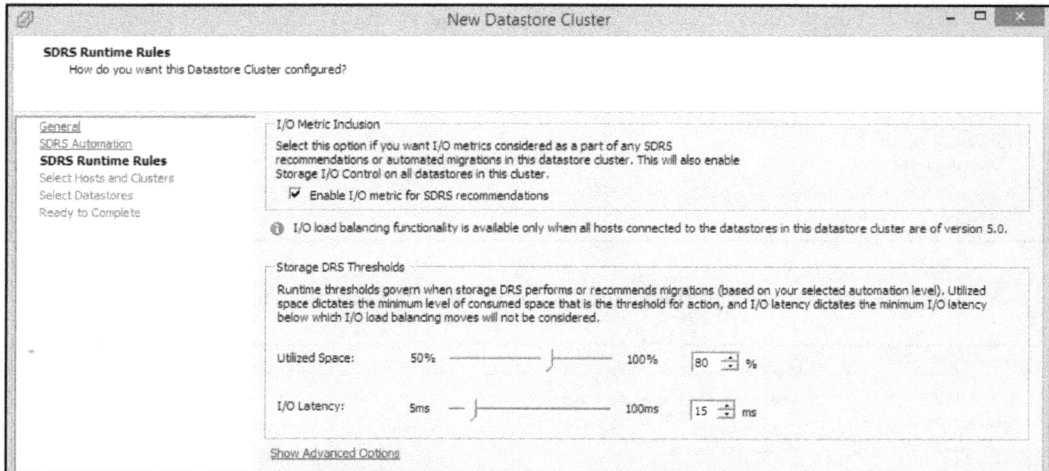

> More information about thresholds can be found in the *Configuring storage load balancing thresholds* recipe in this chapter.

6. Click on **Next**.

7. In the next two steps, select the vSphere cluster and datastores, which will be included in this datastore cluster.

8. Finally, review the configuration and click on **Finish** to create datastore cluster.

## Taking advantage of initial placement

To allow SDRS, decide where to place new VMs, select a datastore cluster instead of an individual datastore during VM creation.

In Web Client, this option will be available in step **2c Select storage**:

In vCenter Client, this step is called **Storage**:

## Adding existing VMs to a datastore cluster

To move the existing virtual machine to a datastore cluster, initiate storage vMotion and select this cluster as the destination.

In Web Client, this can be accomplished by right-clicking on a VM and selecting **Migrate**.

1.  Choose the **Change datastore** option and click on **Next**.

2.  Select a cluster and click on **Next**.

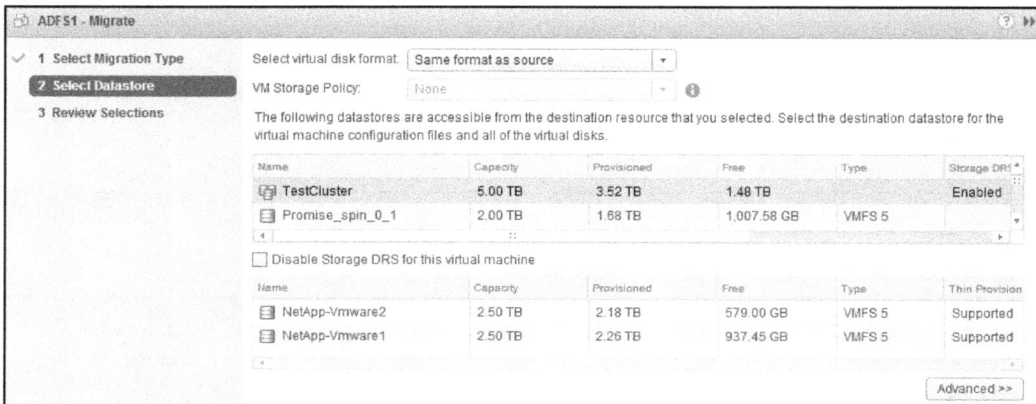

3.  Review selections and click on **Finish** to start migration. SDRS will choose the datastore automatically based on the current load.

The process is similar in vCenter Client:

1.  Right-click on a VM and select **Migrate**.

2.  Switch to the **Change datastore** option and click on **Next**.

3. Select the cluster in the list and click on **Next**.

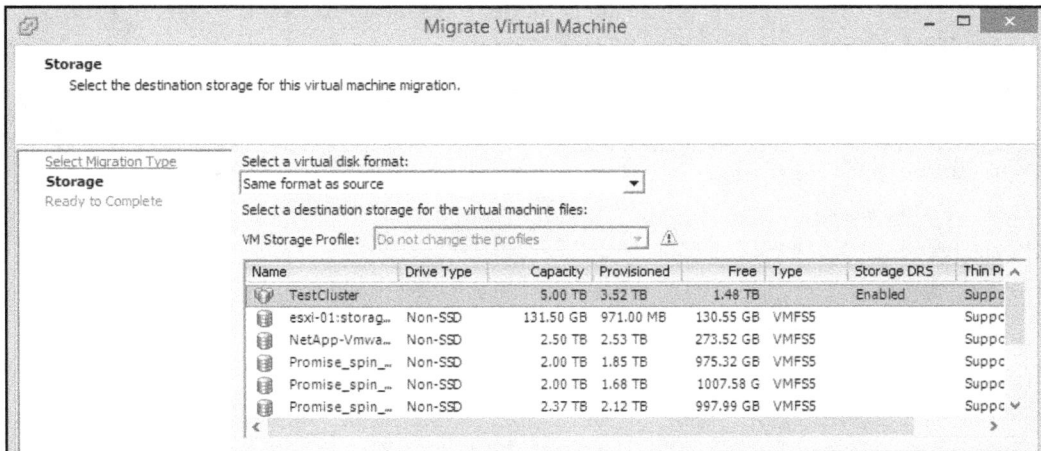

4. Confirm selections and click on **Finish** to start migration.

> VM storage performance can change after the migration.

## Reviewing and applying recommendations

Storage DRS recommendation will be available after SDRS has been enabled for at least one day. If SDRS is in manual mode, the recommendations can be reviewed and applied after selecting the datastore cluster object under **Monitor** | **Storage DRS** | **Recommendations**:

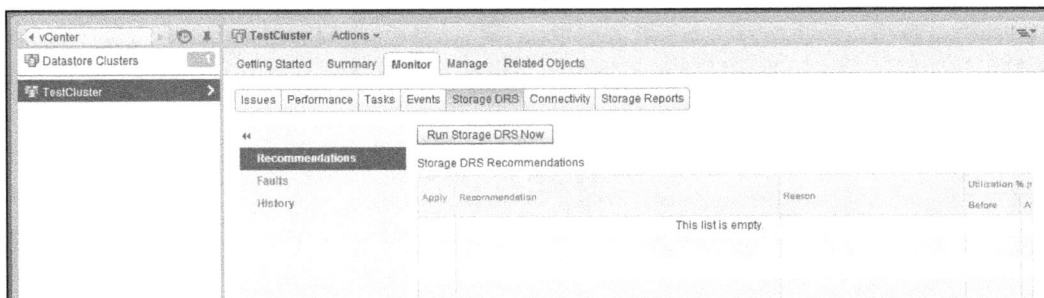

Click on the **Apply Recommendations** button to start VM migrations.

In vCenter Client, these options are available under the **Storage DRS** tab of the datastore cluster object, as shown in the following screenshot:

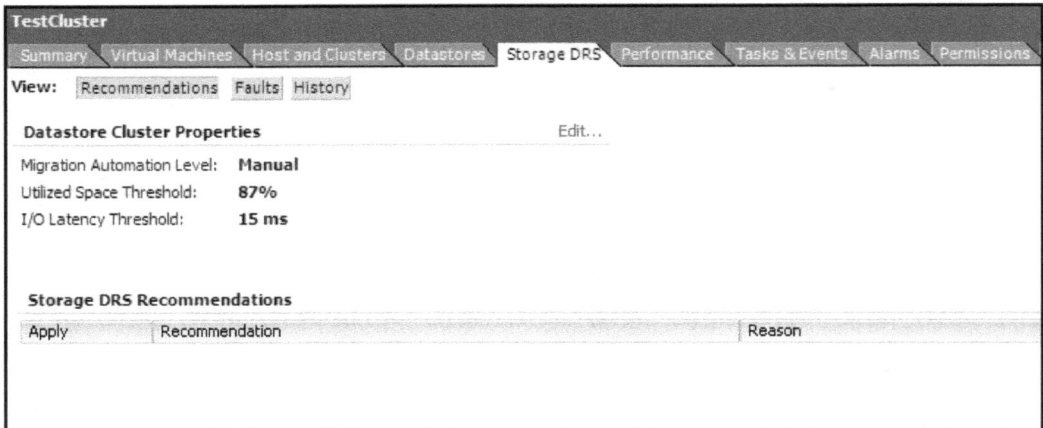

# Configuring storage load balancing thresholds

**Storage distributed resource scheduler** (**SDRS**) has been introduced in vSphere 5. More details about its features and usage can be found in the *Balancing loads between datastores* recipe in this chapter.

SDRS load balancing constantly monitors datastore space utilization and I/O latency. When one of the configured thresholds for these metrics is exceeded on a particular datastore, SDRS calculates the possible options for VM storage migrations and recommends the one that offers the best load distribution.

> The default threshold for space utilization is 80 percent. The default value for I/O latency round trip is 15 milliseconds. Both thresholds can be changed. While the I/O latency threshold can be disabled, the space utilization limit can only be disabled by turning SDRS off.

## How to do it...

Default SDRS thresholds can be changed during datastore cluster creation or can be adjusted later.

### Changing the threshold for new clusters

In Web Client, SDRS threshold options are available in step **3 Storage DRS Runtime Settings**:

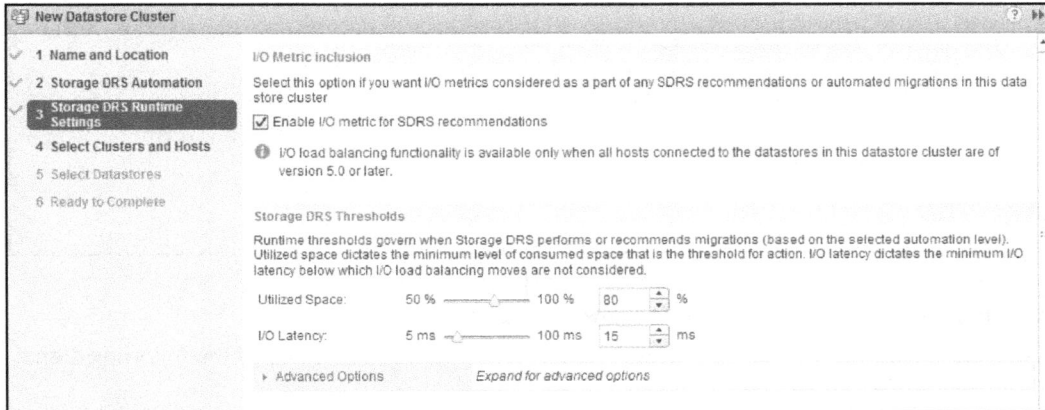

The advanced options explained in the *How to do it* section of this recipe can be changed in the same step:

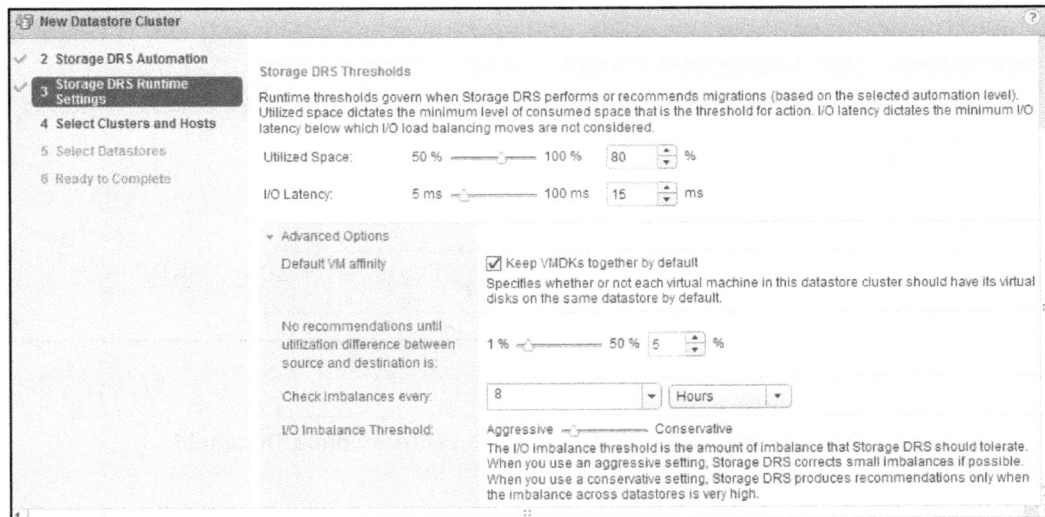

In vCenter Client, this step is called **SDRS Runtime Rules**:

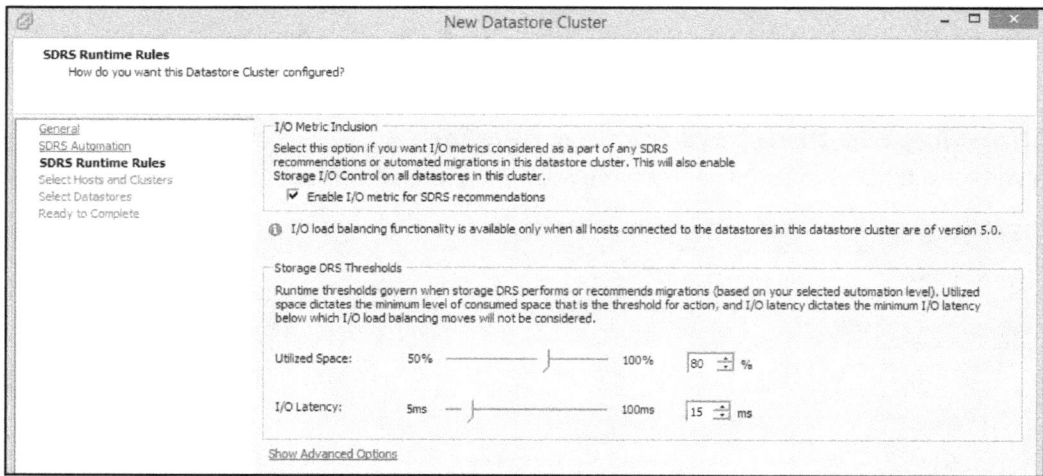

## Changing the threshold for existing clusters

To change SDRS thresholds for the existing cluster in Web Client, perform the following steps:

1. Select the datastore cluster.

2. Go to **Manage** | **Settings** | **Storage DRS**.

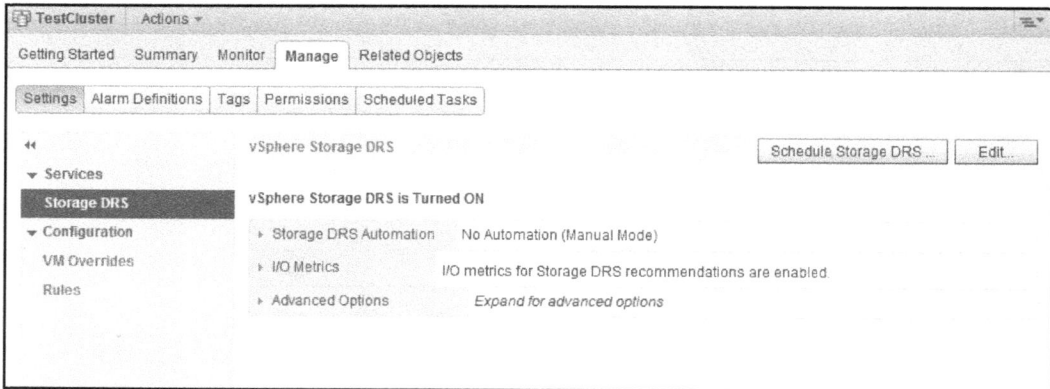

3. Click on **Edit**.

4. Expand **Storage DRS Automation** to change **Utilized Space Threshold**.

5. Expand **I/O Metrics** to enable or disable **I/O Latency Threshold** or change its value.

6. Expand **Advanced Options** to change them if necessary. These advanced settings are explained in the *How it works* section of this recipe.

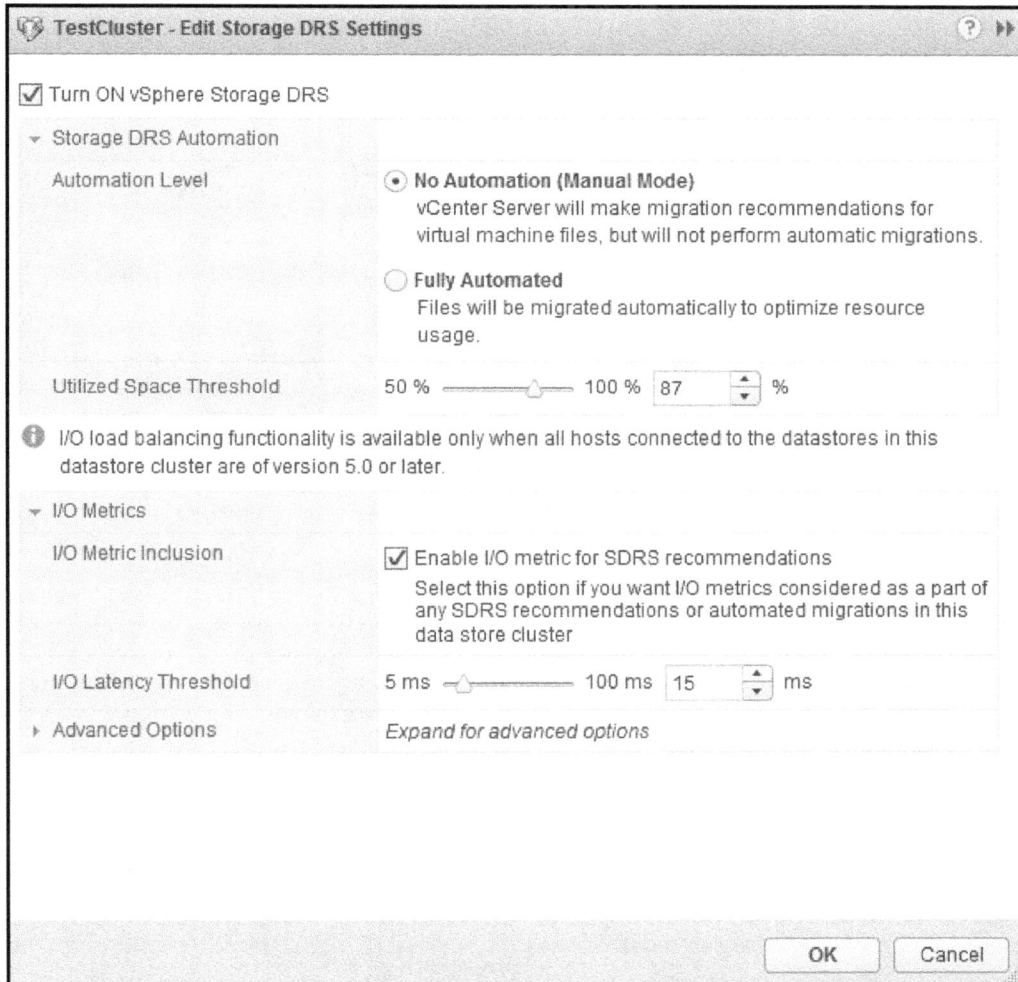

---

**TestCluster - Edit Storage DRS Settings**                                    ⑦ ▶▶

☑ Turn ON vSphere Storage DRS

▼ Storage DRS Automation

Automation Level            ⦿ **No Automation (Manual Mode)**
                            vCenter Server will make migration recommendations for
                            virtual machine files, but will not perform automatic migrations.

                            ◯ **Fully Automated**
                            Files will be migrated automatically to optimize resource
                            usage.

Utilized Space Threshold    50 % ————△———— 100 %  [ 87 ] ▲▼ %

ⓘ  I/O load balancing functionality is available only when all hosts connected to the datastores in this
   datastore cluster are of version 5.0 or later.

▼ I/O Metrics

I/O Metric Inclusion        ☑ Enable I/O metric for SDRS recommendations
                            Select this option if you want I/O metrics considered as a part of
                            any SDRS recommendations or automated migrations in this
                            data store cluster

I/O Latency Threshold       5 ms △———————— 100 ms  [ 15 ] ▲▼ ms

▶ Advanced Options          *Expand for advanced options*

                                                          [ OK ]   [ Cancel ]

---

7. Click on **OK** when done.

In vCenter Client, perform the following steps:

1. Switch to the **Datastore and Datastore Clusters** view.

2. Right-click on datastore cluster and go to **Edit Settings**.

3. Go to **SDRS Runtime Rules** to change both thresholds.

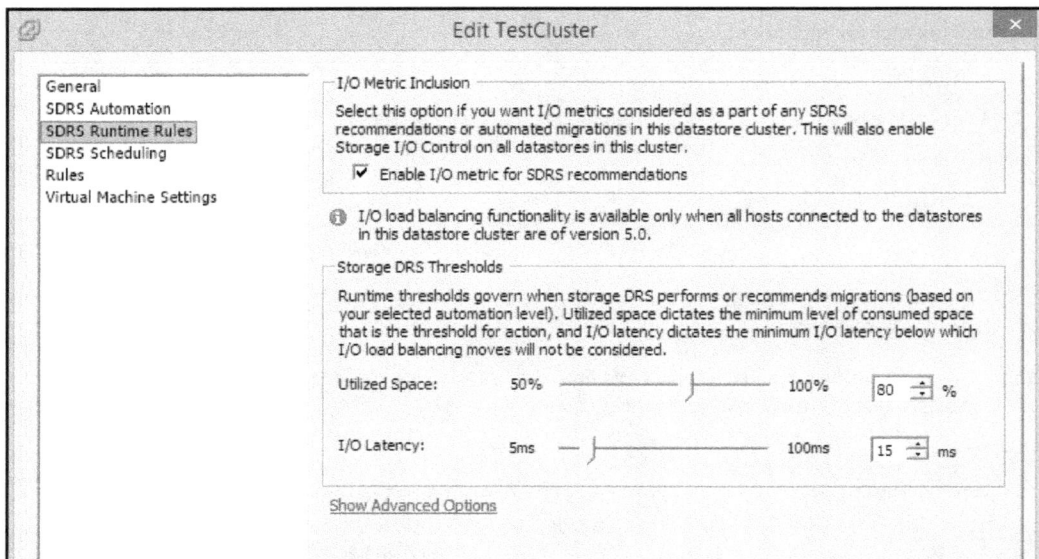

4. Click on **Show Advanced Options** to change the I/O aggressiveness level, difference settings, and schedule. These advanced settings are explained in the *How it works* section of this recipe. Click on **OK** when finished.

## How it works...

Once space usage threshold violation occurs, SDRS starts the load balancing process. It analyses the current VM space usage and creates a utilization report, which takes into account VMs that are not registered.

SDRS then starts evaluating the possible combinations for VM migrations between datastores. Migrations of powered off VMs are preferred over powered on machines. SDRS also considers thin provisioning settings and takes into account migrations that offer more than the defined difference in space utilization. This value is 5 percent by default and can be changed under **Advanced Options** by adjusting the **No recommendations until utilization difference between source and destination is** parameter.

Based on these factors, each possible migration is assigned the goodness metric.

The I/O latency is monitored for a longer period of time. A threshold is considered exceeded when it has been violated for a total of 1.6 hours during at least 16 hours of the current day.

Once exceeded, SDRS evaluates the possible migrations, taking into account datastore correlation factor to avoid migrations within the same physical storage. Based on the aggressiveness level, which can be configured under **Advanced Options** and determines how small imbalances should be fixed, SDRS calculates the weighted sum of improvements for each possible migration. It then assigns the goodness metric to each of these options.

Based on the metrics obtained from two processes described earlier, SDRS generates unified recommendations for VM placement. In fully automated mode, these recommendations are invoked by default every 8 hours. This value can be changed under **Advanced Options** by adjusting the **Check imbalances every** parameter. In manual mode, they have to be reviewed and applied by the administrator.

# Limiting VM storage I/O consumption

Storage I/O Control (SIOC) allows administrators to control the storage I/O consumption by virtual machines.

On the datastore level, SIOC takes care of distributing I/O resources between running VMs so that a single VM cannot monopolize a datastore.

On the VM level, this feature allows limiting the amount of I/O available to a particular virtual machine.

vCenter is required only to enable the SIOC feature. Once enabled, SIOC does not need vCenter to run.

By default, SIOC is disabled. First, it should be enabled for datastores. Unfortunately, it has to be done for each datastore separately. When enabling SIOC, you will be able to configure the latency threshold. SIOC does not engage until this threshold is reached. By default, it is 30 milliseconds.

> SIOC will be enabled automatically for datastores that are members of datastore cluster. Please refer to the *Balancing loads between datastores* recipe in this chapter for more information about SDRS and datastore clusters.

SIOC enabled on datastores will make sure the storage I/O capacity distribution is equal between VMs.

The second step is to enable I/O limits for certain virtual machines as required. This is optional and should be used only when required.

## How to do it...

SIOC configuration involves two tasks. The first one is enabling SIOC on datastores. The second one is configuring the VM limit for storage I/Os. This option requires SIOC to be enabled on datastores.

### Enabling SIOC on a datastore

To accomplish this in Web Client, perform the following steps:

1. Go to **Datastores** and select a datastore.

2. Go to **Manage | Settings | General**.

3. Click on the **Edit...** button beside **Datastore Capabilities.**

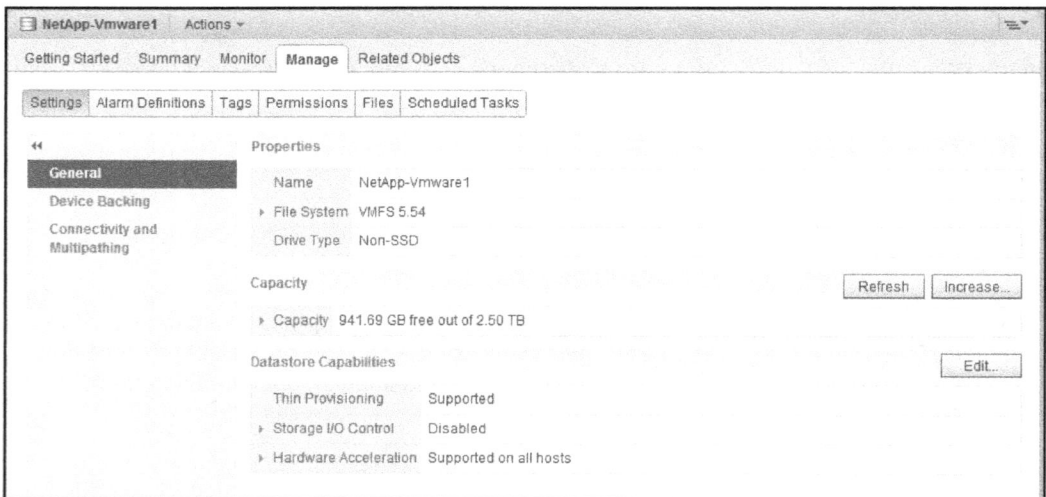

4. Check the **Enable Storage I/O Control** option and click on **OK**.

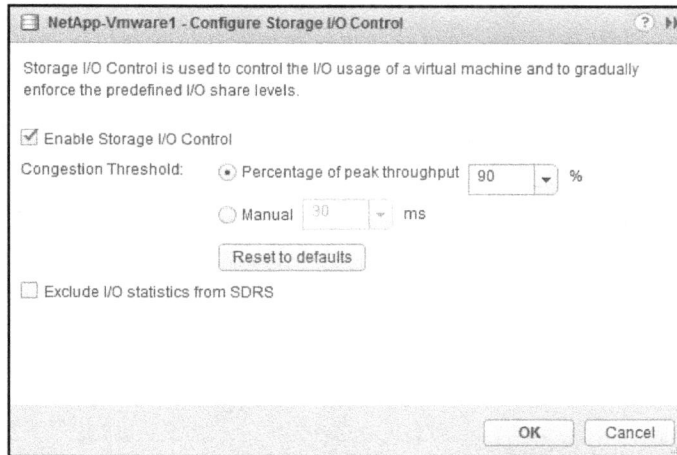

In vSphere Client, perform the following steps:

1. Switch to the **Datastores and Datastore Clusters** view.
2. Select a datastore.
3. Go to **Configuration** and click on **Properties**.
4. Check **Enabled** under the **Storage I/O Control** section and click on **OK**.

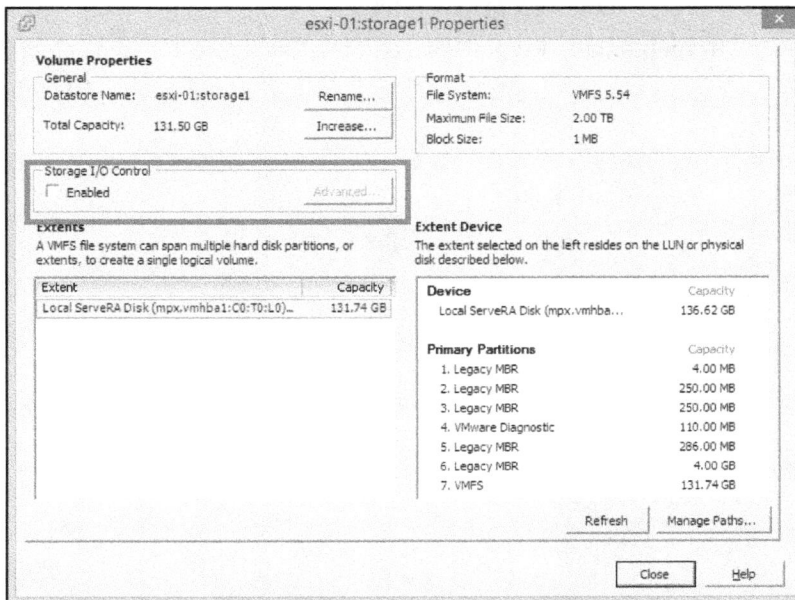

## Limiting I/Os per VM

To set the I/O limit for a virtual machine, do the following:

1. Right-click on a VM and select **Edit Settings**.

2. Under **Virtual Hardware**, expand the hard disk, set IOPs limit, and click on **OK**.

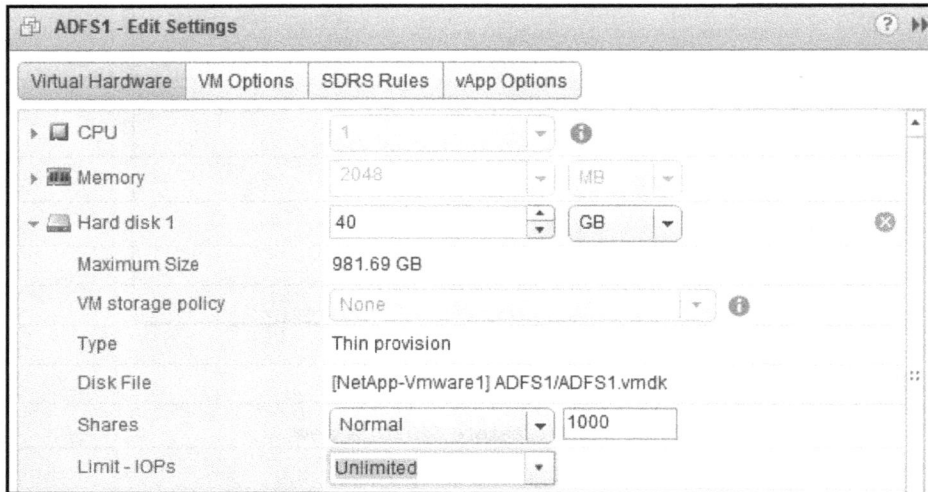

vSphere Client allows setting VM I/O limit by performing the following steps:

1. Right-click on a VM and select **Edit Settings**.

2. Then, in **Virtual Machine Properties**, go to the **Resources** tab and select **Disk**.

3.  Finally, set IOPs number for a virtual disk in the **Limit - IOPs** column.

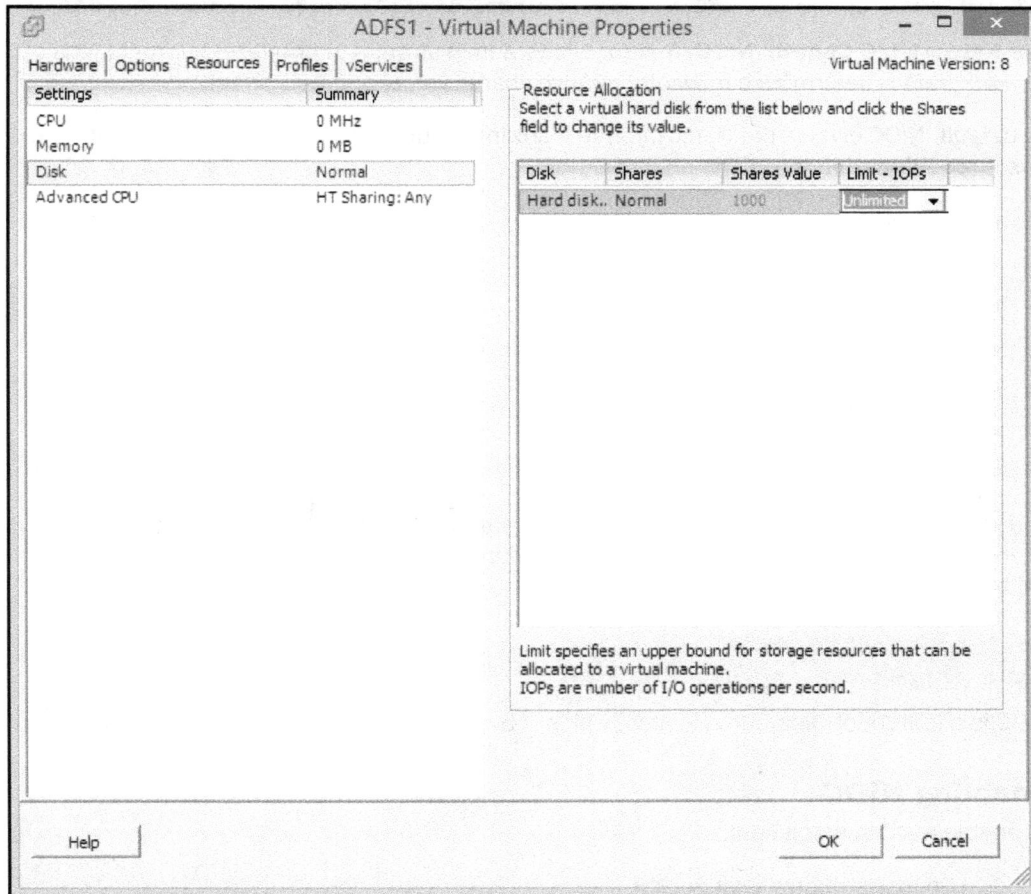

The current I/O consumption level can be checked in vCenter for each VM under the **Performance** tab. Depending on the storage used, there may be tools from the storage vendor available. There are also tools for vSphere performance analysis that can be purchased separately. For example, such tools from VMware are called VMware Operations Manager.

# Limiting VM network I/O consumption

The **Network I/O Control** (**NIOC**) feature allows administrators to prioritize different kinds of network traffic—determine bandwidth, relative shares value, and QoS priority.

By default, NIOC divides the traffic into the following groups, which can be viewed under the **Resource Allocation** tab of Distributed Switch:

- ▸ FT traffic
- ▸ iSCSI traffic
- ▸ vMotion traffic
- ▸ Management traffic
- ▸ vSphere Replication traffic
- ▸ NFS traffic
- ▸ Virtual machine traffic

Administrators can create their own traffic groups and assign virtual switch ports to them. User-defined traffic groups have been introduced in vSphere 5 and are applicable only to VM traffic.

## How to do it...

NIOC is a feature of Distributed Switch, which is available only with the Enterprise Plus license.

### Enabling NIOC

To enable NIOC in Web Client:

1. Go to Distributed Switch.
2. Go to **Manage | Settings | Properties**.
3. Click on **Edit**.
4. Select **Enable** from the **Network I/O Control** drop-down menu.

5.  Click on **OK**.

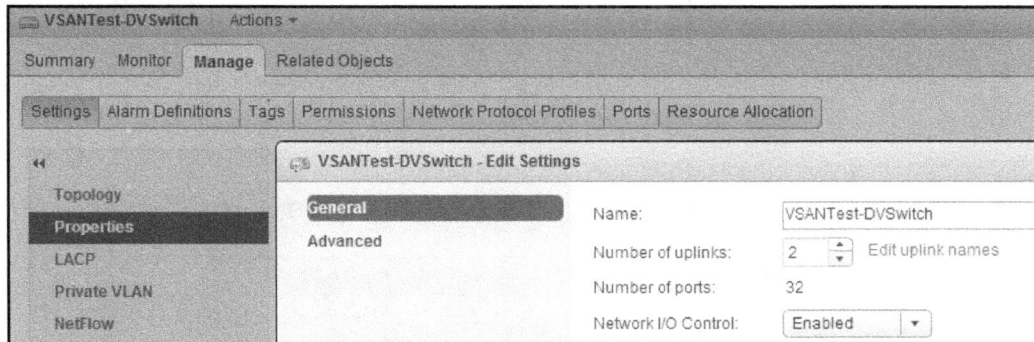

In vCenter Client, perform the following steps:

1.  Switch to the **Networking** view.
2.  Select distributed switch.
3.  Go to the **Resource Allocation** tab and click on **Properties**.
4.  Check **Enable Network I/O Control on this vSphere distributed switch** and click on **OK**.

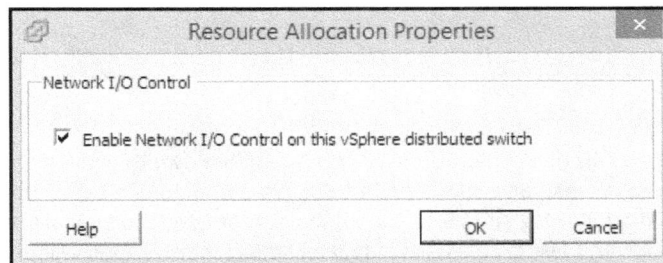

## Creating network resource pool

In Web Client, user-defined network resource pools for NIOC can be created with the following steps:

1.  Under distributed switch, go to **Manage | Resource Allocation**.

2.  Click on **New**.

3.  Type the pool name and optionally its description.

4.  Set values for shares, **Limit**, and the **QoS tag** and click on **OK**.

| VSANTest-DVSwitch - New Network Resource Pool | (?) |
| --- | --- |

| Name: | Limited-10Mbps pool |
| --- | --- |
| Origin: | User-defined network resource pools |
| Description: | |
| Limit (Mbps): | 10 |
| | ☐ Unlimited |
| Physical adapter shares: | Low ▾ 25 |
| QoS tag: | 0 ▾ |

| | OK | Cancel |
| --- | --- | --- |

The **Limit** parameter represents the total bandwidth available to a network resource pool. One of the most common use cases for a limit is the following situation. The administrator needs to allocate only a 2 Gbps bandwidth to a certain type of traffic, for example, vMotion traffic, out of the 10 Gbps total bandwidth available on the network adapter.

The **Share** option is of relative importance to this network pool compared to other pools. The idea is the same as with VM pool shares explained in the *Prioritizing VMs with shares* recipe in this chapter. Share values can be set as follows: low—25, normal—50, and high—100. With the custom option, an administrator can assign a specific number of shares between 1 and 100.

The **QoS tag** allows prioritizing network traffic based on its importance. For example, video streaming traffic should have higher priority than file transfers.

In vCenter Client, perform the following steps:

1. Switch to the **Networking** view.

2. Select distributed switch.

3. Go to the **Resource Allocation** tab and click on **New Network Resource Pool**.

4. Type the pool name and optionally its description.

5. Set values for shares, **Host Limit**, and **QoS priority tag**, and click on **OK**.

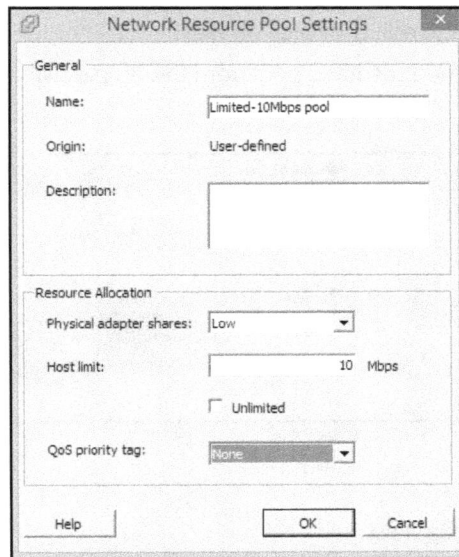

| Network Resource Pool Settings | | |
|---|---|---|
| **General** | | |
| Name: | Limited-10Mbps pool | |
| Origin: | User-defined | |
| Description: | | |
| **Resource Allocation** | | |
| Physical adapter shares: | Low | |
| Host limit: | 10 | Mbps |
| | ☐ Unlimited | |
| QoS priority tag: | None | |
| Help | OK | Cancel |

The **Limit** parameter represents the total bandwidth available for the network resource pool. One of the most common use cases for a limit is the following situation. An administrator needs to allocate only 2 Gbps of bandwidth to a certain type of traffic, for example, vMotion traffic, out of a 10 Gbps total bandwidth available on the network adapter.

The **Share** option is of relative importance to this network pool compared to the other pools. The idea is the same as with VM pool shares explained, which is explained in the *Prioritizing VMs with shares* recipe from this chapter. Share values can be set as follows: low—25, normal—50, and high—100. With the custom option, an administrator can assign a specific number of shares between 1 and 100.

The **QoS tag** allows prioritizing network traffic based on its importance. For example, video streaming traffic should have higher priority than file transfers.

## Assigning port groups to network resource pools

Once the network resource pool has been created, the existing port groups defined for the distributed switch can be added to this resource pool.

To accomplish this in Web Client, perform the following steps:

1. Right-click on distributed switch and select **Manage Distributed Port Groups**.

2. On the **Select port group policies** page, check **Resource allocation**, and check on **Next**.

3. Choose port groups to edit and click on **Next**.

4. Select the user-defined resource pool from the drop-down menu and click on **Next**.

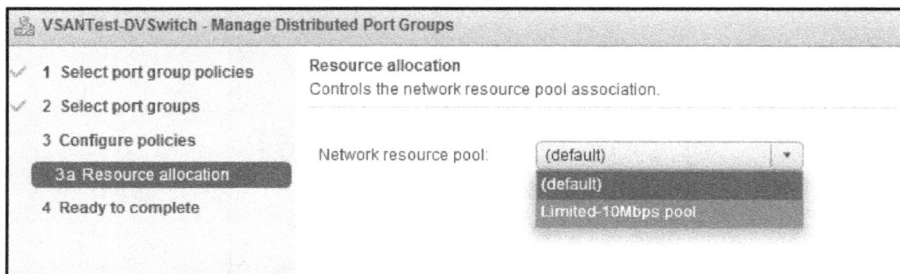

In vCenter Client:

1. Go to the **Networking** view.

2. Select distributed switch and go to the **Resource Allocation** tab.

3. Click on **Manage Port Groups**.

4. Select the network resource pool from the list and click on **OK**.

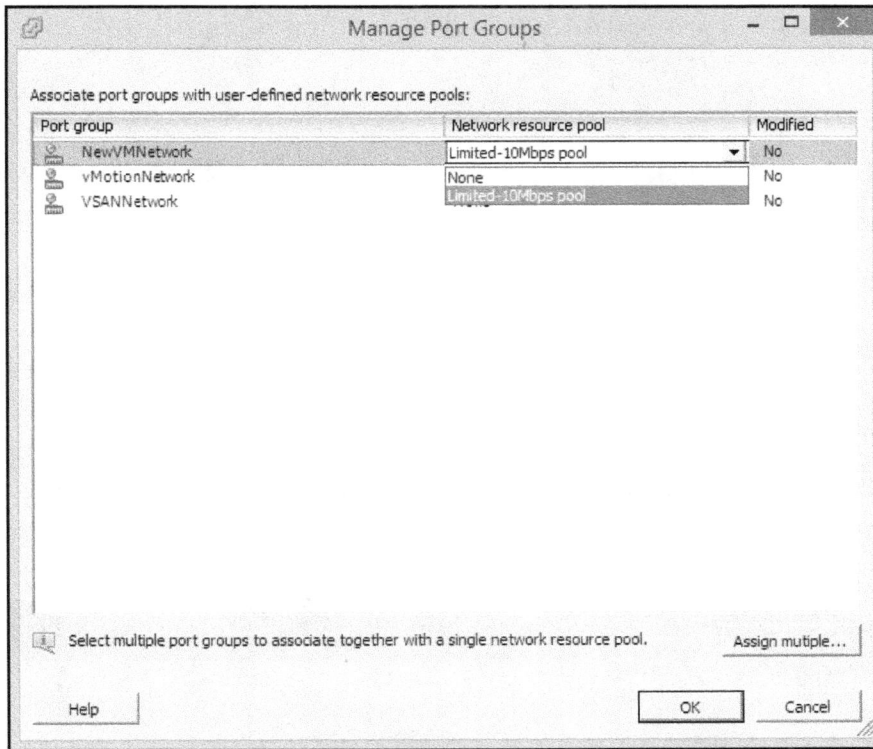

**Manage Port Groups**

Associate port groups with user-defined network resource pools:

| Port group | Network resource pool | Modified |
|---|---|---|
| NewVMNetwork | Limited-10Mbps pool ▼ | No |
| vMotionNetwork | None | No |
| VSANNetwork | Limited-10Mbps pool | No |

Select multiple port groups to associate together with a single network resource pool.  Assign mutiple...

Help        OK        Cancel

## Editing the network resource pool

To edit the network resource pool in Web Client, select it from the list and click on **Edit**.

| VSANTest-DVSwitch | Actions ▾ | | | | | |
|---|---|---|---|---|---|---|

| Summary | Monitor | **Manage** | Related Objects |
|---|---|---|---|

| Settings | Alarm Definitions | Tags | Permissions | Network Protocol Profiles | Ports | Resource Allocation |
|---|---|---|---|---|---|---|

Physical network adapters:    7
Bandwidth capacity:    7.000 Gbit/s
Network I/O Control:    Enabled

➕ | ✏ ✖

| Network Resource Pool | Limit (Mbps) | Physical Adapter Sha... | Shares Value | QoS Priority Tag |
|---|---|---|---|---|
| Virtual S [Edit the properties of the selected network resource pool.] | | gh | 100 | |
| **User-defined network resource pools** | | | | |
| Limited-10Mbps pool | 10 | Low | 25 | |

In vCenter Client, right-click on a network resource pool and select **Edit Settings...**.

**VSANTest-DVSwitch**

| Summary | Networks | Ports | Resource Allocation | Configuration | Virtual Machines | Hosts | Tasks & Events | Alarms | Permissions |
|---|---|---|---|---|---|---|---|---|---|

Total network bandwidth capacity:    **6000 Mbps**
Network I/O Control:    🔵 **Enabled**

| Network resource pool | Host limit - Mbps | Physical adapter shares | Shares value | QoS priority tag |
|---|---|---|---|---|
| Fault Tolerance (FT) Traffic | Unlimited | Normal | 50 | -- |
| ISCSI Traffic | Unlimited | Custom | 20 | -1 |
| Management Traffic | Unlimited | Normal | 50 | -- |
| NFS Traffic | Unlimited | Normal | 50 | -- |
| Virtual Machine Traffic | Unlimited | Custom | 30 | -1 |
| Virtual SAN Traffic | Unlimited | High | 100 | -1 |
| vMotion Traffic | Unlimited | Normal | 50 | -- |
| vSphere Replication (VR) Traffic | Unlimited | Normal | 50 | -- |
| **User-defined network resource pools** | | | | |
| Limited-10Mbps pool | | | 25 | -- |
| | New Network Resource Pool... | | | |
| | Edit Settings... | | | |
| **Network Resource Pool De** | Remove | | | |

# Deleting a network resource pool

If a network resource pool is not in use, it can be deleted. All the distributed port groups must be removed from the pool before this can be done. In Web Client, deletion can be accomplished by selecting a pool and clicking on **Remove**.

In vCenter Client, right-click on the pool and select **Remove**.

In both cases, click on **Yes** to confirm deletion.

# 6

# Basic Administrative Tasks

In this chapter, we will cover the following recipes:

- ▶ Improving visibility with e-mail alerts
- ▶ Controlling the space used by snapshots
- ▶ Controlling datastore space utilization
- ▶ Automating VM placement with storage profiles
- ▶ Automating VM placement with VM affinity
- ▶ Automating VM placement with storage affinity
- ▶ Automating tasks with a scheduler
- ▶ Keeping hosts up to date

## Introduction

This chapter covers administrative tasks that are not directly related to scalability, efficiency, availability, or optimization. The following recipes will help administrators to increase control and visibility in their environment by setting up rules for virtual machine placement, automating basic tasks with a scheduler, keeping track of space utilization by VMs and snapshots, and alerting about important events happening in the environment.

# Improving visibility with email alerts

vCenter has an ability to notify administrators about certain events that happen in the vSphere environment. An administrator can choose from a few hundred events. These events, thresholds, and actions are configurable through alarm definitions in vCenter. One of the possible actions is an email notification.

Examples of alarm configuration for snapshot size and datastore space utilization are described in *Controlling the space used by snapshots* and *Controlling datastore space utilization* recipes further in this chapter.

Before vCenter can send emails, it requires mail server configuration, which is covered further in this chapter.

## How to do it...

To configure vCenter to send email notifications using Web Client, perform the following steps:

1. Select the vCenter Server under **vCenter Servers**.
2. Go to **Manage** | **Settings** | **General**.
3. Click on **Edit** and then on **Mail**.
4. Type the **Mail server** IP address or DNS name and **Mail sender** from the email address.

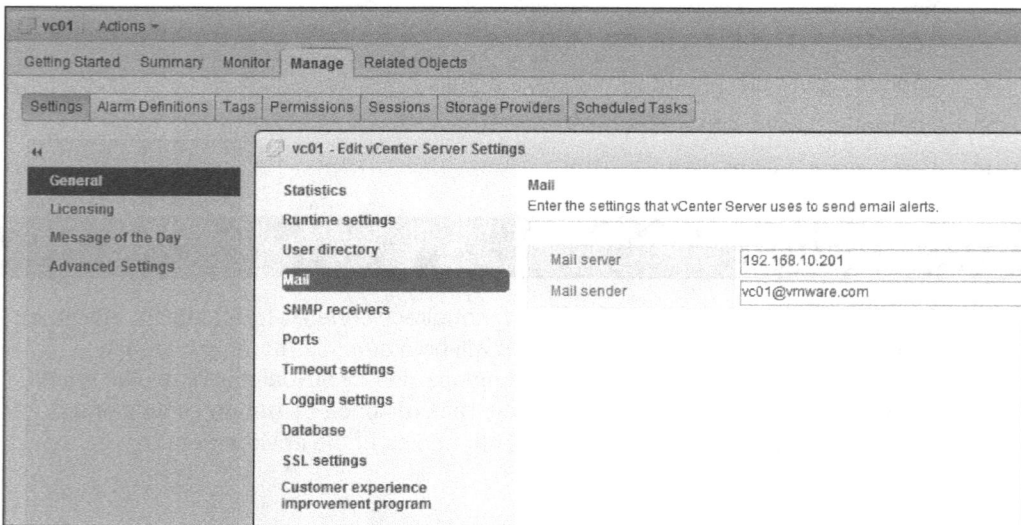

5. Click on **OK** to apply settings.

In vCenter Client, perform the following steps:

1. Go to **Administration | vCenter Server Settings**.
2. Click on **Mail**.
3. Provide **SMTP Server** and **Sender Account** and click on **OK**.

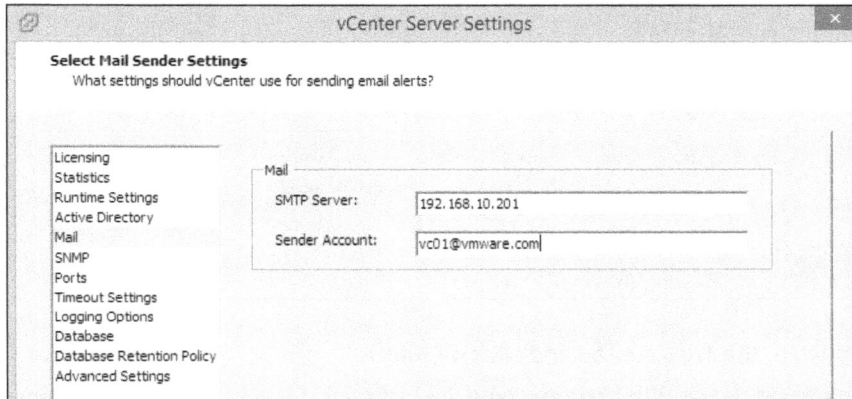

## Testing email alerts

To confirm that vCenter email alerts work, the administrator can initiate an event that triggers a notification. For the purpose of this recipe, we assume that no email alerts have been configured yet. One of the options would be to create an alert that sends an email when a VM changes its power state. We will create this alert on a VM level so it will be valid for this virtual machine only. To do this:

1. Select a VM that can be powered off.
2. Switch to the **Alarms** tab and the **Definitions** view.
3. Right-click anywhere on an empty space and select **New Alarm**.

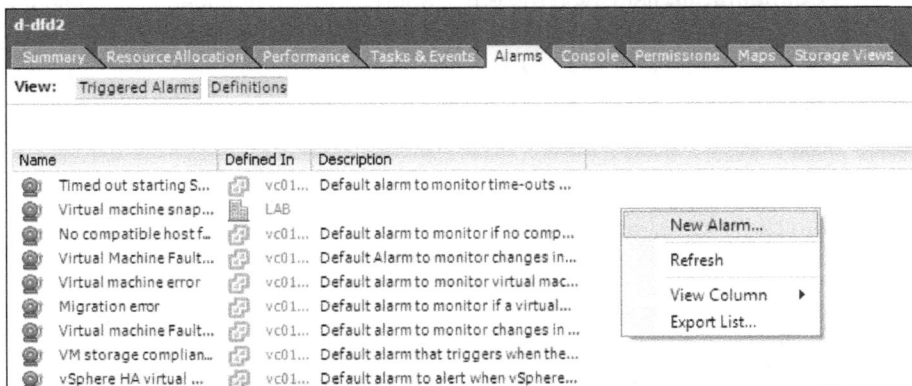

4. Give the new alarm a name and make sure that **Virtual Machine** is selected for the **Monitor** value.

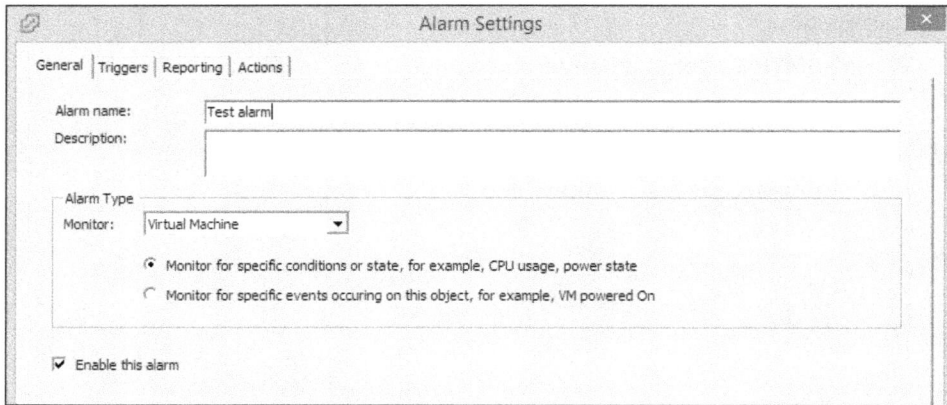

| | |
|---|---|
| | Alarm Settings |

General | Triggers | Reporting | Actions |

Alarm name:  Test alarm
Description:

**Alarm Type**
Monitor:  Virtual Machine  ▼

    ⦿ Monitor for specific conditions or state, for example, CPU usage, power state
    ○ Monitor for specific events occuring on this object, for example, VM powered On

☑ Enable this alarm

5. Switch to the **Triggers** tab and click on **Add**.

6. Select **VM State** in the **Trigger Type** field and set the alert condition to **Powered off**.

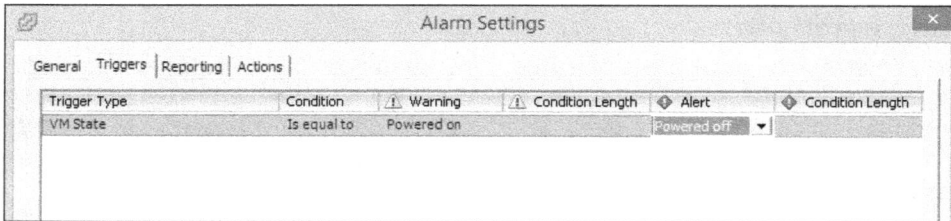

| | |
|---|---|
| | Alarm Settings |

General  Triggers | Reporting | Actions |

| Trigger Type | Condition | ⚠ Warning | ⚠ Condition Length | ◆ Alert | ◆ Condition Length |
|---|---|---|---|---|---|
| VM State | Is equal to | Powered on | | Powered off ▼ | |

7. Switch to the **Actions** tab and click on **Add**.

8. **Send a notification email** should appear by default in the **Action** field.

9. In the **Configuration** field, type the email address where notifications should be sent.

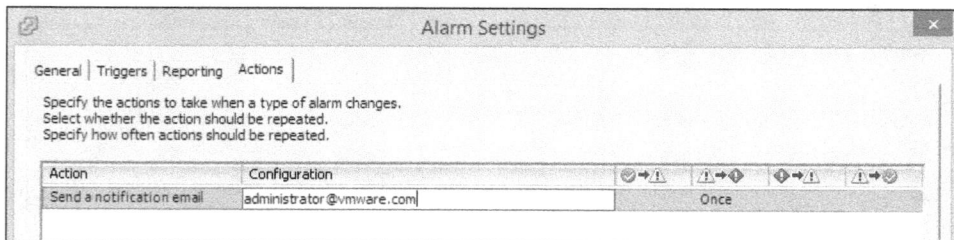

| | |
|---|---|
| | Alarm Settings |

General | Triggers | Reporting  Actions |

Specify the actions to take when a type of alarm changes.
Select whether the action should be repeated.
Specify how often actions should be repeated.

| Action | Configuration | ⊘→⚠ | ⚠→◆ | ◆→⚠ | ⚠→⊘ |
|---|---|---|---|---|---|
| Send a notification email | administrator@vmware.com | | Once | | |

10. Click on **OK** to save the alarm.

11. Shut down the VM and check whether the email has been received.

If the email has not been received after several minutes, please refer to the *There's more* section of this recipe for troubleshooting steps.

## Configuring email alerts for important events

Now, since the mail server has been configured and the mail flow works, notification email actions should be added to events that are important to know about.

Most of the useful alerts already exist in vCenter by default. Adding a notification email action involves the following steps:

1. In Web Client, select the vCenter Server object.
2. Go to **Manage** | **Alarm Definitions**.

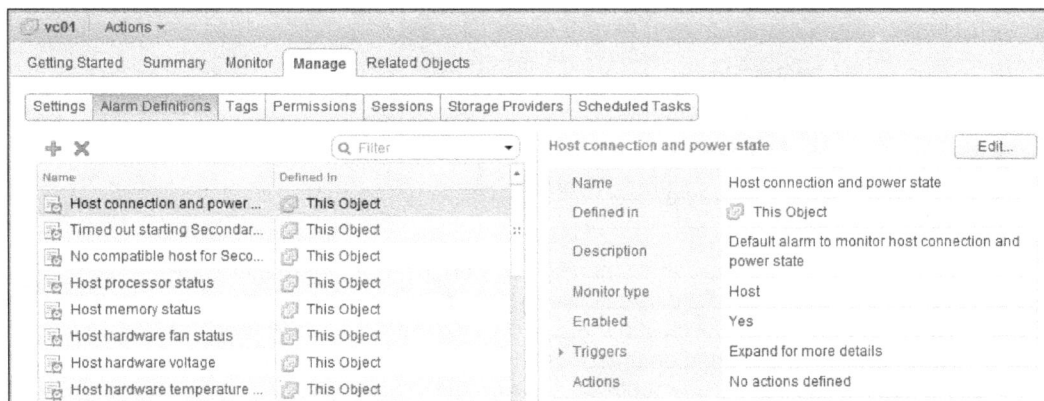

3. Go through the preconfigured alerts in the list.
4. For an event that you want to be notified about, select the alert in the list and click on **Edit**.
5. Go to **Actions**, click on the plus sign to add an action.
6. Select **Send a notification email** in the **Action** field.
7. Type the email address in the **Configuration** field. You can add more than one email address separated by a semicolon.
8. Set conditions as required and click on **Finish**.

The preceding steps should be done for each important event, which most likely includes, but is not limited to:

- ▸ Host connection and power state
- ▸ Host error
- ▸ Virtual machine error
- ▸ Host connection failure
- ▸ Health status changed
- ▸ Host CPU usage
- ▸ Host memory usage
- ▸ Network connectivity lost
- ▸ Health status monitoring
- ▸ vSphere HA host status
- ▸ vSphere HA failover in progress
- ▸ Virtual machine CPU usage
- ▸ Virtual machine memory usage

> Alarm definitions can be modified only on the level where they were created. Most of the default alarm definitions have been defined on the vCenter Server level, and that's why we go there in the first step. If there are alarms defined on the lower level of object hierarchy, for example, for certain hosts, they will not be listed on the vCenter Server level.

## There's more...

When vCenter is not able to send an email, the `vpxd.log` file located under `C:\ProgramData\VMware\VMware VirtualCenter\Logs` contains a message similar to the following:

```
[02536 error 'Default'] [VpxdMail] Failed to send the mail to SMTP
server <mail server> at port 25. Error=The transport failed to
connect to the server.
```

> Please refer to the VMware KB article for information on how to troubleshoot email alerts not being sent from vCenter Server at http://kb.vmware.com/kb/1004070.

# Controlling the space used by snapshots

VM snapshots and concerns related to space usage are described in the *Managing space used by snapshots* recipe in *Chapter 4, Improving Environment Efficiency*. This recipe also has an example of configuring an alarm that can help to identify virtual machines that have a snapshot.

While such an approach is suitable for a cleaning task, it's also helpful to be notified about VMs with large snapshots before they take too much space and start causing performance issues. This can be achieved by creating an alarm with a higher threshold for snapshot size and attaching an email notification to it.

> An alarm definition for snapshot size does not exist by default in vCenter and has to be added manually.

## How to do it...

vCenter has a trigger that monitors VM snapshot size, which can be used to create an alert that will notify the user when the snapshot size reaches a specified threshold.

To accomplish this in vCenter Client:

1.  Go to the **Datacenter** level, switch to the **Alarms** tab, and then to the **Definitions** view.

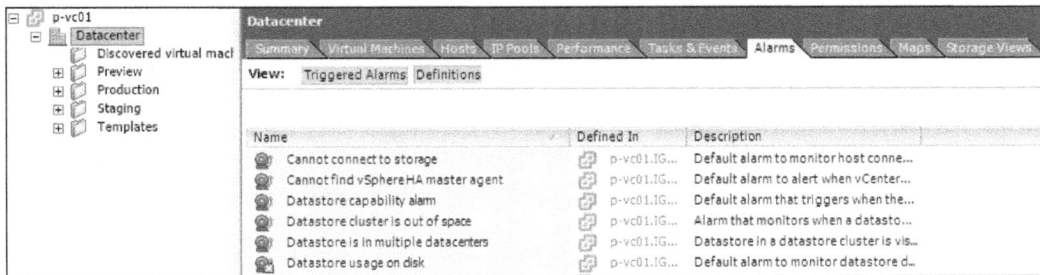

> The level an alarm is created at defines its coverage. The vCenter level alarms cover virtual machines in all datacenters. The **Datacenter** level alarms cover all virtual machines in the particular datacenter, while alarms created for a particular folder will trigger virtual machines placed in this folder or in its child folders.

2.  Go to **File | New | Alarm** or press *Ctrl + M*.

3. In the **General** tab of the **Alarm Settings** dialog, give this alarm a name and make sure that **Virtual Machines** is selected for **Monitor** under the **Alarm Type** section.

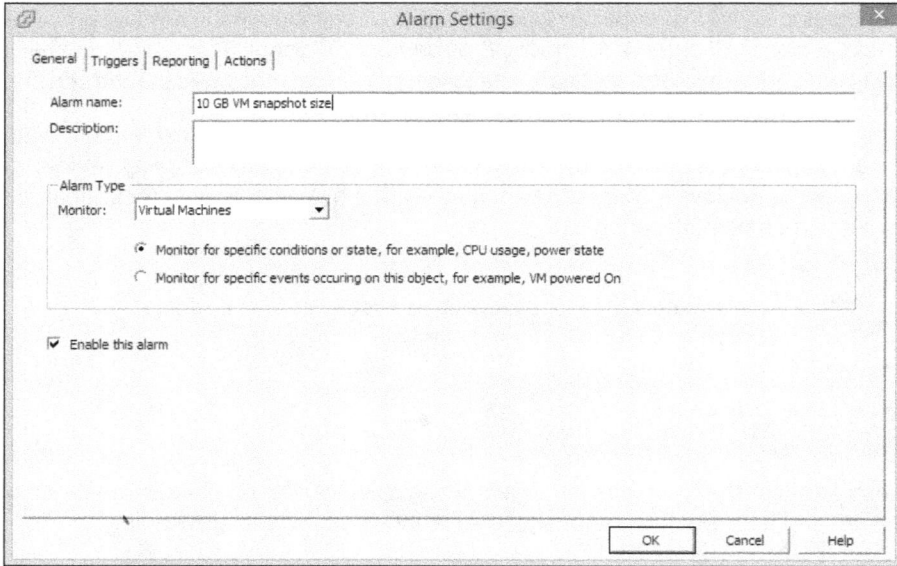

4. In the **Triggers** tab, click on **Add**, select the **VM Snapshot Size** (**GB**) trigger, and configure thresholds.

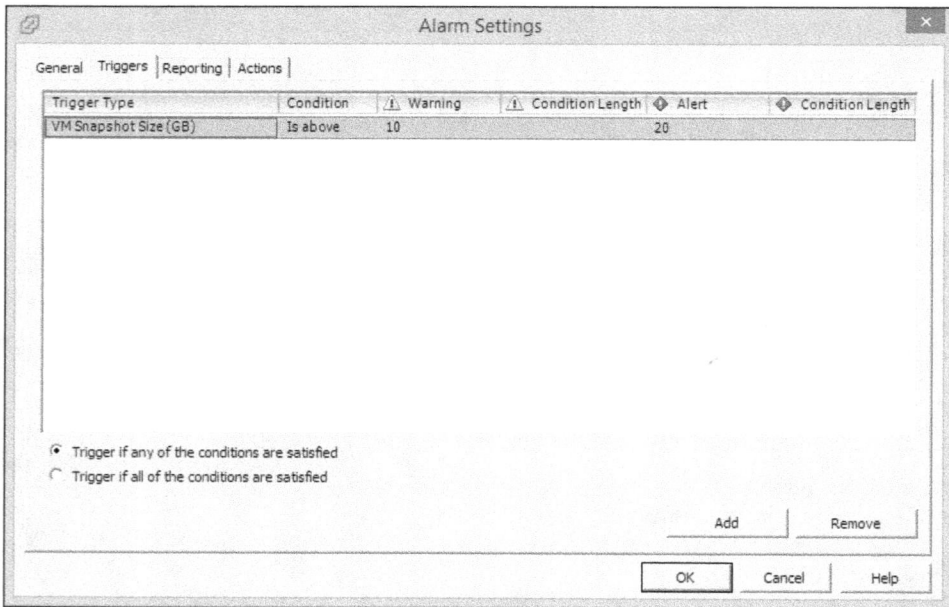

5.  In the **Actions** tab, click on **Add**, select **Send a notification email** in the **Action** field, add email addresses in the **Configuration** field, configure the required actions, and click on **OK**.

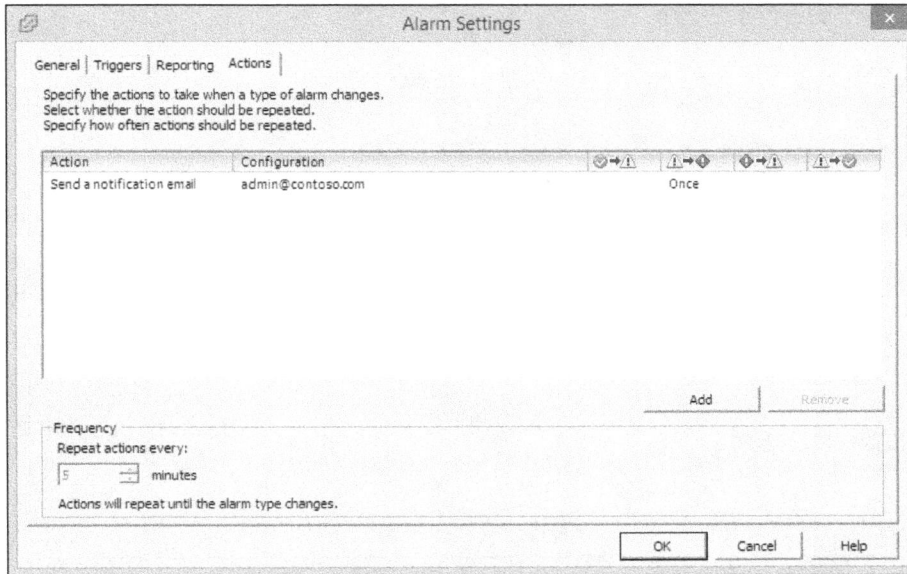

In the previous screenshot, vCenter is configured to send email notifications when the snapshot size exceeds 20 GB.

In Web Client, perform the following steps:

1.  Go to cluster, switch to the **Manage** tab, and click on **Alarm Definitions**.

2.  Click on the plus sign to create a new alarm.

3. Give the new alarm a name and set the **Monitor** value to **Virtual Machines**.

4. Click on **Next**. Click on the plus sign to add a trigger and select **VM Snapshot Size** in the drop-down menu.

5. Click on **Next**, select **Send a notification email** in the **Action** field, add email addresses in the **Configuration** field, configure the required actions, and click on **Finish**.

For email notifications to work properly, mail servers must be configured, which is covered in the *Improving visibility with email alerts* recipe in this chapter.

> Once you receive the snapshot size alert, check whether this snapshot is still needed. Confirm that there is enough free space on the datastore if the snapshot cannot be deleted for some time.

It is important that along with snapshot size alerts, appropriate datastore free space alerts are configured as well, which is covered in the *Controlling datastore space utilization* recipe in this chapter.

## Changing the VM snapshot file location

For cases when a snapshot file does not have to be stored along with virtual machine `.vmdk` files, its default location for a particular VM can be changed. This can be done with the following steps:

1. Turn off the virtual machine.
2. Right-click on the VM and select **Remove from Inventory**.

3. Connect to the ESXi host via SSH to edit the `.vmx` configuration file in vi editor or download the file from the datastore via vCenter Client to edit it locally.

4. Open VM's `.vmx` file in a text editor and add the following lines:

```
workingDir = "new_location"
snapshot.redoNotWithParent = "true"
```

> The value for the new location can be a local path on the ESXi server or any folder on a datastore connected to the server, for example, `/vmfs/volumes/46f1225f-552b0069-e03b-00145e000000/vm-snapshots`.

5. Save the changes to the `.vmx` file, and upload it back if necessary.

6. Add the virtual machine to the inventory by right-clicking on VM's `.vmx` file in vCenter's datastore browser and selecting **Add to inventory**.

7. Follow the wizard to choose a location for the VM.

8. Power the virtual machine on.

From now, all future snapshots of this VM will be created in the folder defined.

# Controlling datastore space utilization

Two approaches can be taken to manage datastore space usage and make sure that there is always enough free space for VMs to run: vCenter space usage alarms and the **Storage Distributed Resource Scheduler** (**SDRS**) feature.

SDRS has been described in the *Balancing storage utilization* recipe in *Chapter 5, Optimizing Resource Usage*. It is a more advanced approach, which allows completely automating VM migrations. At the same time, this feature requires the Enterprise Plus license, which may not be needed for all environments.

A more simple approach is vCenter alarms. vCenter has default alarm definitions related to datastore space usage. Configured with email notifications, they allow administrators to react proactively and move VMs around to avoid "out of free space" situation. Alarms only notify administrators about conditions, so there is no option to automate any actions. At the same time, this feature does not require any additional license.

By default, datastore free space alarms are defined only once on the vCenter Server level. Such configurations may become inconvenient when an environment has datastores of a significantly different size. As the trigger for this alarm is a percentage of the free space left in a datastore, vCenter may generate false positives for larger datastores.

One of the possible solutions in this case is to group datastores that are close by their size and assign separate alarm definitions to each group with different trigger thresholds.

## How to do it...

Datastores can be grouped into folders but the first step is to disable the predefined alarm on the vCenter Server level.

### Disabling default alarm

To disable the vCenter predefined alarm for datastore space utilization:

1. Select the vCenter Server object.
2. Go to **Manage | Alarm Definitions**.
3. Select the **Datastore usage on disk** alarm in the list and click on **Edit**.
4. Uncheck **Enable this alarm** and click on Finish.

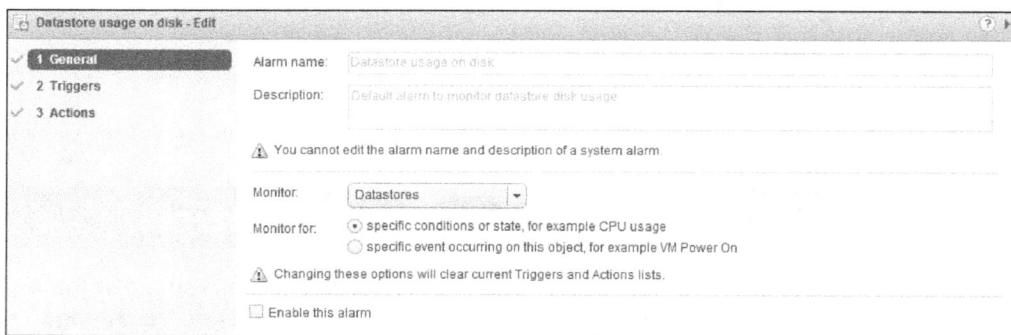

### Creating folders for datastores

The next step is to identify requirements for free space alerts as well as the existing datastores and their size. For example, if the environment consists of 1 TB and 500 GB datastores, at least two groups will be required.

If the administrator needs to be alerted when there is 100 GB of free space left, a trigger for the group of 1 TB datastores should be set to 10 percent. A trigger for the group of 500 GB datastore should be configured as 20 percent.

To group datastores into folders, perform the following steps:

1. Switch to the **Storage** view.
2. Right-click on the **Datacenter** object and go to **All vCenter Actions | New Storage Folder...**.

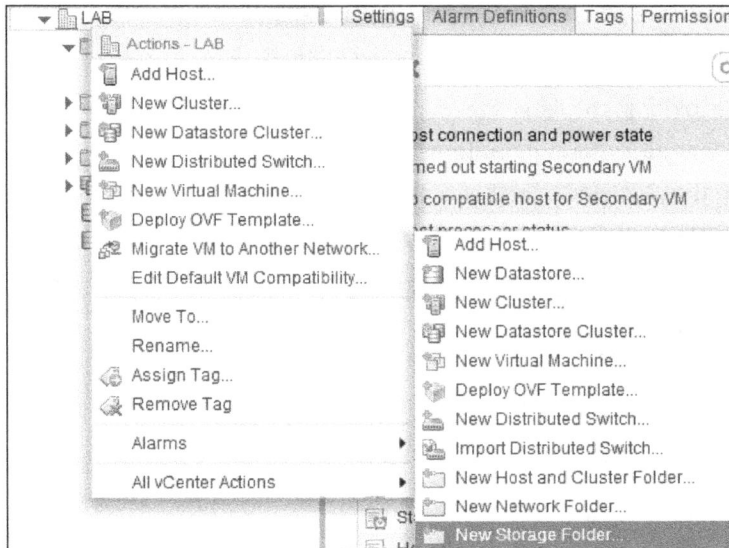

3. Give this folder a name and click on **OK**.

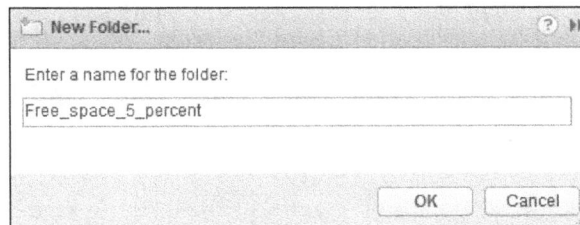

4. Create a separate folder for each datastore group.

5. Drag and drop datastores to the appropriate group. An example of what the end result should look like is shown in the following screenshot:

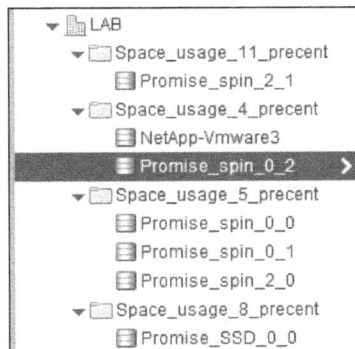

## Creating alarm definitions for each folder

The last step is to create alarm definitions for each folder:

1. Select a folder in the list.

2. Go to **Manage** | **Alarm definitions**.

3. Click on the plus sign to create a new alarm definition.

4. Provide **Alarm name**, select **Datastore** for the **Monitor** field, and click on **Next**.

| Datastore_usage_11_percent - Edit | | ? ►► |
|---|---|---|
| ✓ **1 General** | Alarm name: | Datastore_usage_11_percent |
| ✓ 2 Triggers | Description: | |
| ✓ 3 Actions | | |
| | Monitor: | Datastores ▾ |
| | Monitor for: | ⦿ specific conditions or state, for example CPU usage |
| | | ○ specific event occurring on this object, for example VM Power On |
| | ⚠ Changing these options will clear current Triggers and Actions lists. | |
| | ☑ Enable this alarm | |

5. Click on the plus sign to add a trigger, select **Datastore Disk Usage**, and set the required **Warning Condition** and **Critical Condition** values. Click on **Next**.

| Datastore_usage_11_percent - Edit | | | | ? ►► |
|---|---|---|---|---|
| ✓ 1 General | Trigger if  ANY ▾ of the following conditions are satisfied: | | | |
| ✓ **2 Triggers** | ✚ ✖ | | | |
| ✓ 3 Actions | Trigger | Operator | ⚠ Warning Condition | ◆ Critical Condition |
| | Datastore Disk Usage | is above | 88 % | 89 % |

6. Click on plus sign to add an action, select **Send a notification email**, provide email address, select conditions and click on **Finish**.

| Datastore_usage_11_percent - Edit | | | | | ? ►► |
|---|---|---|---|---|---|
| ✓ 1 General | Specify the actions to take when the alarm state changes. | | | | |
| ✓ 2 Triggers | ✚ ✖ | | | | |
| ✓ **3 Actions** | Action | Configuration | ⊘→⚠ | ⚠→◆ | ◆→⚠ | ⚠→⊘ |
| | Send a notification email | Alerts@vmware.com | Once | Once | Once | Once |

7. Repeat the preceding steps for each folder.

# Automating VM placement with storage profiles

vSphere 5 introduced the so-called **Profile Driven Storage**. This approach allows reducing the administration time required for VM deployment. Instead of manually selecting the correct datastore for new VMs and reviewing periodically if VMs are still placed correctly, Profile Driven Storage automates this.

With the profile driven approach, datastores are labelled according to their characteristics and capabilities. These labels are called datastore **policies**. Policies can be based on storage-defined capabilities, which are available when storage supports **vSphere APIs for Storage Awareness** (**VASA**). These are vendor-defined characteristics, which may differ depending on the storage used.

Storage policies can also be based on user-defined capabilities, which is accomplished with **tags**. Tags are custom labels that can be assigned to many different objects in vSphere, including datastores and datastore clusters. More details about tags can be found in the Categorizing objects in the environment recipe in *Chapter 7, Improving Environment Manageability*.

VMs are assigned datastore policies either during VM deployment or after. If a policy is assigned during VM creation, vCenter will ensure that the VM is placed on a compliant datastore. Later, the administrator can check whether a VM is still compliant to the assigned policies and reapply them if necessary.

The concept of defining storage capabilities and assigning them as compliance requirements to VMs has not changed since vSphere 5 has been introduced and vCenter Client was the primary management tool. Storage policies were called storage profiles, and instead of tags, administrators had to define custom defied capabilities. However, not only names have changed.

Storage policies and capabilities are not interchangeable between vCenter Client and new Web Client. Storage profiles created in vCenter Client are not available in Web Client.

## Getting ready

The Enterprise Plus license is required for this feature to be available.

## How to do it...

Storage profiles are disabled by default so the first step is to enable this feature. With changes to storage profiles introduced in vSphere 5.5, Web Client became a primary means of managing storage capabilities and profiles, so we will use only Web Client in all further configuration examples in this recipe.

## Enable storage profiles and tag datastores

To enable storage profiles in Web Client, perform the following steps:

1. Go to **Home | Rules and Profiles | VM Storage Policies**.

2. Click on the **Enable VM storage policies per compute resource** button.

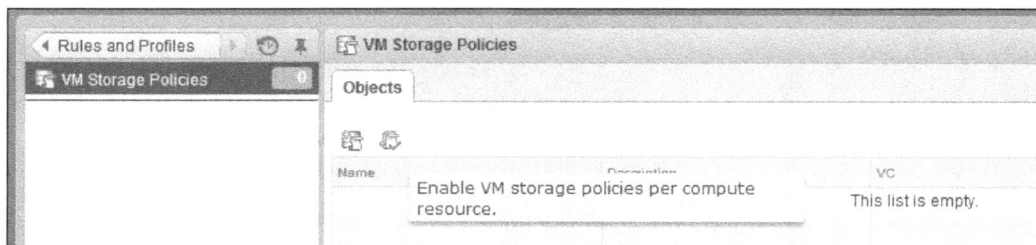

3. Select vCenter Server.

4. Select a host or cluster and click on **Enable**.

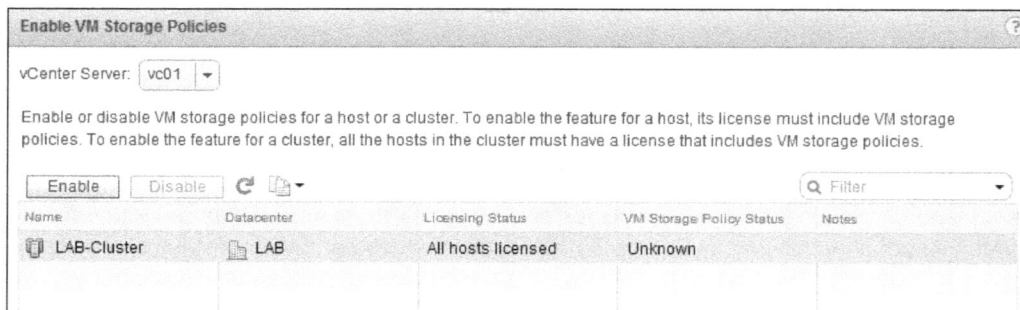

## Creating storage policy

Once datastores and clusters have been tagged as required, the storage policy can be created. To accomplish this, follow the ensuing steps:

1. In Web Client, go to **Home | Rules and Profiles | VM Storage Policies**.

2. Click on the **Create a new VM storage policy** icon.

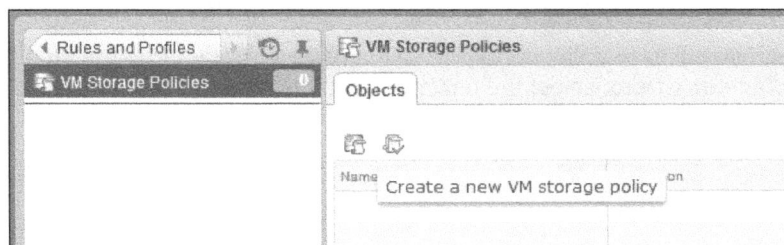

3. Select vCenter Server.

4. Type the storage profile name and click on **Next**.

5. Click on the **Add tag-Based rule** button and select the tag category from the drop-down menu **Categories**.

6. Choose tags and click on **OK**.

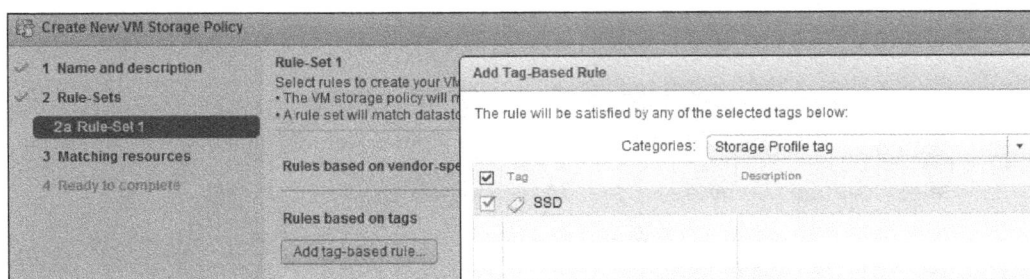

7. Click on **Next** and confirm that the correct datastores and clusters are listed under **Matching resources**.

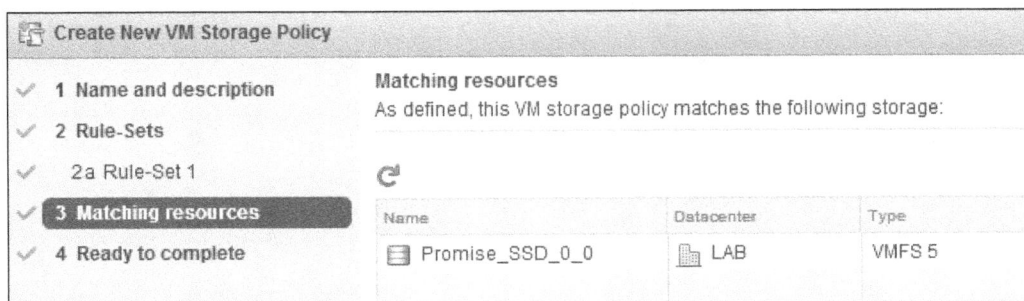

8. Click on **Finish** to create the policy.

All datastores that have selected capabilities will be compliant with this profile.

## Assigning storage policy to a VM

Storage policies can be assigned to VMs either during VM deployment or any time after.

To assign a storage policy to a VM, during creation on the **2c Select storage** step of the **New Virtual Machine** wizard, select the policy from the **VM Storage Policy** drop-down menu instead of an individual datastore.

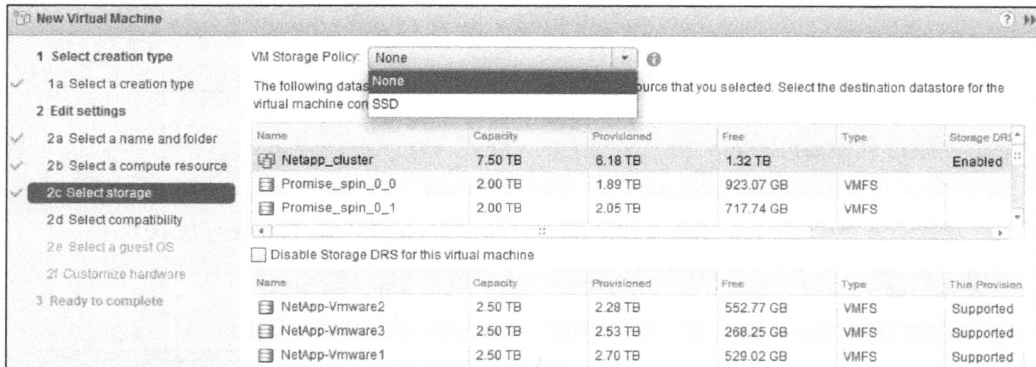

vCenter will place this VM in one of the compliant datastores.

To link an existing VM to a storage policy, perform the following steps:

1. Select a virtual machine and go to **Manage | VM Storage Policies**.

2. Click on the **Manage VM Storage Policies** button and select a policy from the **Home VM storage policy** drop-down menu.

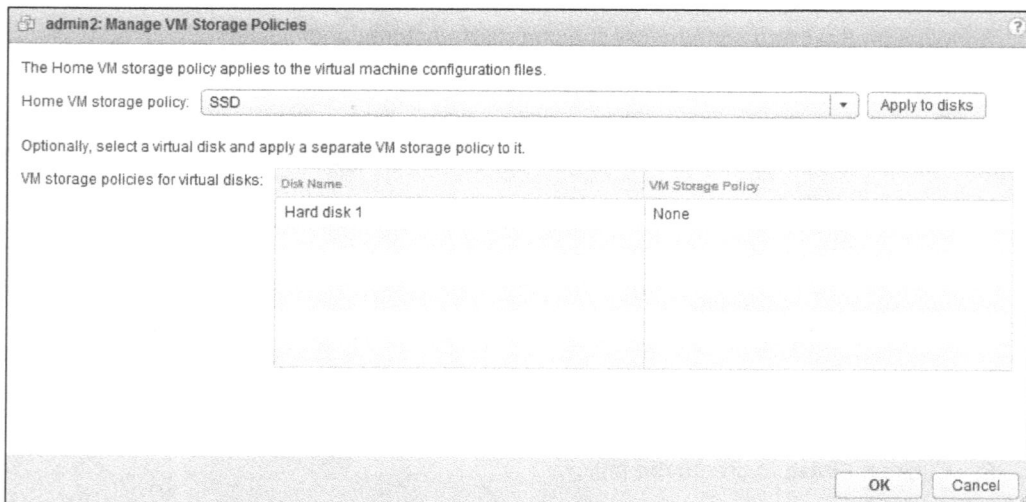

3. Click on **Apply to disks** to apply the selected policy to all virtual disks or select a different policy for each disk under **VM storage policies for virtual disks**

4. Click on **OK**.

Once the storage policy has been assigned, vCenter will report a compliance status for each virtual disk. Click on the **Check the compliance of all VM storage policies of the selected virtual machine** button to rescan for compliance.

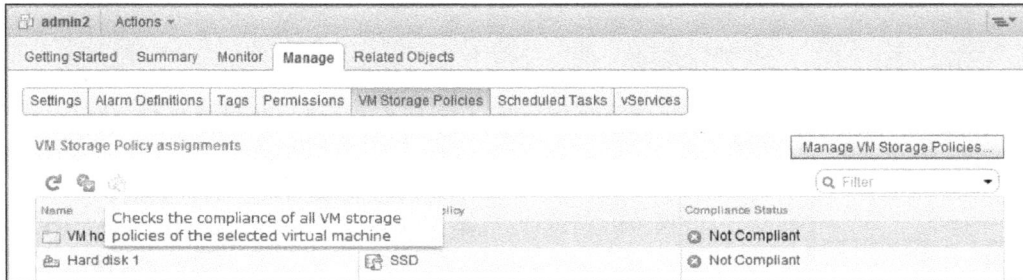

# Automating VM placement with VM affinity

The **Affinity rules** feature is a part of **Distributed Resource Scheduler** (**DRS**) described in the *Balancing loads between hosts* recipe in *Chapter 5, Optimizing Resource Usage*. This feature allows administrators to control the VM placement on cluster hosts. DRS provides its balancing recommendations or migrates VMs automatically if configured, taking into account all the configured affinity rules.

Two types of affinity rules can be created:

▶ VM-to-Host, which controls whether particular groups of VMs can be placed on certain hosts.

▶ VM-to-VM, which define whether VMs can be kept together on the same host.

One of the more common use cases for affinity rules is performance considerations when certain resource-intensive VMs should be run only on hosts with enough resources. Another scenario is related to license restrictions. For example, MS SQL virtual machines licensed for two processors should be placed on hosts with no more than two CPUs.

When a cluster is in violation of an affinity rule, an administrator will be alerted.

## How to do it...

Both VM-to-Host and VM-to-VM affinity rules can be configured under DRS rules.

## Creating VM-to-Host rules

Before VM-to-Host affinity rules can be set up, VM and host groups must be created first under DRS Group Manager:

1.  Select a cluster and go to **Manage | Settings | DRS Groups**.

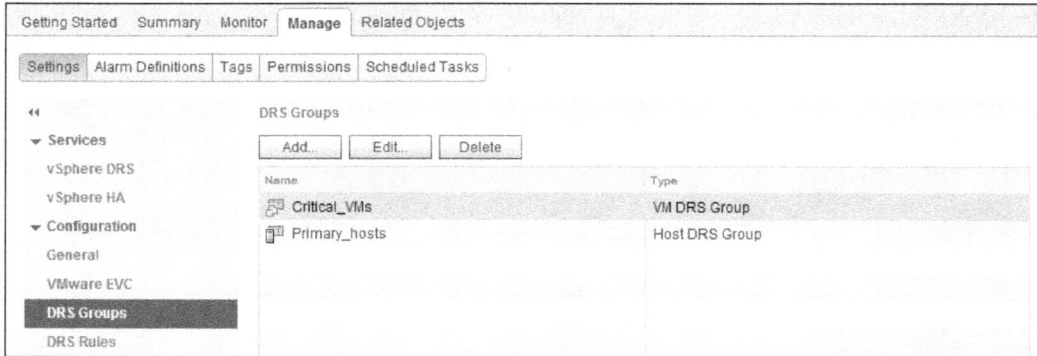

2.  Click on the **Add** button to create a group.
3.  Type the group name and choose type between **VM DRS Group** or **Host DRS Group**.

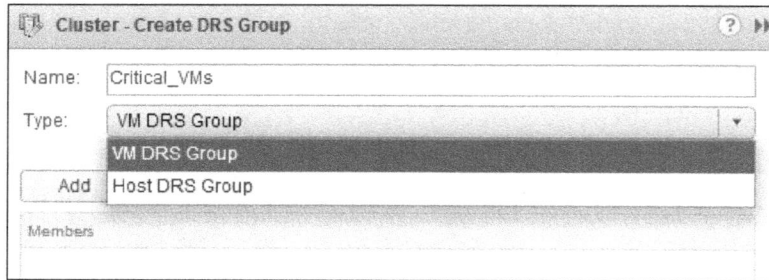

4.  Click on add to add hosts or VMs depending on the type chosen.
5.  Select hosts or VMs and click on **OK** to create the rule.

Once the required host and VM groups exist:

1.  Go to **DRS Rules** click on the **Add** button.
2.  Type the rule name and select **Virtual Machines to Hosts** for **Type**.
3.  Select the VM and Host group and choose the required rule option:

---

**Cluster - Create DRS Rule**

Name: | Rule 1

☑ Enable rule.

Type: | Virtual Machines to Hosts ▾

Description:

Virtual machines that are members of the Cluster DRS VM Group Critical_VMs must run on host group Primary_hosts.

VM Group:

| Critical_VMs ▾ |

| Must run on hosts in group ▾ |

| Must run on hosts in group |
| Should run on hosts in group |
| Must Not run on hosts in group |
| Should Not run on hosts in group |

OK | Cancel

---

The options **Should run on hosts in a group** and **Should Not run on hosts in a group** mean that the rule will be maintained when possible, while the options **Must run on hosts in a group** and **Must Not run on hosts in a group** are required rules. Rules that start with "Must" should be used with caution, especially when more than one rule is being created. Any action that violates "Must" or "Must not" rules will not be performed by vCenter. They include VM migrations, HA failover, and DPM actions.

The older rule always wins in case of a conflict.

If a VM is a part of two or more VM groups assigned to two or more host groups, these VMs will be able to run only on hosts that are members of both groups.

In vCenter Client, perform the following steps:

1. Switch to the **Hosts and Clusters** view.
2. Right-click on a cluster and go to **Edit Settings**.

3.  Create VM and Host groups under **DRS Groups Manager**.

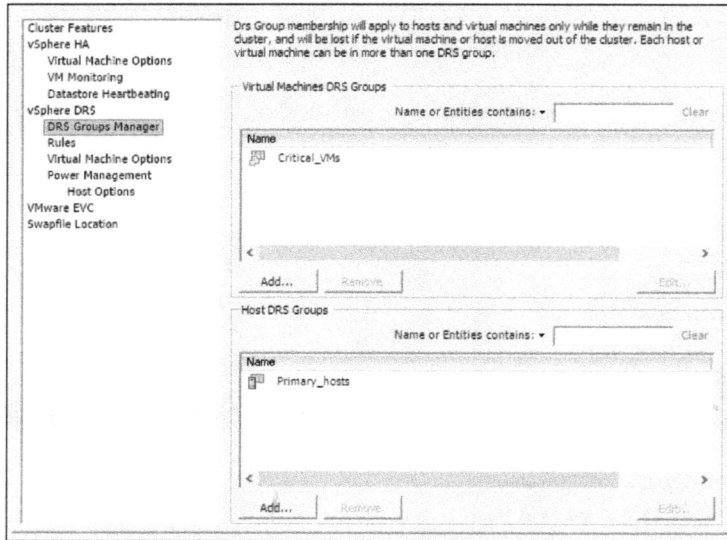

4.  Go to **Rules** and click on the **Add** button.
5.  Type the rule name and select **Virtual Machines to Hosts** under **Type**.
6.  Choose the VM and host groups, as well as the rule option, and click on **OK**.

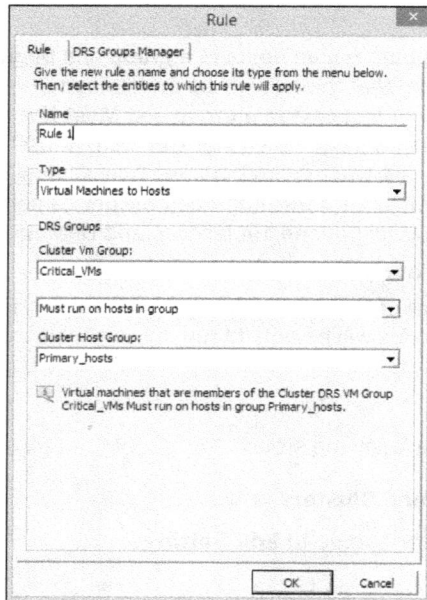

The options **Should run on hosts in a group** and **Should Not run on hosts in a group** mean that the rule will be maintained when possible, while the option **Must run on hosts in a group** and **Must Not run on hosts in a group** are required rules. Rules that start with "Must" should be used with caution, especially when more than one rule is being created. Any actions that violate "Must" or "Must not" rules will not be performed by vCenter. They include VM migrations, HA failover, and DPM actions.

The older rule always wins in case of a conflict.

If a VM is a part of two or more VM groups assigned to two or more host groups, these VMs will be able to run only on hosts that are members of both groups.

## Creating VM-to-VM rules

This type of affinity rules can be created for any existing virtual machines; VM groups are not required. To create such rules in Web Client, perform the following:

1. Select a cluster, go to **Manage** | **Settings** | **DRS Rules**, and click on the **Add** button.

2. Select one of the two options—**Keep Virtual Machines Together** or **Separate Virtual Machines**:

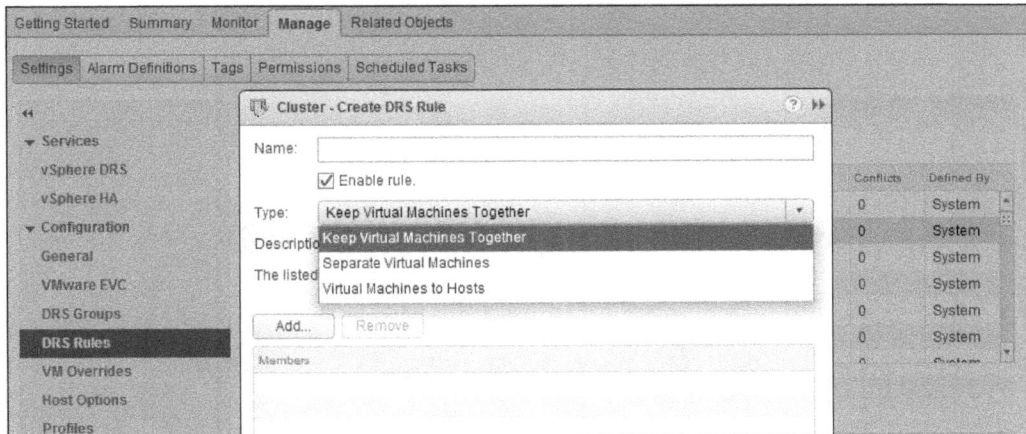

3. Click on **Add**, select the virtual machines, and click on **OK** twice to create a rule.

Only one rule can be enabled in case of a conflict. The older rule always takes precedence; the other rules will be disabled automatically.

In vCenter Client, execute the following steps:

1. Switch to the **Hosts and Clusters** view.

2. Right-click on a cluster and go to **Edit Settings**.

3. Go to **Rules** and click on the **Add** button.

4. Type the rule name and select **Keep Virtual Machines Together** or **Separate Virtual Machines** under **Type**.

5. Click on **Add**, choose VMs from the list, and click on **OK** twice to create a rule:

---

**Rule**   ☒

Rule | DRS Groups Manager

Give the new rule a name and choose its type from the menu below.
Then, select the entities to which this rule will apply.

Name
Rule 2

Type
Keep Virtual Machines Together   ▼

Virtual Machines
OHM
p-admin

Add...   Remove

OK   Cancel

---

Only one rule can be enabled in case of a conflict. The older rule always takes precedence; the other rules will be disabled automatically.

# Automating VM placement with storage affinity

Similar to the DRS affinity rules discussed in *Automating VM placement with VM affinity* recipe in this chapter, Storage DRS affinity rules allow administrators to specify whether certain VMs or virtual drives can be kept in the same datastore.

Before this feature was introduced, nothing except the administrator's manual effort was preventing redundant servers running off from the same datastore. Such redundancy is useless; if this datastore fails, both servers become unavailable.

Two types of SDRS rules are available:

  ▸ Intra-VM, which specifies whether virtual drives that belong to the same VM should be kept together or separately. By default, virtual disks are kept together. This default behavior can be changed.

  ▸ VM-to-VM, which define whether certain virtual machines should be placed in different datastores. The **Affinity** option is not available for this type of rule so it can only separate VMs.

One of the potential use cases for Intra-VM rule is when two disks within a VM are mirrored and keeping them on different datastores adds redundancy.

## Getting ready

The Enterprise Plus license is required for this feature to be available. Also, at least one datastore cluster must exist in the environment.

## How to do it...

SDRS affinity rules can be created in Web Client or in vCenter Client.

### Creating the Intra-VM rule

To create the Intra-VM rule in Web Client, execute the following steps:

  1. Select a datastore cluster and go to **Manage** | **Settings** | **Configuration** | **Rules**.

  2. Click on **Add**.

3. Type the rule name and select **VMDK anti-affinity** from the **Type** drop-down menu.

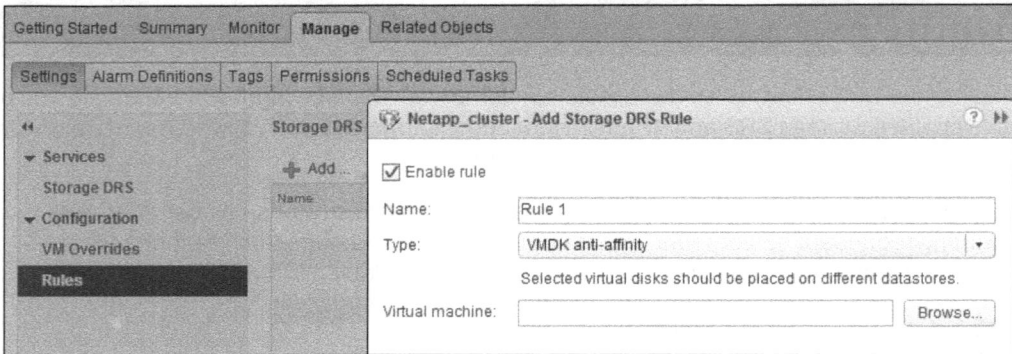

4. Click on **Browse**, select a VM from the list, and click on **OK**.
5. Choose two or more virtual drives and click on **OK** to create the rule.

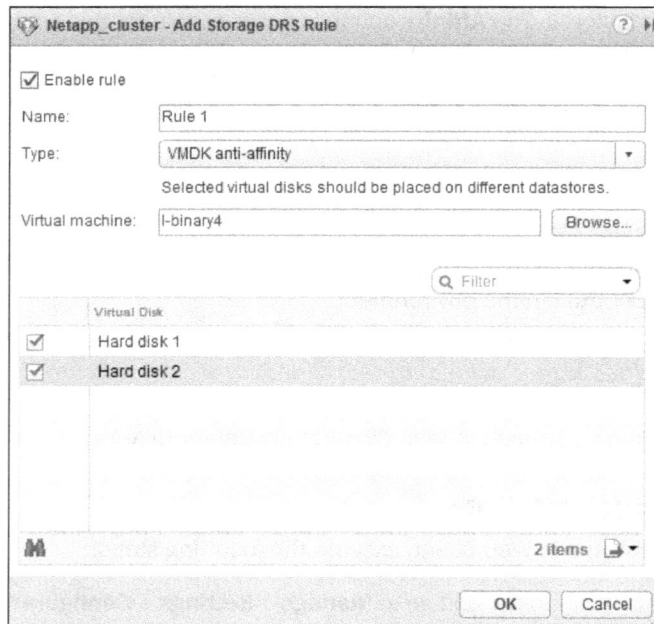

In vCenter Client, follow the ensuing steps:

1.  Switch to the **Datastores and Datastore Clusters** view.
2.  Right-click on the datastore cluster and select **Edit Settings**.
3.  Go to **Rules** and click on **Add**.
4.  Type the rule name and choose **VMDK anti-affinity** from the **Type** drop-down menu.

5.  Click on **Add**.
6.  Click on on **Select Virtual Machine**.

7. Choose a VM, select two or more virtual drives, and click on **OK**.

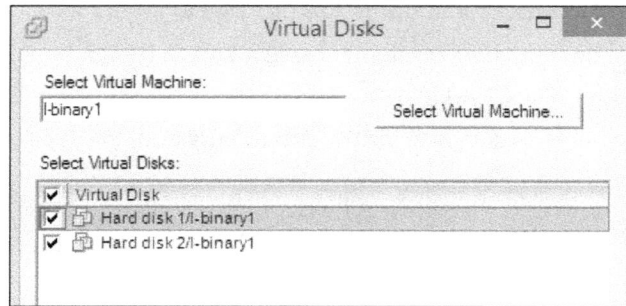

8. Click on **OK** to save the rule.

## Creating a VM-to-VM rule

To create a VM-to-VM rule in Web Client, perform the following steps:

1. Select a datastore cluster and go to **Manage | Settings | Configuration | Rules**.

2. Click on **Add**.

3. Type the rule name and select **VM anti-affinity** from the **Type** drop-down menu.

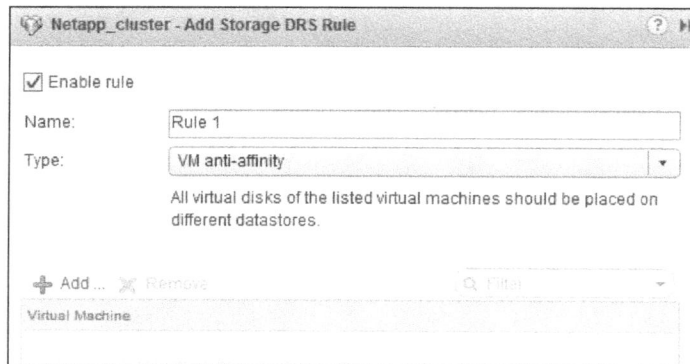

4. Click on **Add**.

5. Choose two or more virtual machines and click on **OK** twice to create the rule.

If you use vCenter Client, perform the following steps:

1. Switch to the **Datastores and Datastore Clusters** view.

2. Right-click on the datastore cluster and select **Edit Settings**.

3. Go to **Rules** and click on **Add**.

4. Type the rule name and choose **VM anti-affinity** from the **Type** drop-down menu.

5. Click on **Add**.

6. Select two or more virtual machines and click on **OK** twice to save the rule.

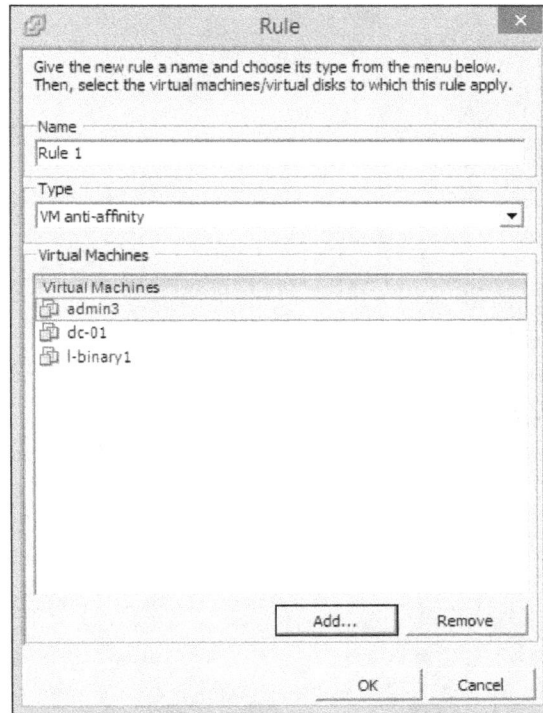

## Changing default affinity rule

If you use Web Client, perform the following steps:

1. Select a datastore cluster and go to **Manage** | **Settings** | **Configuration** | **VM Overrides**.

2. Click on **Add**.

3. Select the VMs with a plus button.

4. Select **No** from the **Keep VMDKs together** drop-down menu.

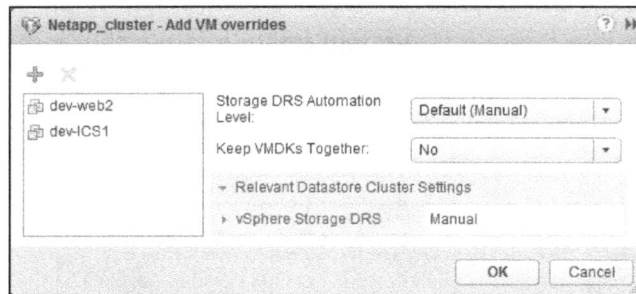

5. Click on **OK**.

In vCenter Client, perform the following steps:

1. Switch to the **Datastores and Datastore Clusters** view.

2. Right-click on the datastore cluster and click on **Edit settings**.

3. Go to **Virtual machine settings**.

4. Uncheck **Keep VMDKs together**.

5. Override this setting for individual machines if necessary by checking the box next to a VM.

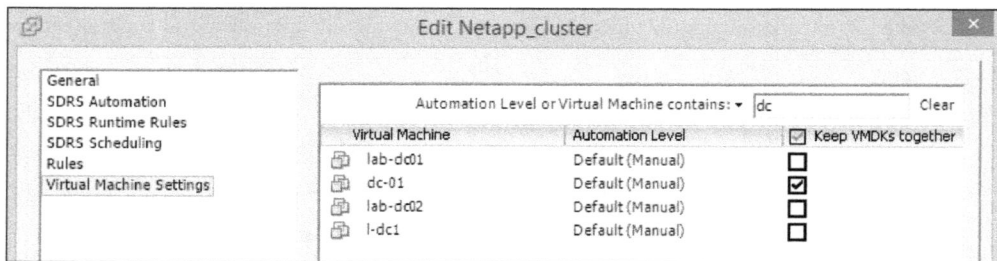

## There's more...

When one of the existing affinity rules applies to a VM:

▶ When a VM violates the rule SDRS provides migration recommendations or migrates the VM automatically if it's configured to do so.

▶ If SDRS is not able to make a recommendation or migrate the VM, it reports a rule violation as a fault.

▶ SDRS follows the rule even if VM migration is mandatory, for example, if migration is required to put a datastore into maintenance mode.

# Automating tasks with a scheduler

vCenter has a **task scheduler** that allows scheduling certain tasks to run in future, either once or multiple times. A task is an event or activity that takes some time to complete. Examples of such events are powering on or off, shutting down, cloning, deploying, or migrating a virtual machine; adding a host; changing the resource pool or VM settings, and so on.

Unfortunately, a vCenter scheduler does not have the ability to schedule tasks for multiple objects. If a few virtual machines have to be turned off, a separate task has to be created for each VM.

Once a scheduled task runs, it stays in the list and can be scheduled to run again by modifying its properties.

## Getting ready

If vCenter Client is used, it has to be connected to the vCenter Server before a task can be scheduled.

The user creating a task has to be granted the `Scheduled Task.Create Tasks` privilege.

## How to do it...

To schedule a task in Web Client, execute the following steps:

1. Select an object the new task will be performed on.
2. Go to **Manage | Scheduled Tasks**.
3. Click on **Schedule a New Task** and select an action from the list.

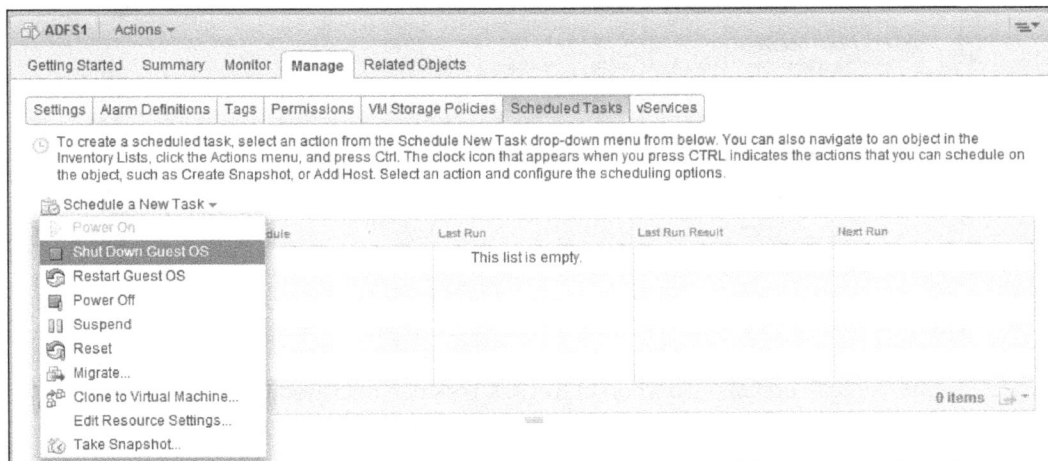

4. Confirm the action.

5. Go to **Scheduling options** and click on **Change**.

6. Set a schedule and click on **OK** twice to create a task.

In vCenter Client, perform the following steps:

1. Go to **Home | Scheduled Tasks**.

2. Click on **New**.

3. Choose a task and click on **OK**.

4. Depending on the task chosen, the wizard will guide you through the process of creating a scheduled task. If **Change a Virtual Machine's Power State** has been chosen, the first step will be to select a VM.

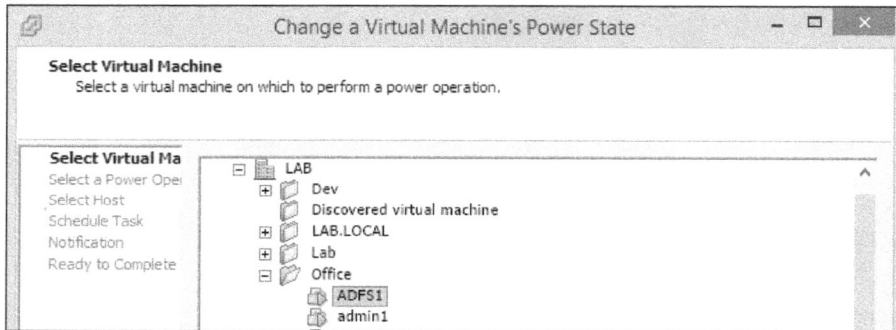

5. Click on **Next**.

6. In this step, select **Power Operation** and click on **Next**.

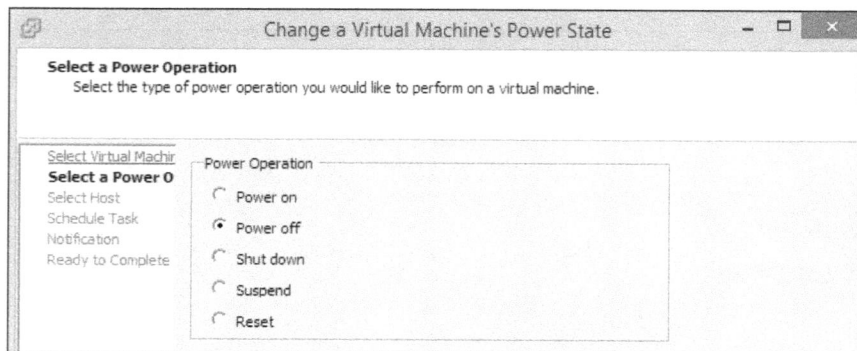

7. Name the task and choose when to run it. A task can be scheduled once—immediately or any time later. There are also options to schedule tasks to run regularly—hourly, daily, weekly, or monthly.

**Change a Virtual Machine's Power State** — □ ×

**Schedule Task**
Select the time and frequency of the task.

| | |
|---|---|
| Select Virtual Machin | Task name: Shut down a VM tasks |
| Select a Power Oper | |
| **Schedule Task** | Task description: |
| Notification | |
| Ready to Complete | Frequency: Once ▼ |

Start Time

○ Now

◉ Later

Time: 9:47 PM

Date: 2017-02-08 ▼

8. Click on **Next**.

9. In this step, you have an option to get notified by e-mail when the task has been completed.

**Change a Virtual Machine's Power State** — □ ×

**Notification**
Request email notification when the task is complete

| | |
|---|---|
| Select Virtual Machin | ☐ Send email to the following addresses when the task is complete |
| Select a Power Oper | |
| Schedule Task | Email addresses: |
| **Notification** | |
| Ready to Complete | Separate multiple email addresses with a semicolon ; |

> The mail server has to be configured before emails can be sent. Please refer to the *Improving visibility with email alerts* recipe in this chapter for more details.

10. Click on **Next**. Review the summary and click on **Finish** to create the task.

Scheduled tasks can be viewed, modified, or deleted in the same place where they are scheduled. In Web Client, go to **Manage | Scheduled Tasks** for a particular object and in vCenter Client, go to **Home | Task Scheduler**.

## There's more...

The following should be considered when using scheduled tasks:

▶ Do not schedule more than one task for the same object at the same time.

▶ The user who is scheduling a task has to have permissions to perform the task on the relevant objects.

▶ A scheduled task will run and fail if the user who created it does not have the required permissions.

▶ When two tasks conflict, the one scheduled to run first wins.

▶ A task will not be run if the object is in a state that prevents this task from executing.

▶ When an object is deleted from vCenter, all the associated tasks are removed.

▶ vSphere Client users see task schedule in their local time, while vCenter uses UTC to determine the start time for the task.

# Keeping hosts up to date

**vSphere Update Manager** allows administrators to manage updates for ESXi hosts. This is a solution for centralized patch management for the whole vSphere environment.

Depending on the client you connect to vCenter with, you will either use the **Update Manager Web Client** plugin or the **Update Manager** plugin for vCenter Client.

The Update Manager Web Client plugin requires the Update Manager server to be installed on the vCenter Server. The Update Manager plugin for vCenter Client requires the Update Manager plugin to be installed on each vCenter Client.

High-level workflow of using Update Manager is as follows:

▶ Create a baseline, which includes patches, hotfixes, and third-party updates if required.

▶ Apply the baseline to one or more hosts and scan them against it.

▶ Update hosts with missing patches and updates from the baseline—remediation.

Update Manager in Web Client does not allow remediating objects.

## Getting ready

The prerequisites for Update Manager server are as follows:

▶ vSphere 5.1 Update 1 or higher.

▶ Oracle or MS SQL database. For small environments with up to five hosts and 50 virtual machines bundled, the SQL Server 2008 R2 Express database can be used.

- ► Microsoft Windows Installer Version 4.5 is required if the bundled SQL Server 2008 R2 Express database is used.
- ► A 32-bit DSN and 32-bit ODBC connection to a database unless a bundled database is used.

The prerequisites for the Update Manager plugin are as follows:

- ► .NET Framework 3.5 or higher
- ► Administrative privileges on the machine with vCenter Client

## How to do it...

Update Manager is an additional component of the vCenter Server. Both the server part and client part, in the case of vCenter Client being used, have to be installed and enabled first.

Once the installation has been completed, the next steps include the following:

- ► Creating a baseline and baseline groups
- ► Attaching baselines or groups to hosts
- ► Scanning hosts and remediate missing objects to install updates

### Installing the Update Manager server

To use Update Manager with Web Client, install the Update Manager server on the vCenter Server. It is a separate component that can be downloaded from `http://vmware.com`. Once it's installed, the **Update Manager** option will appear under the **Monitor** tab for each host.

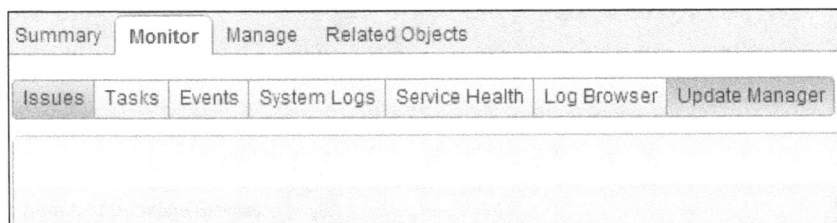

Unfortunately, Update Manager only became available in Web Client starting from vSphere 5.1 Update 1.

The Update Manager server can be installed on the same server as vCenter or on a different one. For detailed steps on the Update Manager server installation process, please refer to the vSphere 5 online documentation at `https://pubs.vmware.com/vsphere-50/topic/com.vmware.vsphere.install.doc_50/GUID-7DB71999-5B42-4D5F-9202-74823BD2BFC6.html`.

## Installing the Update Manager plugin

If you use the vCenter Client, the Update Manager plugin has to be activated first. To do this, perform the following steps:

1.  In vCenter Client, go to **Plug-ins | Manage plug-ins**.

2.  Click on the **Download and Install...** link beside **VMware vSphere Update Manager extension**.

| Plug-in Name | Vendor | Version | Status | Description |
|---|---|---|---|---|
| **Installed Plug-ins** | | | | |
| VMware vCenter Storage Monitoring Service | VMware Inc. | 5.5 | Enabled | Storage Monitoring and Reporting |
| vCenter Service Status | VMware, Inc. | 5.5 | Enabled | Displays the health status of vCenter services |
| vCenter Hardware Status | VMware, Inc. | 5.5 | Enabled | Displays the hardware status of hosts (CIM monitoring) |
| **Available Plug-ins** | | | | |
| VMware vSphere Update Manager Extension | VMware, Inc. | 5.1.0.... | Download and Install... | VMware vSphere Update Manager extension |
| VDP | VMware | 5.1.11... | No client side download is n... | VDP - vSphere Data Protection |
| VDP 5.5 | VMware | 5.5.7.5 | No client side download is n... | VDP - vSphere Data Protection 5. |

*Plug-in Manager*

3.  Go through the VMware vSphere Update Manager installation wizard. You will be required to accept the End User License Agreement and click on the **Install** button to install the client.

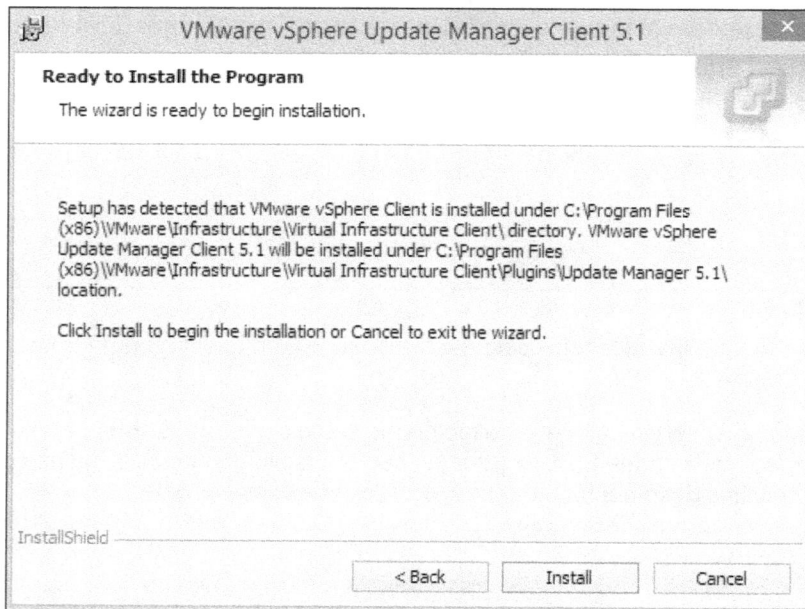

**VMware vSphere Update Manager Client 5.1**

**Ready to Install the Program**

The wizard is ready to begin installation.

Setup has detected that VMware vSphere Client is installed under C:\Program Files (x86)\VMware\Infrastructure\Virtual Infrastructure Client\ directory. VMware vSphere Update Manager Client 5.1 will be installed under C:\Program Files (x86)\VMware\Infrastructure\Virtual Infrastructure Client\Plugins\Update Manager 5.1\ location.

Click Install to begin the installation or Cancel to exit the wizard.

InstallShield

< Back    Install    Cancel

4.  Once the extension is installed, its status in the plugin manager is **Enabled** and the **Update Manager** tab becomes available for each ESXi host.

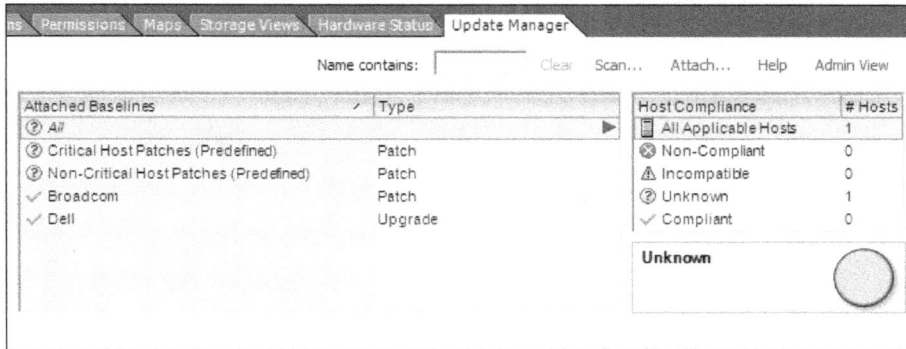

## Creating baselines and groups

Unfortunately, staging and remediation are not available in vSphere 5 Web Client. For the majority of administrators, it means that to update ESXi hosts, they will have to use vCenter Client and for the purpose of this recipe, all further steps and screenshots are considering only the old vCenter Client.

Update Manager comes with predefined baselines. Administrators can create their own baselines or groups. To accomplish this, perform the following steps:

1.  Select a host and go to the **Update Manager** tab.
2.  Switch to **Admin View**.
3.  Right-click on the white space and select **New Baseline...**.

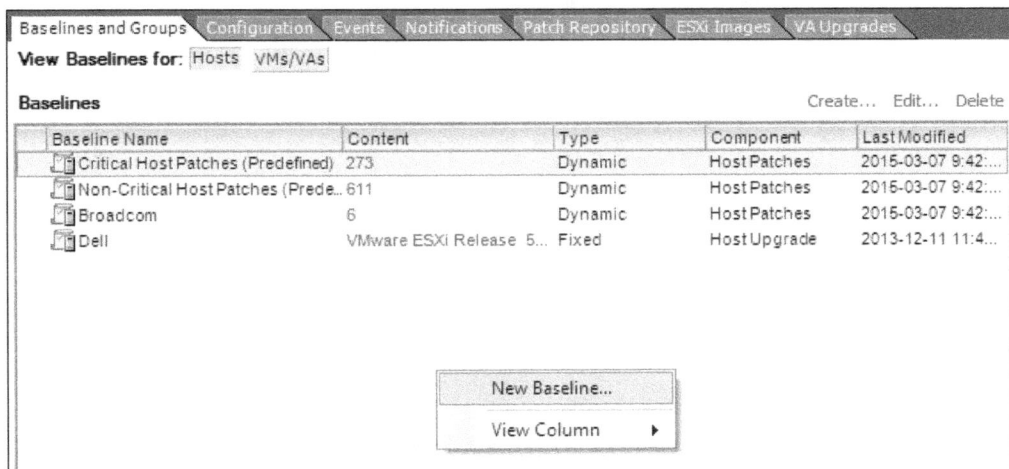

4. Type the baseline name, select **Baseline Type**, and click on **Next**.

5. Choose the patch option for the baseline and click on **Next**.

6. Select the criteria to filter patches and click on **Next**.

7. Select patches to include in this baseline and click on **Next**.

8.  Select the additional patches if available, click on **Next**, review settings, and click on **Finish** to create the baseline.

Two or more non-conflicting baselines can be joined to a baseline group, which allows scanning and remediating objects against more than one baseline at the same time. To do this, perform the following steps:

1.  In **Admin** view, click on **Create** beside **Baseline Groups**.
2.  Select **Baseline Group Type**, give the group a name, and click on **Next**.

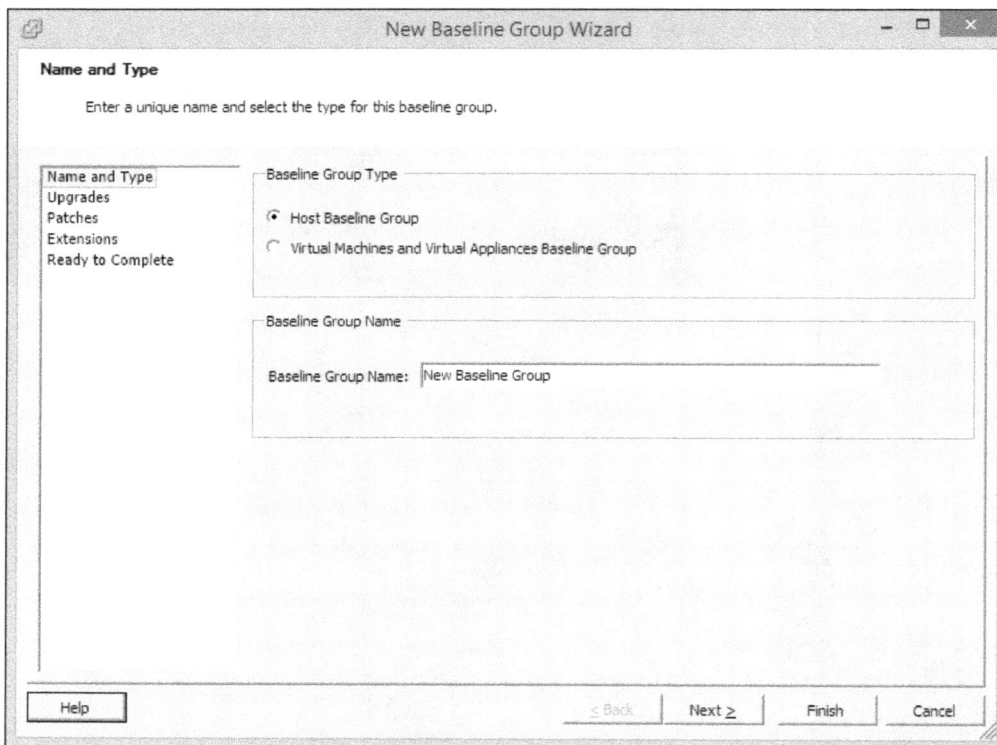

3.  In the next steps of the wizard, add upgrade baselines, patch baselines, and extension baselines, and click on **Finish** when the selections are completed.

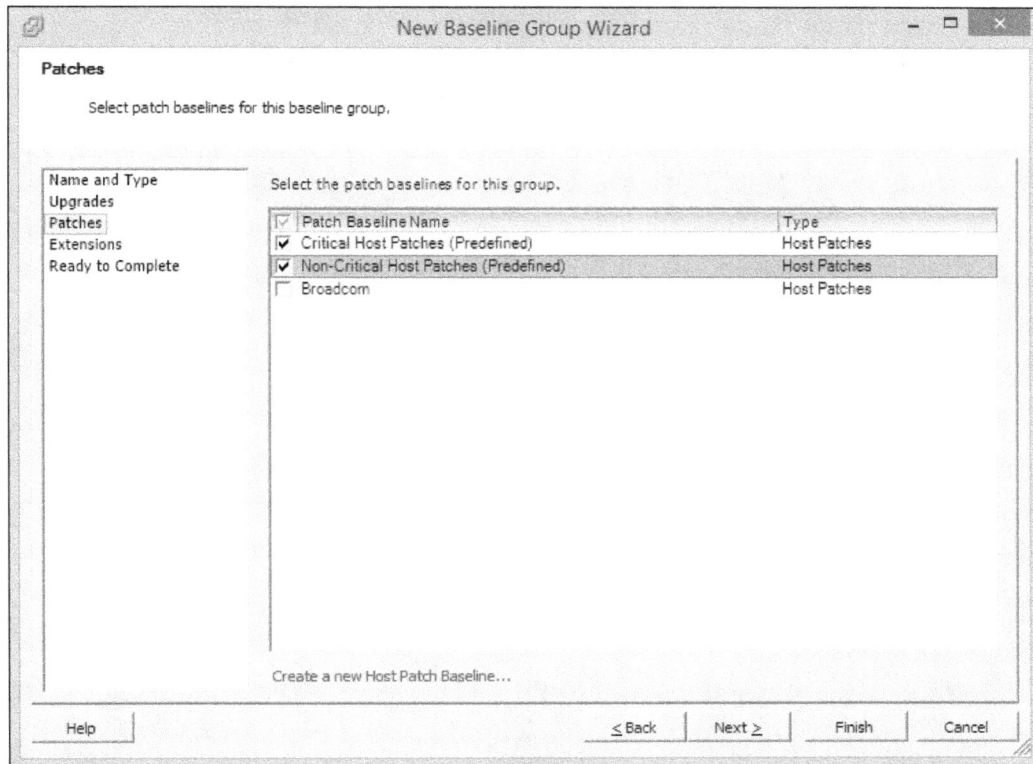

## Attaching baselines or groups to hosts

The existing baselines or groups can be attached to hosts for scanning and remediation against the patches from the attached baselines. To accomplish this, perform the following steps:

1. Select a host and go to the **Update Manager** tab.

2. In **Compliance View**, which should open by default, click on **Attach**.

3.  Select baselines or groups from the list and click on the **Attach** button.

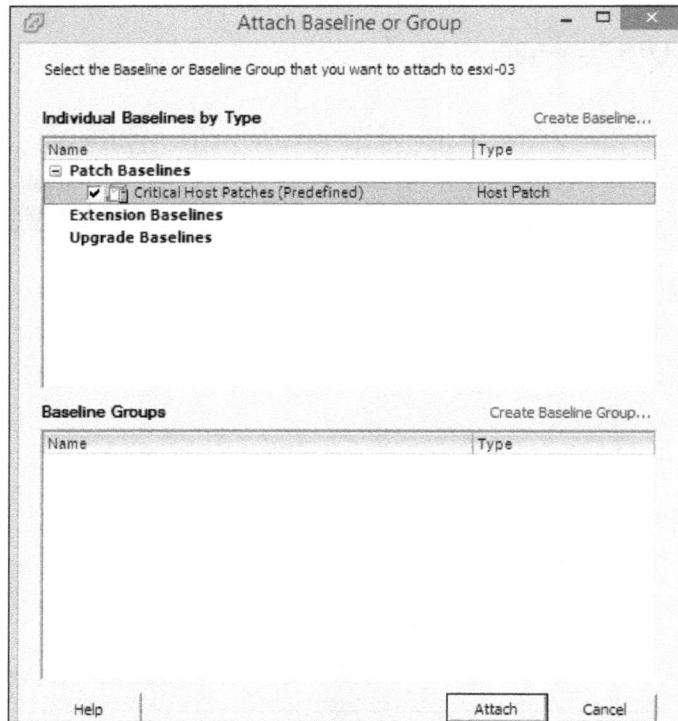

Attached baselines and groups can be reviewed in **Compliance View** under the **Attached Baseline Groups** or **Attached Baselines** sections:

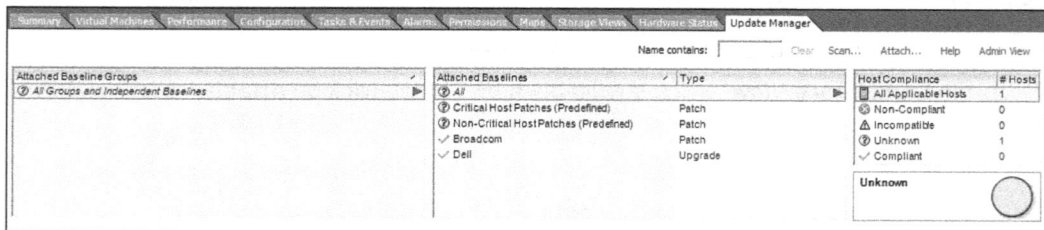

# Scanning and remediating objects

Once the required baselines are attached, perform the following steps:

1. Click on the **Scan** link from the **Compliance** view to check the host against the attached baselines.

2. Select both **Patches and Extensions** and **Upgrades** and click on **Scan**.

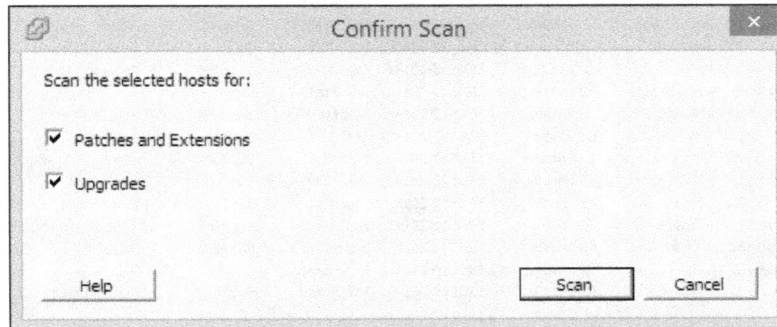

After the scan is completed, instead of question marks next to each attached baseline, The Update Manager will change the icon according to the compliance status:

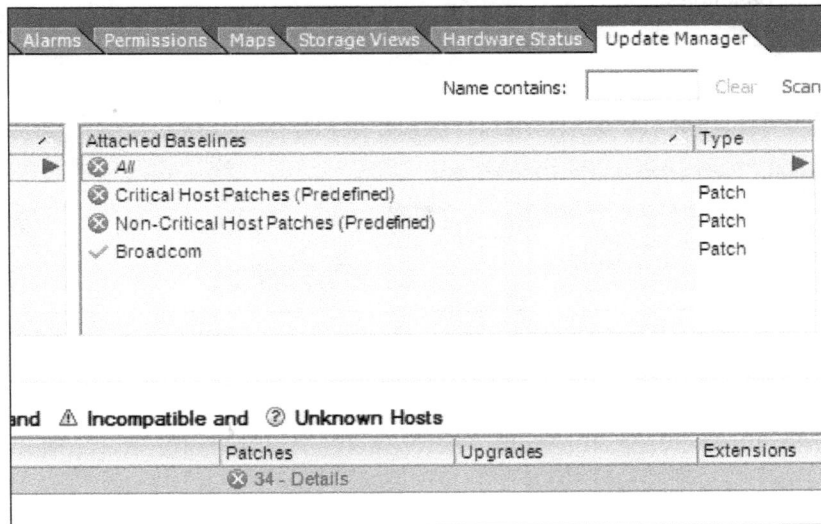

To review the missing patches, click on the link in the **Patches** column. Updates marked **Missing** will be installed during remediation:

To apply missing patches and updates, click on the **Remediate** button and follow the wizard prompts:

1. Select baselines:

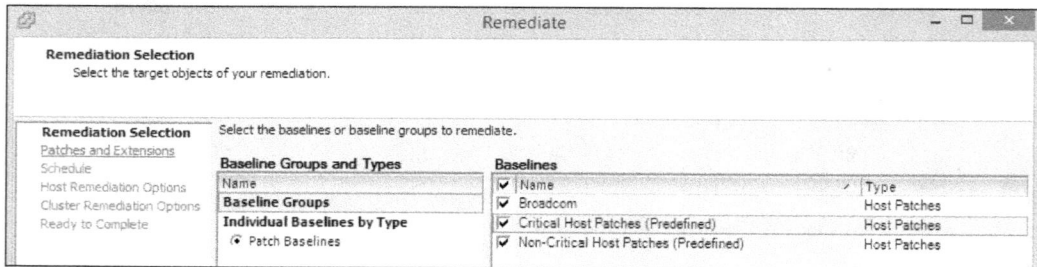

2. Exclude certain patches if necessary:

3. Select when the update will happen:

4. Choose host remediation options and click on **Next**.

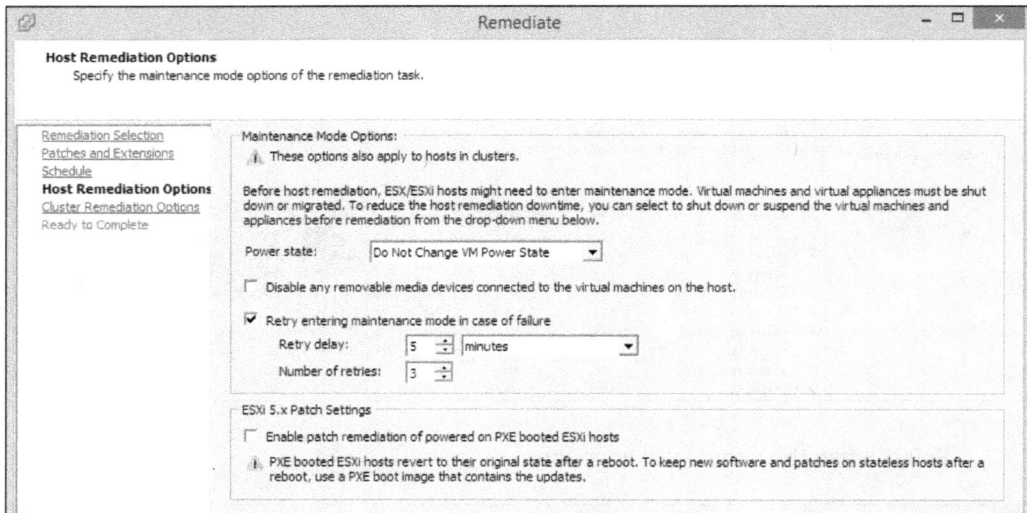

5. Choose cluster remediation options, and click on **Next** and then on **Finish**.

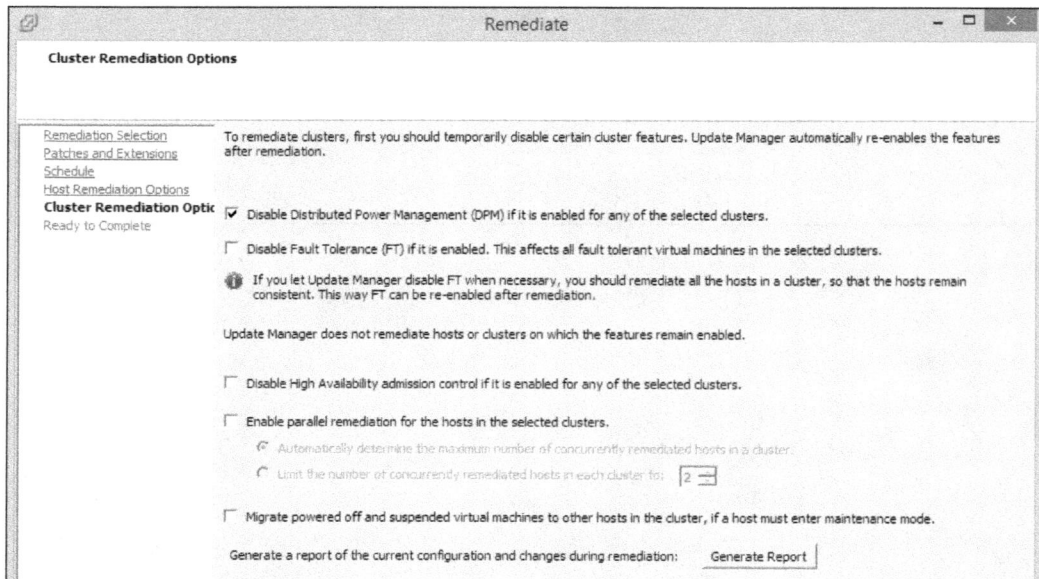

The host will likely require a reboot. Depending on the options chosen, it will be placed in maintenance mode and all virtual machines will be migrated off of it.

# 7
# Improving Environment Manageability

In this chapter, we will cover the following recipes:

- ▶ Categorizing objects in the environment
- ▶ Scheduling the VM clone
- ▶ Redirecting VMkernel dumps to another server
- ▶ Gathering network traffic
- ▶ VDS configuration backup and restore
- ▶ Management network configuration recovery
- ▶ Choosing a MAC address prefix
- ▶ Getting familiar with the new CLI
- ▶ Configuring the firewall from CLI
- ▶ Bypassing "hostd" when it's unresponsive with CLI

## Introduction

This chapter describes small administrative tasks, which play a less important role in the vSphere environment administration compared to tasks discussed in previous chapters. At the same time, they can make an administrator's life easier by improving environment manageability. We will take a look at how to categorize objects in the environment, schedule VM clone, use the command line, and backup and restore virtual switch configuration.

# Categorizing objects in the environment

vSphere 5 and Web Client have introduced a new feature called **Tagging**. Tags are just labels containing metadata information, which can be attached to objects in the vSphere environment for categorization.

Tags can be attached to datastores, datastore clusters, VMs, and so on. Such categorization allows making objects in the environment searchable and sortable, which helps with management and scripting.

Tags can be grouped into categories that define which objects these tags can be applied to.

For example, administrators can categorize virtual machines by a guest OS, or datastores by their characteristics, such as storage speed, redundancy, and so on.

Tags are supported through Web Client and are not interchangeable with user-defined capabilities in vCenter Client, so we will use Web Client to tag objects in the following example.

> If you used attributes in vCenter Client, they can be migrated to tags with the vCenter Attributes migration wizard. The wizard can be started in Web Client by going to **Summary | Custom Attributes | Edit | Migrate** for any object that has custom attributes assigned.
>
> During the migration attribute, names are converted to categories while attribute values become tag names.

Tags must be unique within the vCenter Server. This requirement defines their scope. Objects keep the assigned tags within vCenter Server boundaries. For example, a VM migrated between hosts or clusters and managed by one vCenter will not lose its tags.

## How to do it...

To create a storage tag in Web Client, perform the following steps:

1. Select a datastore, folder, or datastore cluster.
2. Go to **Manage | Tags**.
3. Click on the **New tag** button.
4. Type the name, select **New Category**, choose vCenter Server, type the category name, and make sure that **Datastore** is checked under **Associable Object Types**.

5. Click on **OK**.

To associate a tag with another datastore in Web Client, execute the following steps:

1. Right-click on the datastore and select **Assign tag**.
2. Choose the tag from the list and click on **Assign**.

Once objects have been assigned tags, they can be searched by going to **Home | Search**:

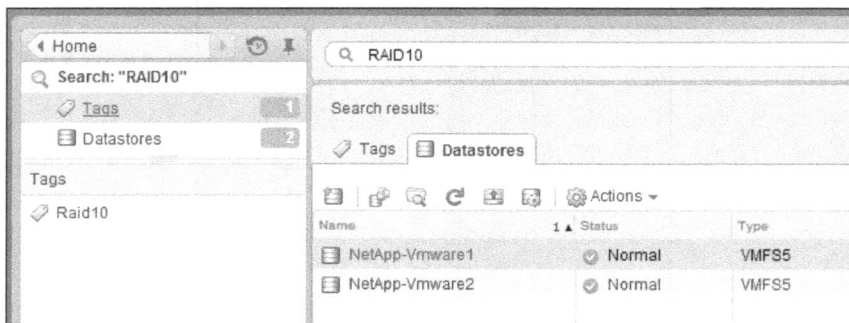

Tags can also simplify filtering and scripting. For example, in PowerCLI, the `get-datastore` command with the tag key can be used to filter only tagged datastores:

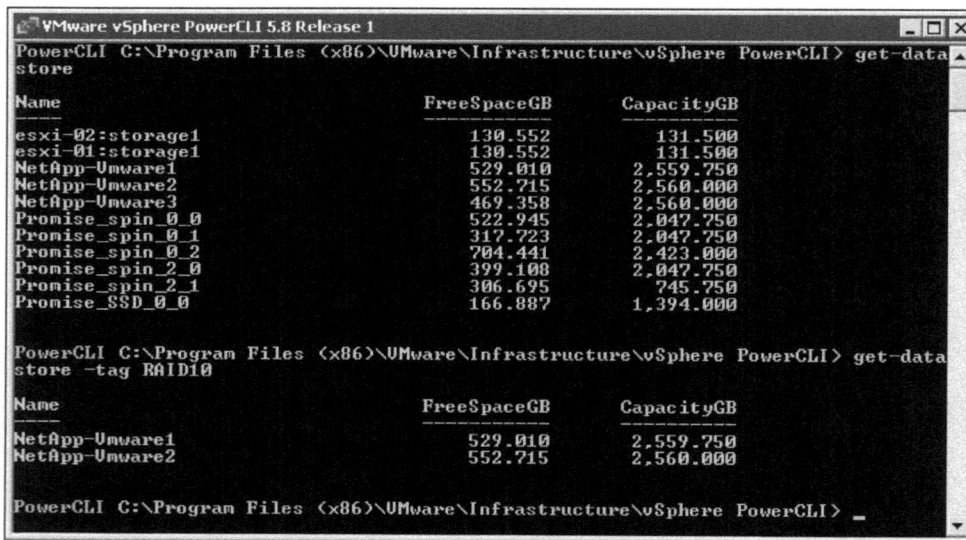

```
VMware vSphere PowerCLI 5.8 Release 1                              _ □ X
PowerCLI C:\Program Files (x86)\VMware\Infrastructure\vSphere PowerCLI> get-data
store

Name                            FreeSpaceGB         CapacityGB
----                            -----------         ----------
esxi-02:storage1                    130.552            131.500
esxi-01:storage1                    130.552            131.500
NetApp-Vmware1                      529.010          2,559.750
NetApp-Vmware2                      552.715          2,560.000
NetApp-Vmware3                      469.358          2,560.000
Promise_spin_0_0                    522.945          2,047.750
Promise_spin_0_1                    317.723          2,047.750
Promise_spin_0_2                    704.441          2,423.000
Promise_spin_2_0                    399.108          2,047.750
Promise_spin_2_1                    306.695            745.750
Promise_SSD_0_0                     166.887          1,394.000

PowerCLI C:\Program Files (x86)\VMware\Infrastructure\vSphere PowerCLI> get-data
store -tag RAID10

Name                            FreeSpaceGB         CapacityGB
----                            -----------         ----------
NetApp-Vmware1                      529.010          2,559.750
NetApp-Vmware2                      552.715          2,560.000

PowerCLI C:\Program Files (x86)\VMware\Infrastructure\vSphere PowerCLI> _
```

# Scheduling the VM clone

The vCenter task scheduler discussed in the *Automating tasks with scheduler* recipe in *Chapter 6, Basic Administrative Tasks*, allows the automation of a lot of management tasks. At the same time, it has limitations. For example, it does not allow scheduling virtual machine clones, which may be necessary when a copy of a VM is needed.

In this, and similar situations, administrators can use Windows Task Scheduler to run the PowerShell script with PowerCLI commands.

## Getting ready

Before creating and testing the following VM deployment script described, make sure that:

- ▸ PowerCLI 5.8 or later is installed on the server, where the script will be executed
- ▸ The user account that will be used has permissions to clone virtual machines

## How to do it...

To accomplish the task, we will create the PowerShell script and schedule it in Windows Task Scheduler.

### Creating the script

The PowerShell script to clone a VM consists of the following commands:

1. Define variables used later in this script:

```
$date = Get-Date
$vcServer = "<vCenter Server address>"
$fromVMname = "<Existing VM>"
$newVMName = "<Name of the clone>"
$tgtEsxName = "<Target host>"
$tgtDatastoreName = "<Target datastore>"
$userName = "<username with appropriate rights>"
$passWord = "<password>"
$notes = ("Clone of: " + $fromVMname + " for backup.
Created on: " + $date)
```

2. Connect to the vCenter Server:

```
Connect-VIServer -Server $vcServer -User $username -
Password $passWord
```

3. Delete the old clone if it exists:

```
$vmExist = Get-VM -Name $newVMname -ErrorAction
SilentlyContinue
if ($vmExist -ne $null)
{
 Remove-VM -deletefromdisk -VM $newVMName -confirm:$false
}
```

4. Clone the VM:

```
$cloneTask = New-VM -Name $newVMName -VM $fromVMname -VMHost
$tgtEsxName -Datastore $tgtDatastoreName -RunAsync
Wait-Task -Task $cloneTask -ErrorAction SilentlyContinue
```

```
Get-Task | where {$_.Id -eq $cloneTask.Id} | %{
    if($_.State -eq "Error"){
        $event = Get-VIEvent -Start $_.FinishTime | where
          {$_.DestName -eq $newVMName} | select -First 1
        $emailFrom = <email address>
        $emailTo = <email address>
        $subject = "Clone of " + $newVMName + " failed"
        $body = $event.FullFormattedMessage
        $smtpServer = <SMTP server IP or FQDN>
        $smtp = new-object
          Net.Mail.SmtpClient($smtpServer)
        $smtp.Send($emailFrom, $emailTo, $subject, $body)
    }
}
```

5. Add notes to the clone:

```
Set-VM -VM $newVMName -Notes $notes -confirm:$false
```

6. Disconnect from the vCenter Server:

```
Disconnect-VIServer -Server $vcServer -Confirm:$false
```

## Creating a scheduled task

To schedule the PowerShell script to run in Windows Task Scheduler, execute the following steps:

1. On the Windows Server, go to **Server Manager | Configuration | Task Scheduler**.

2. Right-click on **Task Scheduler Library** and select **Create Task**.

3. In the **General** tab, provide the task name and user account that will be used to run the task.

4. Select **Run whether user is logged on or not** and check the **Run with highest privileges** option.

5. Go to the **Triggers** tab, click on **New**, and create a schedule for the task.

6. Click on **OK**, go to the **Actions** tab, and click on **New**.

7. Under **Action**, choose **Start a program**.

8. In the **Program/script** field type the following path:

```
C:\Windows\System32\WindowsPowerShell\v1.0\powershell.exe
```

9. In the **Add arguments (optional)** field type the following:

```
-PSConsoleFile "C:\Program Files
(x86)\VMware\Infrastructure\vSphere PowerCLI"\vim.psc1 -
command "&{<path to Power Shell script>}"
```

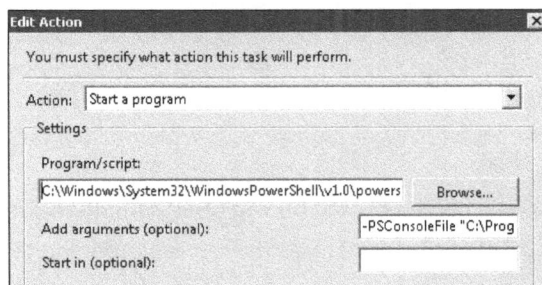

10. Click on **OK** twice to create the task.

# Redirecting VMkernel dumps to another server

vSphere 5 has introduced **VMware vSphere Network Dump Collector**—a service that allows an ESXi host to send diagnostic information to a remote location in case of a failure with the pink diagnostic screen.

Diagnostics information can be sent to a remote host instead, or in addition to the local store. This information is useful for troubleshooting host failures.

> For more information about interpreting the pink screen, refer to the VMware KB article 1004250 at `http://kb.vmware.com/kb/1004250`.

The advantage of sending dump to a remote location is that under certain circumstances, it cannot be saved locally. For example, a failure can be caused by local storage issues. Another case is when the ESXi host does not have a local storage at all. The OS may be running from the USB drive or SD card. The absence of a local storage will also be the case for autodeploy configurations.

Dump Collector is available as a Windows service and has to be installed separately. It can be installed on the same server as vCenter Server. It comes with the vCenter Server Virtual Appliance.

## Getting ready

Before implementing Netdump, administrators should be aware of the following requirements and limitations:

▶ ESXi host administrative access is required to enable the feature.

▶ Core dumps will be sent using the Netdump protocol, which supports only IPv4.

- ▶ Network traffic is not encrypted; it uses UDP/6500 by default.
- ▶ Netdump does not support any authentication or authorization mechanisms, so there is no way to verify the integrity or validity of the data collected.
- ▶ Network Dump Collector is incompatible with VMkernel ports configured for EtherChannel/LACP.
- ▶ Netdump Collector is not supported on vSphere Distributed Switch.
- ▶ By default, only 2 GB of diagnostic information is stored and older dumps are deleted.
- ▶ The default timeout to receive files is 60 seconds. Any partial files are deleted once it expires. Unfortunately, this value is not configurable.

## How to do it...

Before core dump collection can occur, both sides have to be configured—remote collector service and the ESXi host.

### Configuring the Netdump collector service

The Dump Collector service installed on the Windows Server can be configured by making changes to the `vmconfig-netdump.xml` configuration file located in the following directory:

`C:\ProgramData\VMware\VMware ESXi Dump Collector\`

An administrator can change:

- ▶ `defaultDataPath`: This is the value that defines a folder where dumps will be stored
- ▶ `port`: This is the UDP port the service is listening on
- ▶ `maxSize`: This is the amount of disk space allocated to core dumps in GB

The Dump Collector service has to be restarted after any changes to `vmconfig-netdump.xml`. To do this from the Windows-elevated Command Prompt, run the following command:

```
net stop vmware-network-coredump
```

```
net start vmware-network-coredump
```

The Dump Collector service comes preconfigured with vCenter Virtual appliance. Its settings can be changed using the web interface:

1. Log in to `https://<vCenter appliance address>:5480/` with the administrative account.
2. Go to **Services | NetDump**.
3. Change the UDP port and maximum disk space allocated to core dumps as required.

4. Click on **Save Settings**.
5. Go to the **Status** tab.
6. Click on **Stop ESXi Services**.
7. Click on **Start ESXi Services**.

## Configuring the ESXi host for Netdump

ESXi hosts can be configured to send core dumps to the remote network location either through the host profile or with the ESX command line (esxcli).

To configure the host profile in Web Client, perform the following steps:

1. Go to **Home | Rules and Profiles | Host Profiles**.
2. Select the existing profile and go to **Actions | Edit Settings**.

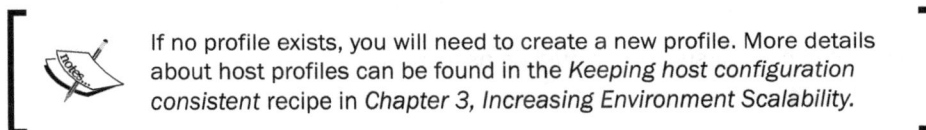

> If no profile exists, you will need to create a new profile. More details about host profiles can be found in the *Keeping host configuration consistent* recipe in *Chapter 3, Increasing Environment Scalability.*

3. Go to the **2 Edit Host Profile** step.
4. Go to **Networking configuration | Network Coredump Settings**, and perform the following steps:
   - Enable the feature
   - Specify the network interface to be used for outbound traffic
   - Type the IP address of the remote server and port it's listening on

| Network Coredump Settings | | |
| --- | --- | --- |
| Fixed Network Coredump Policy | Network Coredump settings | ▼ |
| | *Network Coredump enabled | ☑ Enabled |
| | Host NIC to use | vmk0 |
| | Network Coredump Server IP | 192.168.0.56 |
| | Network Coredump Server Port | 6500 |

5. Click on **Next** and **Finish** to save changes.

To configure hosts for Netdump with the command line, perform the following steps:

1.  Open a console session to the host or connect remotely via SSH.

2.  Review the current settings:

    ```
    esxcli system coredump network get
    ```

3.  Specify the outbound interface, IP address, and UDP port of the remote collector:

    ```
    esxcli system coredump network set --interface-name
    <VMkernelInterface> --server-ipv4 <IPAddress> --server-port
    PortNumber
    ```

4.  Enable the configuration:

    ```
    esxcli system coredump network set --enable true
    ```

5.  Check the functionality of the collector server:

    ```
    esxcli system coredump network check
    ```

6.  Output in case of success should be as follows:

    ```
    Verified the configured netdump server is running
    ```

7.  Save the configuration permanently:

    ```
    /sbin/auto-backup.sh
    ```

# Gathering network traffic

Often, for troubleshooting or auditing purposes, the network traffic has to be mirrored to a remote collector. The most common solution is to use the **NetFlow** protocol, which collects the IP traffic as records and sends them to the remote server for analysis.

In vSphere 5, NetFlow Version 10 is supported by vSphere Distributed Switch. vSphere Distributed Switch requires the Enterprise Plus license.

Traffic which can be collected includes the following:

*   VM-to-VM traffic within one host
*   VM-to-VM traffic between hosts
*   VM to physical network traffic

## How to do it...

To configure NetFlow in Web Client, execute the following steps:

1. Select Distributed Switch.
2. Go to **Manage | Settings | NetFlow**.
3. Click on **Edit**.
4. Specify the IP address and port of the NetFlow collector.

5. Specify the IP address of Distributed Switch, change **Advanced Settings** if required, and click on **OK**.

> More information on **Advanced Settings** is available in the *There's more...* section of this recipe.

In vCenter Client, NetFlow settings are available in Distributed Switch settings:

1. Right-click on Distributed Switch.
2. Click on **Edit Settings**.

3.  Go to the **NetFlow** tab. Specify the IP address and port of the NetFlow collector.

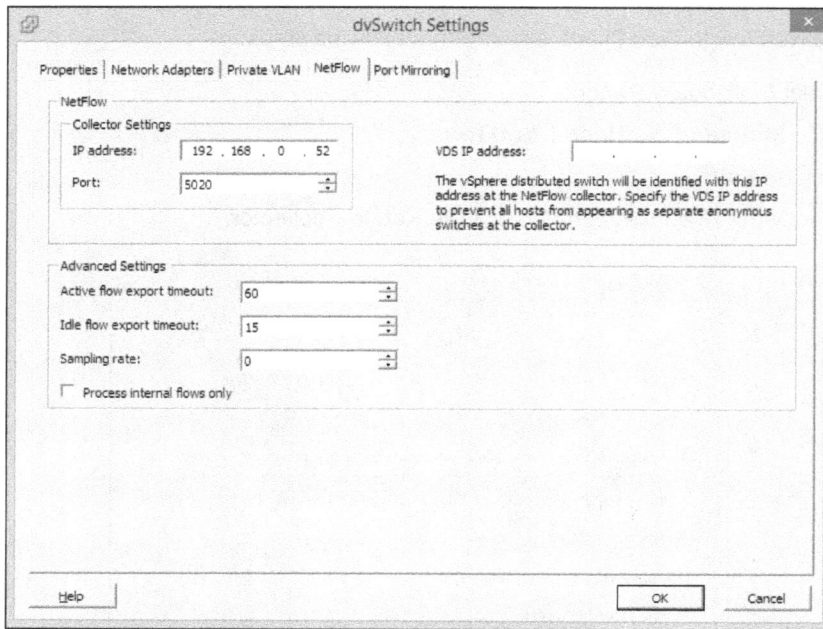

4.  Specify the IP address of Distributed Switch, change **Advanced Settings** if required, and click on **OK**.

## There's more...

The VDS IP address is required to differentiate the traffic collected from different switches in one environment.

Advanced settings control the sampling rate and export timeouts for active and idle flows.

Timeouts define how often gathered data is sent to the NetFlow collector. To generate alerts and view troubleshooting data, the **Active flow export timeout** setting should be close to 1 minute. Increasing this value may cause spikes in traffic reports.

**Idle flow export timeout** is used to ensure that finished flows are being sent to the collector periodically. The default setting will be sufficient for most environments. Increasing this value to more than 250 seconds may cause traffic levels that are too low in the reports.

Enabling NetFlow will have an impact on the host CPU usage. The significance of this impact depends on the number of flows in the environment. If enabling NetFlow increases CPU utilization to an unacceptable level, change the sampling rate or choose to monitor only internal flows.

The sampling rate defines the amount of information collected for a flow, for example, a rate of 1 means that data from every second packet will be collected. A rate of *x* means that *x* number of packets will be dropped after each collected packet.

**Internal flows** are the network activity between virtual machines running on the same host. When this setting is chosen, only such traffic will be collected.

# VDS configuration backup and restore

vSphere 5 offers the administrator an option to back up and restore the virtual switch configuration. This feature may be useful for backup purposes in case of configuration corruption. It can also be helpful if the same switch configuration has to be created in another environment.

## How to do it...

To export the Distributed Switch configuration in Web Client, perform the following steps:

1. Right-click on the switch and go to **All vCenter Actions | Export Configuration**.

2. Select either the **Distributed switch only** or **Distributed switch and all port groups** option.

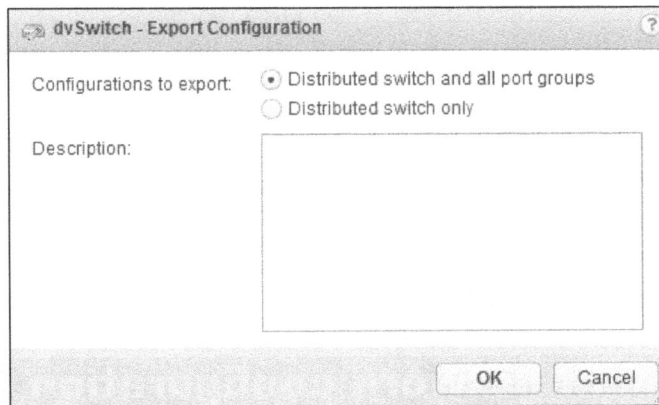

3. Click on **OK** and then on **Yes**.

4. Select the location to save the backup, make sure it's `.zip`, and click on **Save**.

Use switch configuration restore to reset any changes made or to recover the corrupt configuration; it can be accomplished with the following steps:

1. Right-click on the switch and go to **All vCenter Actions | Restore Configuration**.

2. Click on **Browse** and select the backup file.

3. Select either the **Restore distributed switch and all port groups** or **Restore distributed switch only** option.

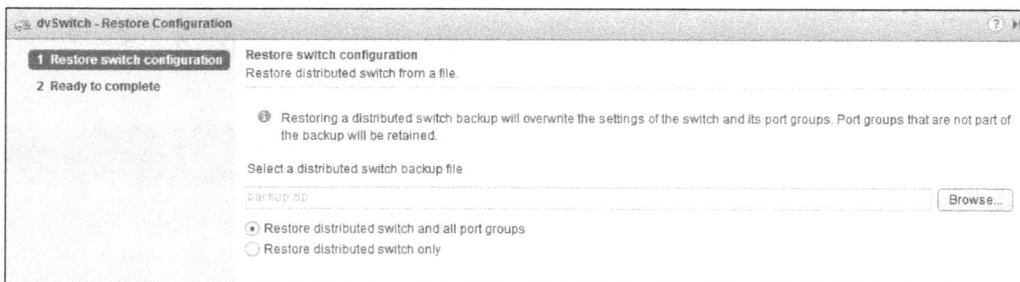

4. Click on **Next** and then on **Finish**.

To import the backup that creates a new Distributed Switch, and can be done in the same, or a different environment, perform the following steps:

1. Right click on the datacenter and go to **All vCenter Actions | Import Distributed Switch**.

2. Click on **Browse** and select the backup file.

3. Select **Preserve original distributed switch and port group identifiers**.

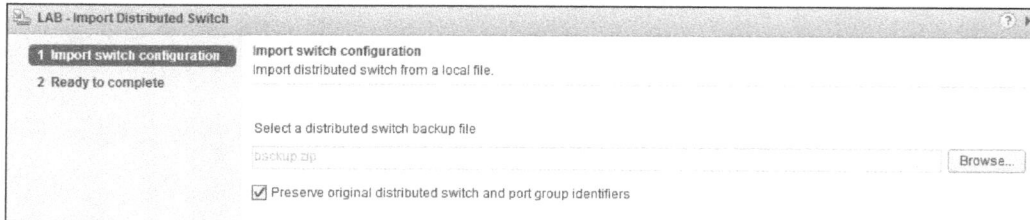

4. Click on **Next** and then on **Finish**.

# Management network configuration recovery

The vSphere Distributed Switch backup and restore functionality has been discussed in the *VDS configuration backup and restore* recipe of this chapter. One of the additional features of this functionality introduced in vSphere 5.1 is the ability to recover settings for a single port group instead of restoring configuration for the whole virtual switch.

This feature is useful in situations when the Distributed Switch has been misconfigured, which causes interruption or outage. **Network rollback** is enabled by default but can be disabled, which is not recommended.

## How to do it...

If a change has been made to the virtual switch port group that unexpectedly broke, the required functionality administrator can perform the following steps to revert the port group configuration to the previous state:

1. Right-click on the Distributed Switch port group.

2. Go to **All vCenter Actions** and select **Restore Configuration**.

3. Choose the **Restore to previous configuration** option.

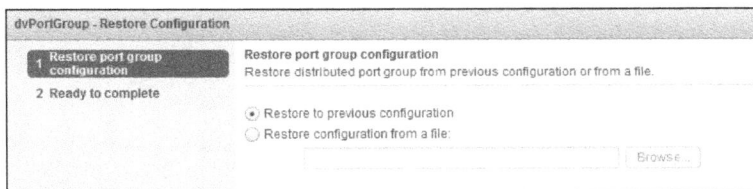

4. Click on **Next** and then on **Finish**.

To disable the Network Rollback feature completely:

1. Select vCenter Server in the Web Client navigator.

2. Go to **Manage | Settings | Advanced Settings** and click on **Edit**.

3. Select the **config.vpxd.network.rollback** key and change its value to **false**.

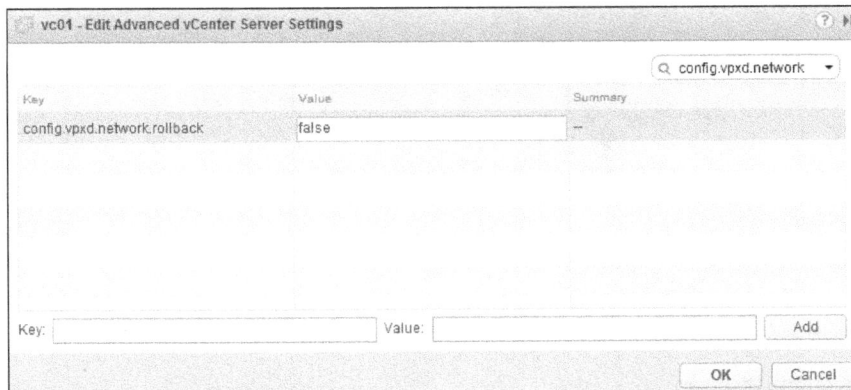

4. Click on **OK** to apply changes.

# Choosing a MAC address prefix

Under normal circumstances, network adapters of virtual machines get their MAC address assigned automatically by vCenter. This happens when a VM is created or when the virtual network adapter is being added to an existing VM. vCenter keeps the MAC address prefix consistent across virtual machines in the environment. Also, this prefix belongs to the VMware range.

Such behavior can be an issue in certain situations. One of them is when a physical machine has been converted to virtual and there is software whose license is tied to the MAC address.

vSphere allows changing MAC addresses assigned to virtual machines. If the whole MAC address needs to be different, it should be changed in the guest OS and requires a reboot.

The MAC address can also be changed in **VM Settings** if the default prefix, which belongs to the VMware, is acceptable.

## How to do it...

In vSphere 5.1 and later, Distributed Switch has the default security policy enabled that prevents virtual machines from changing their MAC addresses. This setting makes sure that VMs are not able to send packets on behalf of other virtual machines.

If a MAC change is required, this setting has to be turned off. To do this, perform the following steps:

1. Right-click on a port group that allows MAC address changes and click on **Edit Settings**.

2. Go to **Security** and switch the **Forged transmits** setting to **Accept**.

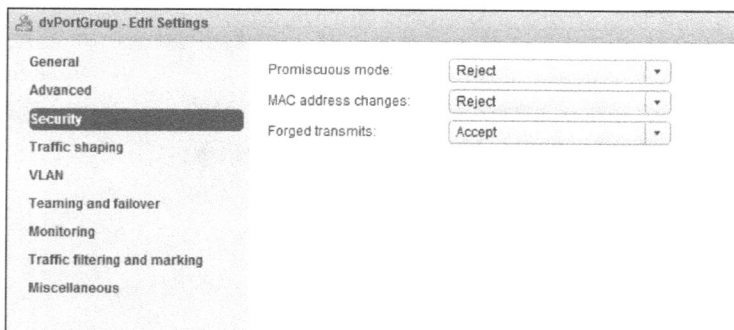

3. Click on **OK**.

To change the MAC address in Windows virtual machine, perform the following steps:

1. Go to **Control Panel | Administrative Tools | Computer Management | Device Manager**.

2. Expand **Network Adapters**.

3. Right-click on the VMware network adapter and go to **Properties**.

4. Go to the **Advanced** tab

5. Select **Mac Address** or **Locally Administered Address** depending on the network adapter type installed.

6. Switch to **Value**.

7. Type the new MAC address.

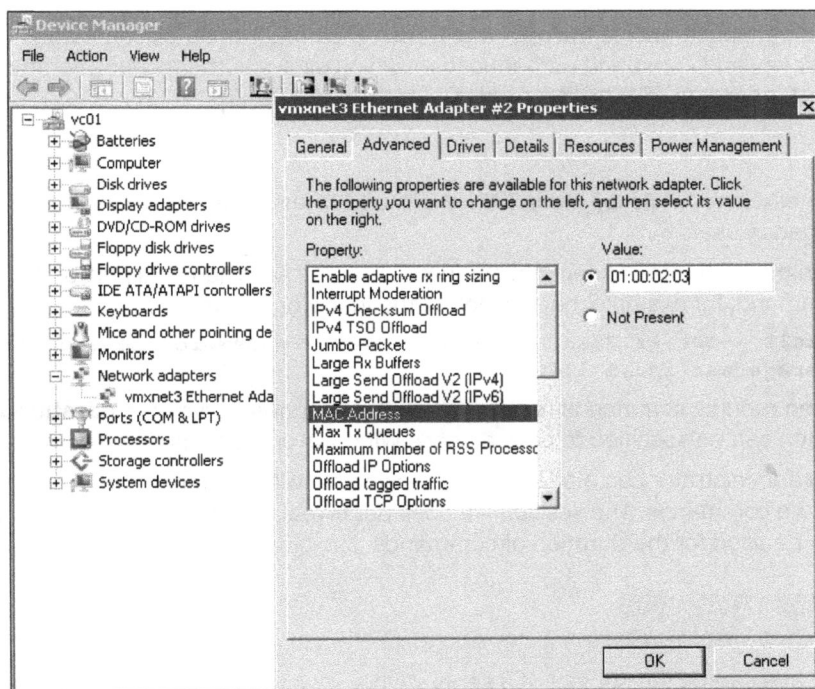

8. Click on **OK** and restart the virtual machine to apply changes.

# Getting familiar with new CLI

In vSphere 5, the new command-line interface has been introduced. The tools are called **esxcli**; it offers a structured and intuitive interface with real-time discovery of syntax options.

The esxcli is the first attempt to standardize multiple command-line tools required; which before, were different depending on the way the administrator connects to hosts. The new tool has improved syntax and additional functionalities, which were not available before. Among them are network and security policies, firewalls, and VIN management.

Esxcli can be used to manage hosts via the ESXi shell, with the vCLI package, which can be installed on Windows or Linux servers, and through **vSphere Management Assistant** (**vMA**).

The general command structure is as follows:

```
esxcli <connect options> <namespace> <cmd options>
```

For example, have a look at the following command:

```
esxcli --server 192.168.1.25 network ip interface list
```

Among other enhancements is the option to format the output of esxcli commands with the formatter key and command authentication, which allows authenticating commands either against individual ESXi hosts or the vCenter Server.

User authentication works in the following way:

- ▶ The esxcli ran while logged in locally to the ESXi shell will use credentials of logged-in user.
- ▶ Within the remote connection, credentials can be specified as a part of the command, for example, have a look at the following command:

```
esxcli --server ESXi --username user --password 'password'
storage san iscsi list
```

- ▶ When running commands remotely from the Windows Server, the **passthroughauth** option can be specified to pass a user's Windows credentials to the command.
- ▶ The administrator can also provide a session file with credentials as a parameter for the commands. The session file does not reveal the password information and can be used for the duration of commands. It expires after 30 minutes if not used.

## How to do it...

The esxcli usage can be the subject of a separate book, so in this recipe, let's take a look at a few examples on how to use the utility. We will look at power and management operations and some examples of the networking configuration.

### Formatter options

The Esxcli formatter allows modifying the command output for simplicity, visibility, or report generation purposes.

The output can be formatted as .xml, .csv or key-value pair. An administrator can also filter fields that will be displayed.

For example, the default list of network interfaces looks as follows:

```
~ # esxcli network ip interface list
```

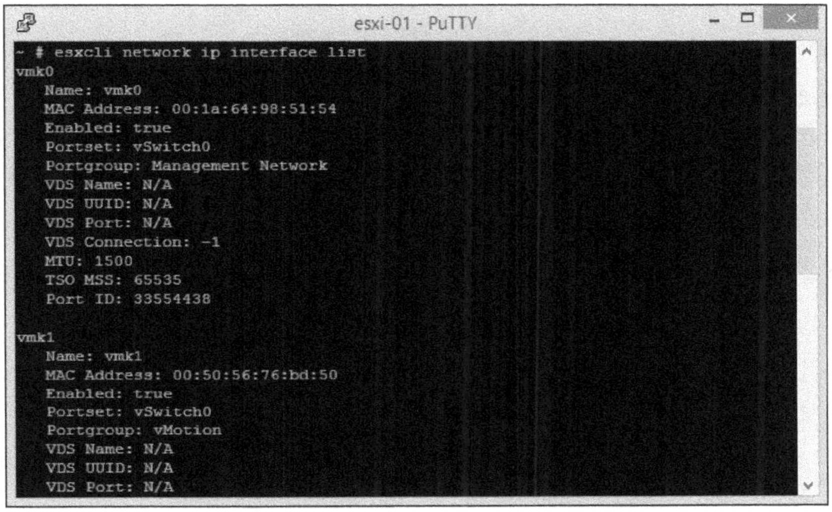

The formatted output is easier to read, as shown in the following screenshot:

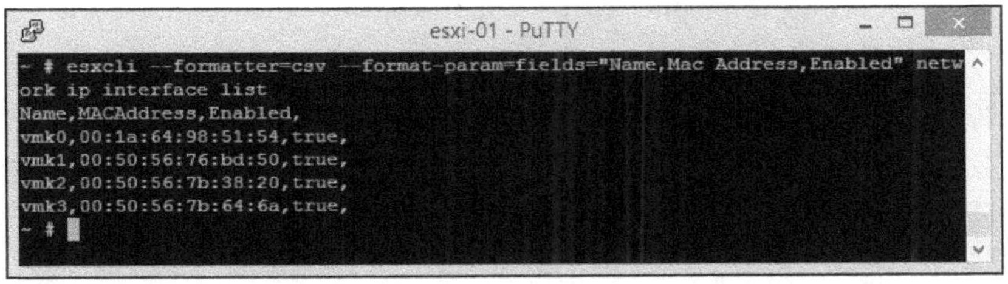

## Management operations

Esxcli has the `maintenanceMode` option, which allows the administrator to put hosts in and out of maintenance mode.

To get the current state of the host run:

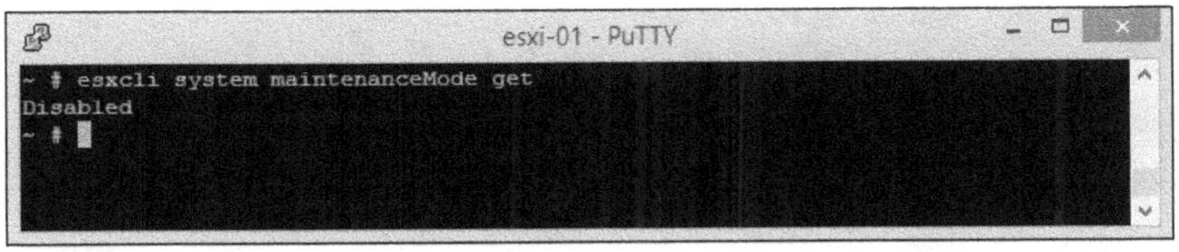

To put the host in maintenance mode, execute the following command:

```
~ # esxcli system maintenanceMode set -e true -t 0
~ # esxcli system maintenanceMode get
Enabled
```

## Power operations

With the shutdown command available in esxcli, administrators can reboot or shut down the ESXi host. The hosts have to be in maintenance mode for these operations to be allowed.

To shut down a host run, execute the following command:

```
~ # esxcli system shutdown poweroff --delay=10 --reason="Maintenance"
```

A host can be rebooted with the following command:

```
~ # esxcli system shutdown reboot -d 10 -r "Updates"
```

In both cases, the reason is the required option, which clarifies the reason for shutdown or reboot. Delay is also a required option that represents the time interval in seconds before the host starts the shutdown process.

## Networking operations

In ESXi Shell, regular Linux commands to manage the network configuration are not available. Administrators can use esxcli instead.

The DNS server configuration can be reviewed or changed with the following commands:

```
~ # esxcli network ip dns server list
   DNSServers: 192.168.10.10, 192.168.10.11
~ # esxcli network ip dns server add --server=192.168.10.12
~ # esxcli network ip dns server list
   DNSServers: 192.168.10.10, 192.168.10.11, 192.168.10.12
~ #
```

The DNS search suffix list can be managed with the following commands:

```
~ # esxcli network ip dns search list
   DNSSearch Domains: lab.pvt
~ # esxcli network ip dns search add --domain=test.local
~ # esxcli network ip dns search list
   DNSSearch Domains: lab.pvt, test.local
~ # esxcli network ip dns search remove --domain=test.local
~ # esxcli network ip dns search list
   DNSSearch Domains: lab.pvt
~ #
```

The network interfaces can be listed using the following command:

```
esxcli network ip interface list
```

IPv4 and IPv6 settings for an individual vmknic can be set or listed with the following commands:

```
esxcli network ip interface list
esxcli network ip interface ipv4 get -n vmk<X>
esxcli network ip interface ipv6 get -n vmk<X>
```

The esxcli equivalent to netstat looks as follows:

```
~ # esxcli network ip connection list
Proto  Recv Q  Send Q  Local Address      Foreign Address      State         Wo
rld ID  World Name
-----  ------  ------  ---------------    ---------------      -----------   --
------  ---------------
tcp        0       0  127.0.0.1:8307      127.0.0.1:54014      ESTABLISHED    1
186978  hostd-worker
tcp        0       0  127.0.0.1:54014     127.0.0.1:8307       ESTABLISHED
585253  rhttpproxy-work
tcp        0       0  127.0.0.1:443       127.0.0.1:50491      ESTABLISHED    8
142377  rhttpproxy-work
```

Finally, to list the ARP table, use the following command:

```
~ # esxcli network ip neighbor list
Neighbor        Mac Address         Vmknic      Expiry        State
-----------     -----------------   ------      ------        -----
192.168.2.22    00:a0:98:12:5d:f0   vmk2         277 sec
192.168.10.10   00:50:56:ba:00:00   vmk0        1182 sec
192.168.10.11   00:50:56:95:45:d5   vmk0        1198 sec
192.168.10.30   00:1a:64:98:51:54   lo0     4283116810 sec
192.168.10.32   b8:ca:3a:ee:da:af   vmk0         807 sec
```

# Configuring the firewall from CLI

General information about esxcli can be found in the *Getting familiar with new CLI* recipe in this chapter. It is a very powerful tool to manage ESXi hosts remotely or locally; it can be used for configuration tasks and scripting.

vSphere 5 introduced many changes to esxcli. One of them is a separate namespace for the ESXi firewall configuration.

> The ESXi firewall between the management interface and network is available in ESXi 5 and later. It is service oriented and not based on iptables as it was in earlier versions. The ESXi firewall is enabled by default and often requires changes in the configuration, as default settings may not be sufficient.

The command structure for the namespace is as follows:

```
esxcli network firewall (get | set | refresh | load | unload)
esxcli network firewall ruleset (list | set)
esxcli network firewall ruleset allowedip (add | list | remove)
esxcli network firewall ruleset rule list
```

## How to do it...

The firewall `get` can be used to display the general firewall configuration:

With firewall `set` command default action and enabled values can be changed. The administrator can use the following commands:

```
esxcli network firewall set --enabled=(true | false)
esxcli network firewall set --default-action=
```

To load or unload the firewall module, including the rules, use the following command:

```
esxcli network firewall (load | unload)
```

After making changes to the rules, run the following command to apply them:

```
esxcli network fire+wall refresh
```

### Working with rules

To see the existing rules and their status use, execute the command as shown in the following screenshot:

Alternatively, for a specific rule, execute the command as shown in the following screenshot:

Rules can be enabled or disabled with the following command:

```
esxcli network firewall ruleset set --ruleset-id=sshClient --
enabled=(true | false)
```

To verify which IP addresses are allowed by the rule, run the command as shown in the following screenshot:

Specific IP addresses instead of all can be allowed with the sequence of the following command:

# Bypassing "hostd" when it's unresponsive with CLI

The VMware-hostd service is the main interface between the ESXi host and VMkernel. It is required for most of the management tasks, including connections from vCenter, the VIC client directly, or remote command-line connections with esxcli or PowerCLI.

If the hostd service fails, the ESXi host becomes unmanageable. Fortunately, ESXi is still aware of all the running VMs, datastores, and so on, so the hostd failure does not affect virtual infrastructure availability. At the same time, most of the management operations are performed through vCenter, and the ability to power VMs on and off, vMotion, and so on, is vital for the administrator.

For rare cases, when the hostd service does not respond and cannot be restarted with standard means, vSphere 5 offers a new utility called localcli.

This tool works similar to esxcli but does not go through hostd, which makes it ideal to make changes in emergency situations. Any changes made with the tool will not be reflected in the user's interface or hostd internal state.

> VMware warns administrators that localcli can bring hosts into an inconsistent state and should be used carefully, only as a means to recover from failure. To be on the safe side, it's advised that the utility should be used only under the direction of VMware support.

## How to do it...

As localcli is an equivalent to esxcli, it csan be used with the same commands:

```
~ # esxcli network nic list
Name     PCI Device      Driver  Link  Speed  Duplex  MAC Address          MTU   Des
------   -------------   ------  ----  -----  ------  -----------------    ----  ---
vmnic0   0000:004:00.0   bnx2    Up    1000   Full    00:1a:64:98:51:54    1500  Bro
vmnic1   0000:006:00.0   bnx2    Up    1000   Full    00:1a:64:98:51:56    1500  Bro
vmnic6   0000:009:00.0   bnx2    Up    1000   Full    00:10:18:ae:98:b0    1500  Bro
vmnic7   0000:009:00.1   bnx2    Up    1000   Full    00:10:18:ae:98:b2    1500  Bro
vmnic8   0000:00a:00.0   bnx2    Up    1000   Full    00:10:18:ae:98:b4    1500  Bro
vmnic9   0000:00a:00.1   bnx2    Up    1000   Full    00:10:18:ae:98:b6    1500  Bro
~ # localcli network nic list
Name     PCI Device      Driver  Link  Speed  Duplex  MAC Address          MTU   Des
------   -------------   ------  ----  -----  ------  -----------------    ----  ---
vmnic0   0000:004:00.0   bnx2    Up    1000   Full    00:1a:64:98:51:54    1500  Bro
vmnic1   0000:006:00.0   bnx2    Up    1000   Full    00:1a:64:98:51:56    1500  Bro
vmnic6   0000:009:00.0   bnx2    Up    1000   Full    00:10:18:ae:98:b0    1500  Bro
vmnic7   0000:009:00.1   bnx2    Up    1000   Full    00:10:18:ae:98:b2    1500  Bro
vmnic8   0000:00a:00.0   bnx2    Up    1000   Full    00:10:18:ae:98:b4    1500  Bro
vmnic9   0000:00a:00.1   bnx2    Up    1000   Full    00:10:18:ae:98:b6    1500  Bro
~ #
```

VMware recommends using this command only as the last resort. If possible, it's advised to restart the hostd process and start using esxcli. This can be done with the following command:

```
/etc/init.d/hostd restart
```

Alternatively, to restart all management agents, execute the following command:

```
services.sh restart
```

Please refer to KB 1002849 for more information about troubleshooting an unresponsive hostd process at `http://kb.vmware.com/kb/1002849`.

# Index

## Symbols

**100 percent uptime**
ensuring, for critical VMs 50-53
**.vmdk files**
backing up 63-68
restoring 63-68

## A

**Admission Control**
enabling 58
**Advanced Configuration and Power
   Interface (ACPI) 147**
**affinity rules**
types 215
feature 215
**alarm**
creating, in vCenter Client 134
**application monitoring 40**
**Application Program Interface (API) 94**

## B

**backup retention policy**
configuring 71, 72
**Baseboard Management
   Controller (BMC) 142**
**baselines**
attaching, to hosts 237, 238
creating 233-236
**behavior, Lockdown mode 29**
**behavior, Normal mode 29**
**Blue Screen of Death (BSOD) 40**

## C

**Changed Block Tracking (CBT) 63**
**CLI 259**
**CPU, VM**
increasing 109-112
**customizations**
about 81
creating 81, 82
troubleshooting 84, 85
using 82-84
**custom policy 148**

## D

**database cluster**
about 74
cons 74
pros 74
**datastore cluster**
creating 171-174
**datastores**
grouping, into folders 208
tagging 212
**datastore space utilization**
alarm definitions, creating 210
controlling 207
default alarm, disabling 208
folders, creating for datastores 208, 209
**direct-to-host restore option 68**
**disk formats**
converting 132, 133
**disk provisioning**
selecting, for new VMs 131

# [PACKT] PUBLISHING   enterprise 🞡
## professional expertise distilled

## Thank you for buying
## VMware vCenter Cookbook

# About Packt Publishing

Packt, pronounced 'packed', published its first book, *Mastering phpMyAdmin for Effective MySQL Management*, in April 2004, and subsequently continued to specialize in publishing highly focused books on specific technologies sand solutions.

Our books and publications share the experiences of your fellow IT professionals in adapting and customizing today's systems, applications, and frameworks. Our solution-based books give you the knowledge and power to customize the software and technologies you're using to get the job done. Packt books are more specific and less general than the IT books you have seen in the past. Our unique business model allows us to bring you more focused information, giving you more of what you need to know, and less of what you don't.

Packt is a modern yet unique publishing company that focuses on producing quality, cutting-edge books for communities of developers, administrators, and newbies alike. For more information, please visit our website at www.PacktPub.com.

# About Packt Enterprise

In 2010, Packt launched two new brands, Packt Enterprise and Packt Open Source, in order to continue its focus on specialization. This book is part of the Packt Enterprise brand, home to books published on enterprise software – software created by major vendors, including (but not limited to) IBM, Microsoft, and Oracle, often for use in other corporations. Its titles will offer information relevant to a range of users of this software, including administrators, developers, architects, and end users.

# Writing for Packt

We welcome all inquiries from people who are interested in authoring. Book proposals should be sent to author@packtpub.com. If your book idea is still at an early stage and you would like to discuss it first before writing a formal book proposal, then please contact us; one of our commissioning editors will get in touch with you.

We're not just looking for published authors; if you have strong technical skills but no writing experience, our experienced editors can help you develop a writing career, or simply get some additional reward for your expertise.

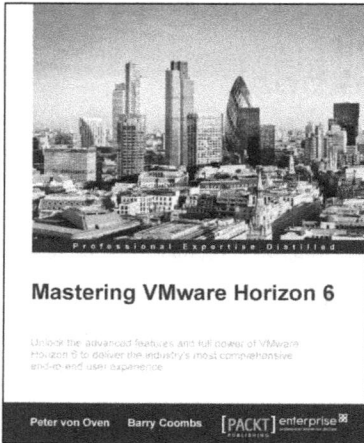

## Mastering VMware Horizon 6

ISBN: 978-1-78439-923-8          Paperback: 640 pages

Unlock the advanced features and full power of VMware Horizon 6 to deliver the industry's most comprehensive end-to-end user experience

1. Learn why a EUC strategy is important, what it can deliver, and the approach you should take when starting out with your own project.

2. Understand the key architecture components, new capabilities, and how to build, install, and configure an optimized delivery platform for end-user computing services.

3. Build your own environment for VDI and hosted applications with the help of screenshots, real-life scenarios, and best practices.

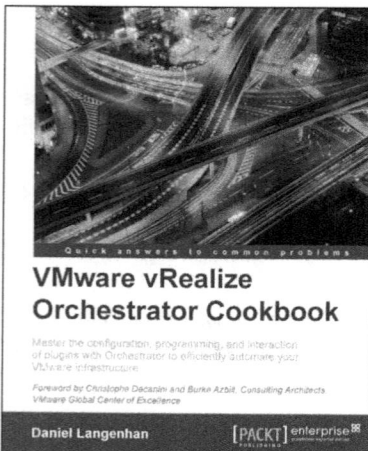

## VMware vRealize Orchestrator Cookbook

ISBN: 978-1-78439-224-6          Paperback: 382 pages

Master the configuration, programming, and interaction of plugins with Orchestrator to efficiently automate your VMware infrastructure

1. Program with Orchestrator to automate and synchronize your infrastructure.

2. Integrate the base plug-ins into your workflows.

3. Packed with over 100 example workflows, packaged for download and reuse.

Please check **www.PacktPub.com** for information on our titles

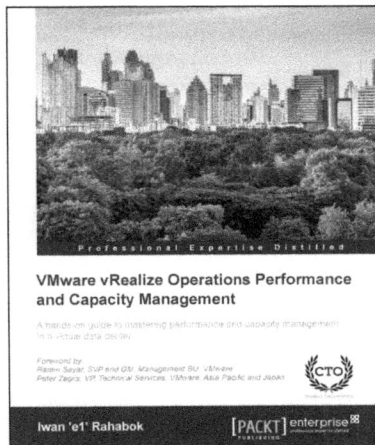

# VMware vRealize Operations Performance and Capacity Management

ISBN: 978-1-78355-168-2          Paperback: 276 pages

A hands-on guide to mastering performance and capacity management in a virtual data center

1. Understand the drawbacks of traditional paradigm and management that make performance and capacity management difficult in SDDC.

2. Master the counters in vCenter and vRealize Operations by discovering what they mean and their interdependencies.

3. Build rich dashboards using a practical and easy-to-follow approach supported with real-life examples.

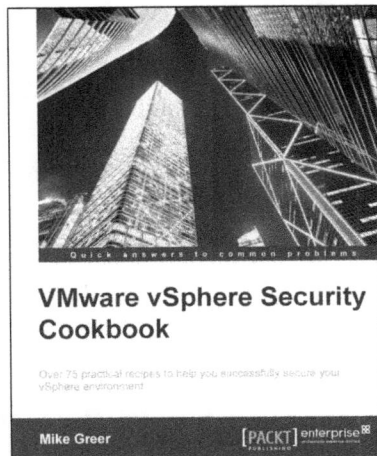

---

# VMware vSphere Security Cookbook

ISBN: 978-1-78217-034-1          Paperback: 334 pages

Over 75 practical recipes to help you successfully secure your vSphere environment

1. Secure your vSphere environment from the ground up, with step-by-step instructions covering all major vCenter components.

2. Eliminate pesky certificate errors in a conventional and secure manner.

3. Get acquainted with the new features of vSphere through a practical, recipe-based approach.

Please check **www.PacktPub.com** for information on our titles

www.ingramcontent.com/pod-product-compliance
Lightning Source LLC
Chambersburg PA
CBHW082108220326
41598CB00066BA/5846